P9-EKS-142

Fodor's 92
San Francisco

Fodor's Travel Publications, Inc.
New York and London

ISBN 0-679-02088-8

Fodor's San Francisco

Editor: Larry Peterson
Contributors: John Burks, Toni Chapman, Laura Del Rosso, Vicky Elliott, Pamela Faust, Sheila Gadsden, Tara Hamilton, Jacqueline Killeen, Marcy Pritchard, Aaron Shurin, Dan Spitzer, Robert Taylor, Casey Tefertiller
Art Director: Fabrizio La Rocca
Cartographer: David Lindroth
Illustrator: Karl Tanner
Cover Photograph: Wim Swann/FPG International

Design: Vignelli Associates

Special Sales

MANUFACTURED IN THE UNITED STATES OF AMERICA
10 9 8 7 6 5 4 3 2 1

Contents

Maps

Contents

Foreword

While every care has been taken to assure the accuracy of the information in this guide, the passage of time will always bring change and, consequently, the publisher cannot accept responsibility for errors that may occur.

All prices and opening times quoted here are based on information supplied to us at press time. Hours and admission fees may change, however, and the prudent traveler will avoid inconvenience by calling ahead.

Fodor's wants to hear about your travel experiences, both pleasant and unpleasant. When a hotel or restaurant fails to live up to its billing, let us know and we will investigate the complaint and revise our entries where the facts warrant it.

Send your letters to the editors of Fodor's Travel Publications, 201 E. 50th Street, New York, NY 10022.

Highlights '92 and Fodor's Choice

Highlights '92

For the first time in 40 years, San Franciscans can stand at the foot of Market Street and take in an unobstructed view of the sparkling waterfront and its sentinel, **The Ferry Building.** The 1989 earthquake finally did something nice: it shook loose the foundations of the ungainly elevated Embarcadero Freeway, causing its ultimate dismantling, and revealing the Ferry Building's graceful **clock tower,** modeled on the Seville cathedral's campanile, at the **Embarcadero** promenade. If, as planned, the freeway is replaced with a subterranean highway, San Francisco will have an appropriate gateway to the inner bay, with an open-air park in which a traveler can breathe in the salt air, and take refuge from the downtown concrete canyons. Drivers, however, may find this area problematic for a few more years.

The city continues its tradition of imaginative redevelopment a few blocks west of the waterfront. The area known as Rincon Hill, once an enclave of English-style town houses but long since given over to industrial warehouses, has blossomed into a sharply contemporary living and dining complex, **Rincon Center.** The soaring towers and atrium are actually built on top of and around an old post office. They house two of San Francisco's finest new restaurants. **Wu Kong** has inspired three-star raves for its bustling Hong Kong ambience and spicy Shanghai cuisine. Across the way, **Etrusca** happily marries Italian regional cooking with elegant, streamlined decor.

Fisherman's Wharf, nearly done in by its age-old formulas for tourist success, is also showing refreshing signs of new life. **Kimco Hotels,** which is responsible for a wave of small, intimate, and carefully appointed new hotels, frequently with their own fine restaurants, has just opened the **Tuscan Inn** at Fisherman's Wharf. With 199 airy rooms, many with pristine views of the bay, the Tuscan offers Old World elegance, Italian-style, and houses the **Cafe Pescatore,** a classic trattoria. A block away, the **Hyatt at Fisherman's Wharf** brings that chain's reputation to its 313 user-friendly rooms. Both of these developments are part of a new master plan to bring comfort and spontaneity (and maybe even locals) back to this ever-popular tourist area.

If you want to leave the city in comfort and style, you can hop the new **Sierra 49er Express** to Lake Tahoe and Reno. This luxury train has more in common with a cruise ship than with a regular passenger train. Its cars include enormous windows providing panoramic views and electrostatically cleaned air. A three-level entertainment car provides live music and dancing. Best of all, the train glides through some of the most spectacular scenery that California has to offer: the marshlands of the Sacramento delta, the Sierra foothills' Gold Country, and the majestic High Sierras. For a shorter trip, Grayline Tours can connect you with the **Napa Wine Train,** where you can enjoy lunch or dinner (and wine, of course) while riding through the North Bay's loveliest wine-producing region.

In a city noted for an abundance of restaurants, the newest place to see and be seen (as well as to eat) is the **Cypress Club** on Jackson Street, and no wonder: situated on the edge of the sober Financial District, this elegantly bizarre space seems to have dropped down from Hollywood's skies with dramatic oversized fixtures and gigantic swooping lights. It is enormously popular so if you can't get a reservation for a table, go in for a look anyway.

Fodor's Choice

No two people will agree on what makes a perfect vacation, but it's fun and helpful to know what others think. We hope you'll have a chance to experience some of Fodor's Choices yourself while visiting San Francisco. For more information about each entry, refer to the appropriate chapters within this guidebook.

Special Moments

Enjoying the sunset view and a drink at the Carnelian Room, Bank of America Building

Picnicking on sourdough bread and California wine on the shores of the lagoon at the Palace of Fine Arts

Attending a classic double feature at the last of San Francisco's great movie palaces, the Castro Theater, when the organist closes the intermission with a chorus of "San Francisco"

Browsing in the City Lights bookstore in North Beach, a cultural landmark from San Francisco's beatnik era

Lunching at Postrio when chef Wolfgang Puck is presiding over the kitchen

Walking across the Golden Gate Bridge

Watching the Giants beat the Dodgers at Candlestick Park

Memorable Sights

The view of the city and her bridges from one of the ferries in the bay

Flower stands at Union Square

Fog rolling into the city over Twin Peaks

The fresh food displays in the Chinatown markets

The sea lions howling in the surf at Cliff House

Restaurants

Masa's (*Very Expensive*)

Stars (*Expensive*)

The Mandarin (*Moderate–Expensive*)

Corona Bar & Grill (*Moderate*)

Fog City Diner (*Moderate*)

Greens at Fort Mason (*Moderate*)

Khan Toke Thai House (*Inexpensive–Moderate*)

Top Seasonal Events

The Chinese New Year's parade in February

Golden Gate Park when the rhododendron dell blooms in April

The Bay to Breakers race in May

The Gay Freedom Parade in June

Opera in the Park in September

Hotels

Campton Place (*Very Expensive*)

Four Seasons (*Very Expensive*)

The Sherman House (*Very Expensive*)

Stanford Court (*Very Expensive*)

Petite Auberge (*Expensive*)

Galleria Park (*Inexpensive*)

Night Spots

Fillmore Auditorium

Great American Music Hall

Kimball's

Pier 23

Plush Room

San Francisco

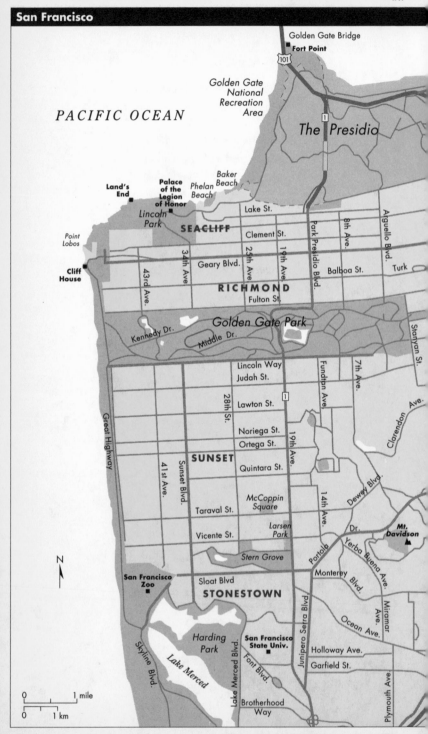

Golden Gate Bridge

Fort Point

101

Golden Gate National Recreation Area

The Presidio

1

PACIFIC OCEAN

Baker Beach

Land's End

Palace of the Legion of Honor

Phelan Beach

Lake St.

Point Lobos

Lincoln Park

SEACLIFF

Clement St.

Cliff House

34th Ave.

Geary Blvd.

25th Ave.

19th Ave.

Park Presidio Blvd.

8th Ave.

Arguello Blvd.

Balboa St.

Turk

43rd Ave.

RICHMOND

Fulton St.

Kennedy Dr.

Golden Gate Park

Middle Dr.

Stanyan St.

Lincoln Way

Judah St.

Fundian Ave.

7th Ave.

28th St.

Lawton St.

1

Clarendon Ave.

Noriega St.

Ortega St.

SUNSET

Quintara St.

19th Ave.

14th Ave.

Dewey Blvd.

Great Highway

41st Ave.

Sunset Blvd.

McCoppin Square

Taraval St.

Larsen Park

Dr.

Mt. Davidson

Vicente St.

Stern Grove

Portola

Yerba Buena Ave.

Miramar Ave.

N

San Francisco Zoo

Sloat Blvd

STONESTOWN

Monterey Blvd.

Ocean Ave.

Skyline Blvd.

Harding Park

Lake Merced

San Francisco State Univ.

Lake Merced Blvd.

Font Blvd.

Junipero Serra Blvd.

Holloway Ave.

Garfield St.

Plymouth Ave.

Brotherhood Way

0   1 mile

0   1 km

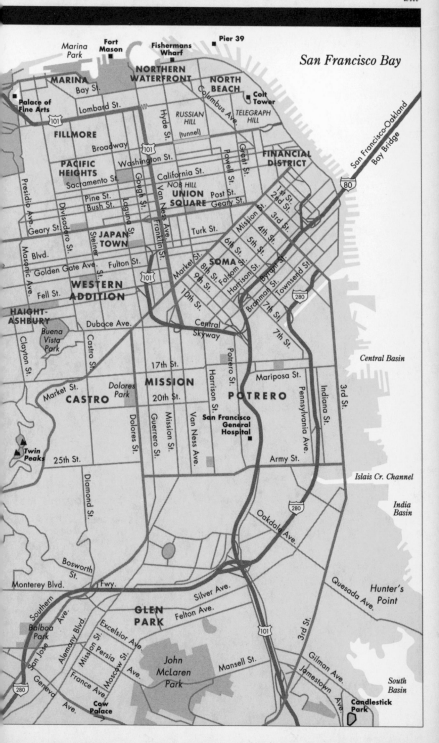

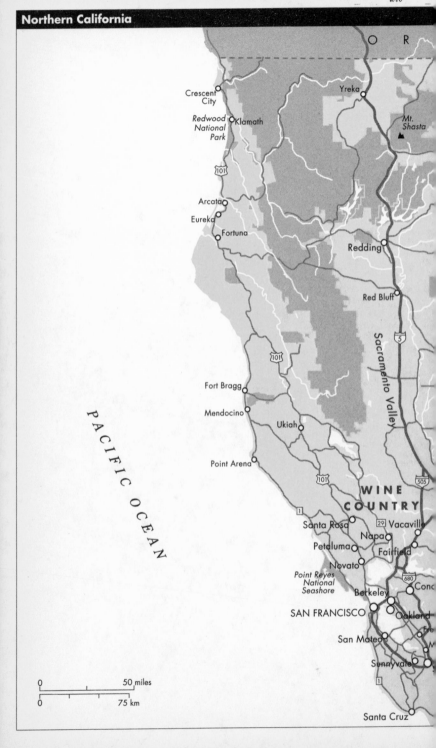

Northern California

Crescent City

Redwood National Park

Klamath

Yreka

Mt. Shasta

Arcata

Eureka

Fortuna

Redding

Red Bluff

Sacramento Valley

PACIFIC OCEAN

Fort Bragg

Mendocino

Ukiah

Point Arena

WINE COUNTRY

Santa Rosa

Vacaville

Napa

Petaluma

Fairfield

Novato

Point Reyes National Seashore

Berkeley

Conc

SAN FRANCISCO

Oakland

San Mateo

Sunnyvale

Santa Cruz

0   50 miles
0   75 km

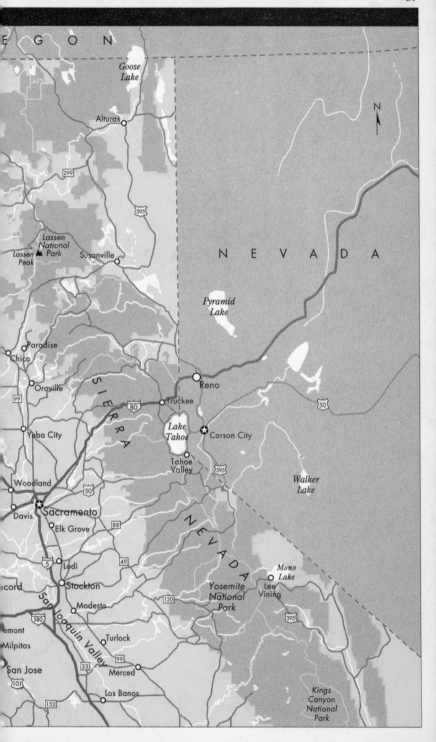

World Time Zones

MONDAY
SUNDAY

International Date Line

+12 +13   -9

-10

-11

-10

+11

+12

+11 +12 -   -11   -10   -9   -8   -7   -6   -5   -4   -3   -2

-4

-3

-7

-5   -4

-6

-5   -4   -3

-5

-4   -3

-3

Numbers below vertical bands relate each zone to Greenwich Mean Time (0 hrs.).
Local times frequently differ from these general indications,
as indicated by light-face numbers on map.

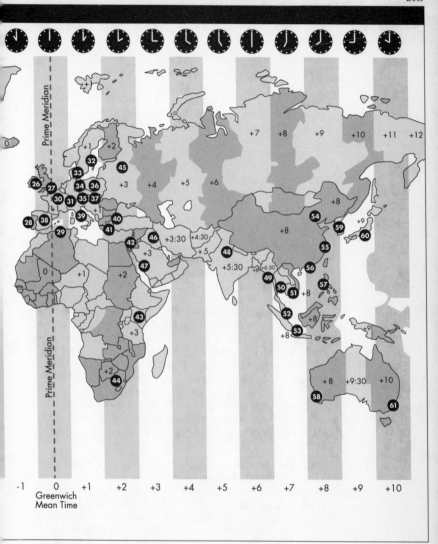

Prime Meridian

Prime Meridian

+1 +2 +3 +4 +5 +6 +7 +8 +9 +10 +11 +12

+3:30 +4:30 +5:30 +6:30

+8 +9:30 +10

-1 0 +1 +2 +3 +4 +5 +6 +7 +8 +9 +10
Greenwich
Mean Time

Mecca, **47**
Mexico City, **12**
Miami, **18**
Montreal, **15**
Moscow, **45**
Nairobi, **43**
New Orleans, **11**
New York City, **16**

Ottawa, **14**
Paris, **30**
Perth, **58**
Reykjavík, **25**
Rio de Janeiro, **23**
Rome, **39**
Saigon, **51**

San Francisco, **5**
Santiago, **21**
Seoul, **59**
Shanghai, **55**
Singapore, **52**
Stockholm, **32**
Sydney, **61**
Tokyo, **60**

Toronto, **13**
Vancouver, **4**
Vienna, **35**
Warsaw, **36**
Washington, DC, **17**
Yangon, **49**
Zürich, **31**

Introduction

an Franciscans tend to regard the envy of visitors as
a matter of course and to look on whatever brought
them to settle here (there's probably never been a
time when the majority of the population was native born)
as a brilliant stroke of luck. Certain local problems can be
traced to this warm contentment with the city and to the
attendant fear that somebody might do something to
change it. The skyline, for example, which in recent decades has become clotted with high rises, has turned into a
source of controversy. The city's Financial District is dominated by the dark, looming Bank of America—the sculpted
lump of black granite out front has been nicknamed "The
Banker's Heart"—and by the Transamerica Building, the
glass-and-concrete pyramid that has made the city's skyline instantly recognizable. (Nearly two decades after
its construction, San Franciscans still argue vehemently
about its merits, or its utter lack of them. But nobody
claims it isn't distinctive.) Admirers of the skyline defend
the skyscrapers as evidence of prosperity and of San
Francisco's world-class stature; detractors grumble about
the "Manhattanization" that's ruining a unique place. His-
torically, San Francisco is a boomtown, and various periods
of frantic building have lined the pockets of developers for
whom the city's beauty was no consideration at all. Nevertheless, in 1986 the voters set limits on downtown construction; now the controversy has moved out to the
neighborhoods, where entrepreneurs want to knock down
single-family houses to make room for profitable apartment
buildings.

The boom began in 1848. At the beginning of that year, San
Francisco wasn't much more than a pleasant little settlement that had been founded by the Spaniards back in the
auspicious year of 1776. The natural harbor of the bay (so
commodious that "all the navies of the world might fit" inside it, as one visitor wrote) made it a village with a future.
The future came abruptly when gold was discovered at
John Sutter's sawmill in the Sierra foothills, some 115 miles
to the northeast. By 1850, San Francisco's population had
zoomed from 500 to 30,000, and a "western Wall Street"
sprang up as millions upon millions of dollars' worth of gold
was panned and blasted out of the hills. The gold mines
began to dry up in a few years; but in 1859 prospectors
turned up a fabulously rich vein of silver in the Virginia
Range, in what is now Nevada; and San Francisco—the nearest financial center—prospered again. The boom made
labor a precious commodity, especially since most of the
able-bodied men were rushing off to the mountains to make
their fortunes. San Francisco has remained a strong
labor town, though not always happily so: During rough

times, the unions found a scapegoat in the immigrant Chinese workers.

But contentiousness is part of the price San Francisco pays for variety. Consider, as an indicator, the makeup of the city's chief administrative body, the 11-member Board of Supervisors: Past boards have included a healthy mix of Chinese, Hispanics, gays, blacks, and women. The city is a bastion of what it likes to refer to as "progressive" politics. Leftish *Mother Jones* magazine publishes from an office on Mission Street; the Sierra Club, founded here by its first president, John Muir, in 1892, has its national headquarters on Polk Street. The two daily newspapers, on the other hand, lean heavily right, at least on their editorial pages. (William Randolph Hearst, whose father gave him the *Examiner* in 1887, turned the paper into a laboratory of yellow journalism; today the name at the top of the masthead is William R. Hearst III.) Political bitterness has sometimes led to violence, most spectacularly with the "Bloody Thursday" face-off between striking longshoremen and scab labor in 1934, and in the 1978 assassinations of the city's liberal mayor, George Moscone, and its first gay supervisor, Harvey Milk, by a vindictive right-wing ex-supervisor. (On a more eccentric note, San Francisco is also the city where, in 1974, the Symbionese Liberation Army and its most famous victim/inductee, Patty Hearst, held up the Sunset District branch of the Hibernia Bank.) But, despite a boomtown tendency toward raucousness, and a sad history of anti-Asian discrimination, the city today prides itself on its tolerance. The mix, everybody knows, is what makes San Francisco. On any given night at the Opera House—a major civic crossroads—you can see costumes ranging from torn denim and full leather to business suits, dinner jackets, and sequined, feathered gowns—expensive originals gracing society dowagers and the occasional goodwill-store find on a well-dressed drag queen.

Geographically, San Francisco is the thumbnail on a 40-mile thumb of land, the San Francisco Peninsula, which stretches northward between the Pacific Ocean and San Francisco Bay. Hemmed in on three sides by water, the land area (less than 50 square miles) is relatively small; the population, at about three-quarters of a million, is small, too. Technically speaking, it's only California's third-largest city, behind Los Angeles and San Diego and no longer very much ahead of nearby San Jose. But that statistic is misleading: The Bay Area, which stretches from the bedroom communities north of Oakland and Berkeley south through Silicon Valley (the cluster of Peninsula cities that have become the center of America's computer industry) and San Jose, is really one continuous megacity, with San Francisco as its heart—its hub.

Not so many centuries ago the area that was to become San Francisco was a windswept, virtually treeless, and, above all, sandy wasteland. Sand even covered the hills. The sand is still there, but—except along the ocean—it's well hidden. City Hall is built on 80 feet of it. The westerly section of the city—the Sunset and Richmond districts and Golden Gate Park—seems flat only because sand has filled in the contours of the hills.

But the hills that remain are spectacular. They provide vistas all over the city—nothing is more common than to find yourself staring out toward Angel Island or Alcatraz, or across the bay at Berkeley and Oakland. The hills are also exceptionally good at winding pedestrians. (The cable cars didn't become instantly popular because they were picturesque.) The city's two bridges, which are almost as majestic as their surroundings, had their 50th birthdays in 1986 and 1987. The Golden Gate Bridge, which crosses to Marin County, got a bigger party, but the San Francisco–Oakland Bay Bridge got a better present: a necklace of lights along its spans. They were supposed to be temporary, but the locals were so taken with the glimmer that bridge boosters started a drive to make them permanent; radio DJs and newspaper columnists put out daily appeals, drivers gave extra quarters to the toll takers, various corporations put up shares, and—close to a million dollars later—the lights on the Bay Bridge now shine nightly.

First-time visitors to San Francisco sometimes arrive with ideas about its weather gleaned from movie images of sunny California or from a misinformed 1967 song that celebrated the "warm San Franciscan nights." Sunny, perhaps; warm—not likely. That's *southern* California. (A perennially popular T-shirt quotes Mark Twain's apocryphal remark: "The coldest winter I ever spent was a summer in San Francisco.") Still, it almost never freezes here, and heat waves are equally rare. Most San Franciscans come to love the climate, which is genuinely temperate—sufficiently welcoming for the imposing row of palms down the median of Dolores Street but seldom warm enough for just a T-shirt at night. The coastal stretch of ocean may look inviting, but the surfers you sometimes see along Ocean Beach are wearing wetsuits. (The beach, though, can be fine for sunning.) And, of course, there's the famous fog—something that tourists tend to find more delightful than do the residents. It's largely a summer phenomenon; San Francisco's real summer begins in September, when the fog lifts and the air warms up for a while. November brings on the rains.

The city has three trademarks: the fog, the cable cars, and the Victorians. Bay-windowed, ornately decorated Victorian houses—the multicolor, ahistorical paint jobs that have become popular make them seem even more ornate—are the city's most distinguishing architectural feature. They date mainly from the latter part of Queen Victoria's reign, 1870 to the turn of the century. In those three decades, San

Francisco more than doubled in population (from 150,000 to 342,000); the transcontinental railway, linking the once-isolated western capital to the east, had been completed in 1869. That may explain the exuberant confidence of the architecture.

Over the years, plenty of the Victorians have gone under the wrecker's ball to make way for such commercial projects as shopping complexes, or for the low-income housing projects that went under the rubric of "urban renewal" but quickly degenerated into slums. The decrepit old houses were out of favor for a while, but once the era of gentrification arrived, those that were left standing were snatched up, fixed up, and sold at exorbitant prices. Parts of the city that not so long ago were considered ghettos are becoming expensive places to live. (Five years ago the corner of Haight and Fillmore streets was a dubious place to wait for a bus. Now it's chic.)

By far the biggest annihilator of San Francisco's older buildings, of course, was the April 18, 1906 earthquake—or, more precisely, the fire that followed it. San Francisco doesn't lie precisely on the San Andreas Fault, and the violent shaking of the earth accounted for only about 20% of the total damage. The Victorians, in fact—most of them redwood, an ideally tractable medium for all the gingerbread—swayed and bent and withstood the quake admirably. But they were natural fodder for the blaze. Some 28,000 buildings—80% of the city's property—went up, and well over half the city's population were left homeless. But San Francisco bounded back quickly. The *Chronicle* observed that the people who had been burned out of their homes were "taking things as happily and philosophically as if they were out on a summer's camping trip." Entrepreneurs began rebuilding so rapidly that the city missed a golden opportunity to right some of its long-standing design blunders. (The streets have never followed the contours of the hills; they were laid out on a grid pattern that had—and still has—nothing to do with the natural features of the landscape. Hence their sometimes unbelievable steepness.) The catastrophe left its deepest mark on the city's imagination. San Franciscans are sensitive to the sudden rattle of dishes on the shelves, and no one who has lived here for any length of time hasn't heard it.

In terms of both geography and culture, San Francisco is about as close as you can get to Asia in the continental United States. (The city prides itself on its role as a Pacific Rim capital, and overseas investment has become a vital part of its financial life.) The first great wave of Chinese immigrants came during the Gold Rush, in 1852. Chinese workers quickly became the target of race hatred and discriminatory laws; Chinatown—which began when the Chinese moved into old buildings that white businesses seeking more fashionable locations had abandoned—

developed, as much as anything else, as a refuge. Chinatown is still a fascinating place to wander, and it's a good bet
for late-night food, but it's not the whole story by any
means. The Asian community, which now accounts for a
fifth of San Francisco's population, reaches into every San
Francisco neighborhood, and particularly into the Sunset
and Richmond districts, out toward the ocean. Clement
Street, which runs through the center of the Richmond, has
become the main thoroughfare of a second Chinatown.
Southeast Asian immigrants, many of them ethnic Chinese,
are transforming the seedy Tenderloin into a thriving Little Indochina. There was heavy Japanese immigration
earlier in this century, but most of it went to southern
California, where organized labor had less of a foothold and
where there were greater opportunities for Asian workers.
Still, San Francisco has its Japantown, with its massive Japan Center complex and scads of shops and restaurants
clustered in and around it. In the past, Asians have tended
toward a backseat—or at least an offstage—role in the
city's politics; but like so much else on the city's cultural/
political landscape, that, too, seems to be changing.

San Francisco has always been a loose, tolerant—
some would say licentious—city. As early as the
1860s, the "Barbary Coast"—a collection of taverns,
whorehouses, and gambling joints along Pacific Avenue
close to the waterfront—was famous, or infamous. Bohemian communities seem to thrive here. In the 1950s, North
Beach, the city's Little Italy, became the home of the Beat
Movement. (Herb Caen, the city's best-known columnist,
coined the term "beatnik.") Lawrence Ferlinghetti's City
Lights, a bookstore and publishing house that brought out,
among other titles, Allen Ginsberg's *Howl* and *Kaddish*,
still stands on Columbus Avenue as a monument to the era.
(Across Broadway, a plaque identifies the Condor as the
site of the nation's first topless and bottomless performances, a monument to a slightly later era.) The Bay Area
was the epicenter of '60s ferment, too. The Free Speech
Movement began at the University of California in Berkeley
(where, in October 1965, Allen Ginsberg introduced the
term "flower power"), and Stanford's David Harris, who
went to prison for defying the draft, numbered among the
nation's most famous student leaders. In San Francisco,
the Haight-Ashbury district was synonymous with hippie-
dom and gave rise to such legendary bands as the Jefferson
Airplane, Big Brother and the Holding Company (fronted
by Janis Joplin), and the Grateful Dead. Twenty years later, the Haight has become a peculiar mix. Haight Street itself is a shopping strip, replete with boutiques and nail-
care salons and noted especially for its vintage-clothing
stores. The once-funky Victorians that housed the com-
munes have been restored and purchased by wealthy
yuppies. The neighborhood's history, and its name, however, still draw neo-hippies, as well as New Wavers with black

lips and blue hair, and some rather menacing skinheads. The transients who sleep in nearby Golden Gate Park make panhandling one of the street's major business activities. It's not a completely happy mix; still, most of the residents remain committed to keeping the Haight the Haight. There's especially bitter resentment against the chain businesses (McDonald's, The Gap) that have moved in. In 1988 a chain drugstore's attempt to open a huge outlet sparked furious protest and, eventually, arson. The question of who set the fire, which gutted not only the unfinished store but several nearby apartments and businesses as well, has never been answered, but the fire accomplished its purpose: The chain pulled out.

Southwest of the Haight is the onetime Irish neighborhood known as the Castro, which during the 1970s became identified with lesbian and gay liberation. Castro Street is dominated by the elaborate Castro Theatre, a 1923 vision in Spanish Baroque, which presents one of the best repertory movie schedules in the city. (The grand old pipe organ still plays during intermissions, breaking into "San Francisco" just before the feature begins.) There's been much talk, most of it exaggerated, about how AIDS has chastened and "matured" the Castro; it's still an effervescent neighborhood, and—as housing everywhere has become more and more of a prize—an increasingly mixed one. At the same time, gays, like Asians, are moving out of the ghetto and into neighborhoods all around the city.

The Lesbian and Gay Freedom Day Parade, each June, vies with the Chinese New Year Parade, in February, as the city's most elaborate. They both get competition from Japantown's Cherry Blossom Festival, in April; the Columbus Day and St. Patrick's Day parades; the June Carnaval in the Hispanic Mission District; and the May Day march, a labor celebration in a labor town. The mix of ethnic, economic, social, and sexual groups can be bewildering, but the city's residents—whatever their origin—face it with aplomb and even gratitude. Everybody in San Francisco has an opinion about where to get the best burrito or the hottest Szechuan eggplant or the strongest cappuccino. The most staid citizens have learned how to appreciate good camp. Nearly everyone smiles on the fortunate day they arrived on, or were born on, this windy, foggy patch of peninsula.

1 Essential Information

Before You Go

Visitor Information

For general information and free booklets and maps, contact the **San Francisco Convention and Visitors Bureau** (201 3rd St., Suite 900, 94103, tel. 415/974–6900). The bureau also publishes an attractive 80-page guide, *The San Francisco Book*, in three editions a year; it includes up-to-date information on theater offerings, art exhibits, sporting events, and other special happenings. Send $1 for postage and handling to SFCVB, Box 6977, 94101.

The **Redwood Empire Association Visitor Information Center** (785 Market St., 15th floor, 94103, 415/543–8334) will provide a wealth of free information on San Francisco and surrounding areas, including the wine country, the redwood groves, and northwestern California. For a dollar's postage they will also send *The Redwood Empire Visitor's Guide*.

The San Francisco Bay Area encompasses dozens of towns, and many of them have chambers of commerce that are happy to provide travelers with information. Here are the addresses of a few of the largest:

Berkeley Chamber of Commerce (1834 University Ave., Box 210, Berkeley, CA 94703, tel. 415/549–7000).
Oakland Convention and Visitors Bureau (1000 Broadway, Suite 200, Oakland, CA 94607, tel. 510/839–9000 or 800/444–7270).
San Jose Convention and Visitors Bureau (333 W. San Carlos St., Suite 1000, San Jose, CA 95110, tel. 408/295–9600).

A detailed 208-page book, *Discover the Californias*, which includes an informative section on the Bay Area, is available free through the **California Office of Tourism** (tel. 800/862–2543). In addition, the California Office of Tourism (801 K St., Suite 1600, Sacramento, CA 95814, tel. 916/322–1397) can answer many questions about travel in the state.

Tour Groups

Joining a tour group has some advantages: Someone else worries about travel arrangements, accommodations, and baggage transfer; you are likely to save money on airfare, hotels, and ground transportation; and you will probably cover a lot of territory. The major disadvantages, of course, are that you'll have to adjust to someone else's time schedule and pacing, and you won't be as free for independent explorations.

When considering a tour, be sure to find out (1) exactly what expenses are included (particularly tips, taxes, side trips, additional meals, and entertainment), (2) ratings of all the hotels on your itinerary and the facilities they offer, (3) cancellation policies for both you and the tour operator, (4) the number of travelers in your group, and (5) if you are traveling alone, the cost of the single supplement. Many tour operators request that bookings be made through a travel agent; there is no additional charge for doing so.

General-Interest Tours A sampling of options is listed here; check with your travel agent or the San Francisco Convention and Visitors Bureau (tel. 415/974–6900) for additional possibilities. Most group tours combine San Francisco with a number of other California cities.

Casser Tours (46 W. 43rd St., New York, NY 10036, tel. 212/840–6500 or 800/251–1411).

Domenico Tours (751 Broadway, Bayonne, NJ 07002, tel. 800/554–8687 or 201/823–8687).

Gadabout Tours (700 E. Tahquitz Way, Palm Springs, CA 92262, tel. 619/325–5556).

Globus-Gateway (150 S. Los Robles Ave., Pasadena, CA 91101, tel. 818/449–0919 or 800/556–5454).

Maupintour (Box 807, Lawrence, KA 66044, tel. 913/843–1211 or 800/255–4266).

Talmage Tours (1223 Walnut St., Philadelphia, PA 19107, tel. 215/923–7100).

Tauck Tours (11 Wilton Rd., Westport, CT 06881, tel. 203/226–6911 or 800/468–2825).

Special-Interest Tours   **American Express Vacations** (Box 5014, Atlanta, GA 30302, tel. 800/241–1700 or 800/282–0800 in GA) offers "Northern California Wine Country," a seven-day tour to delight the eye and the palate. **Wine Adventures, Inc.** (Box 3273, Yountville, CA 94599, tel. 707/944–8468) puts together customized tours of the Napa and Sonoma valleys just north of San Francisco; many of their tour leaders are vintners themselves. **HMS Tours** (1057 College Ave., Suite 206, Santa Rosa, CA 95404, tel. 707/526–2922 or 800/367–5348) sets up tours from San Francisco to the Sonoma and Napa wine valleys that might include hot-air ballooning and the Napa Valley Wine Train. **Sierra Club** (730 Polk St., San Francisco, CA 94109, tel. 415/776–2211) offers naturalist-led tours and excursions of the regions surrounding San Francisco.

If touring by bicycle appeals to you, **Sobek's International Explorers Society** (Box 1089, Angels Camp, CA 95222, tel. 209/736–4524 or 800/777–7939) offers a variety of free-wheeling tours in the Bay Area.

Package Deals for Independent Travelers

Most airlines have packages that include car rentals and lodging along with your flight. **American Fly Away Vacations** (tel. 817/355–1234 or 800/433–7300) offers a city package with discounts on hotels and car rental. The four-day "city spree" packages from **Delta Dream Vacations** (tel. 800/872–7786) include round-trip airfare, accommodations, car rental, and two-for-one admission to the San Francisco Experience. Also check with **United Airlines** (tel. 312/952–4000 or 800/328–6877) and **Continental Airlines** (tel. 800/634–5555) for their offerings. **SuperCities West** (7855 Haskell Ave., 3rd floor, Van Nuys, CA 91406, tel. 818/988–7844 or 800/556–5660) offers similar city packages.

Amtrak offers tours to major attractions in California. For a brochure and specific information, call 800/USA–RAIL or write to Amtrak Public Affairs, 1 California Street, Suite 1250, San Francisco, CA 94111-5466.

Hotels often offer packages for weekends, on- or off-season. Always ask about package options when making reservations. Travel agents, chambers of commerce, and visitors bureaus are also good sources of information.

Tips for British Travelers

Passports and Visas You will need a valid 10-year passport (cost £15). You do not need a visa if you are staying for less than 90 days, have a return ticket, and are flying with a participating airline. There are some exceptions to this, so check with your travel agent or with the **United States Embassy** (Visa and Immigration Dept., 5 Upper Grosvenor St., London W1A 2JB, tel. 071/499–3443). No vaccinations are required.

Customs Visitors 21 or over can take in (1) 200 cigarettes or 50 cigars or 2 kilograms of smoking tobacco, (2) 1 liter of alcohol, and (3) duty-free gifts to a value of $100. Do not try to take in meat or meat products, seeds, plants, or fruits. Avoid illegal drugs like the plague.

Returning to the United Kingdom, you may take home (1) 200 cigarettes or 100 cigarillos or 50 cigars or 250 grams of tobacco; (2) 2 liters of table wine and (a) 1 liter of alcohol over 22% by volume (most spirits) or (b) 2 liters of alcohol under 22% by volume (fortified or sparkling wine) or (c) 2 more liters of table wine; (3) 60 milliliters of perfume and 250 milliliters of toilet water; and (4) other goods up to a value of £32 but not more than 50 liters of beer or 25 lighters.

Insurance We recommend that you insure yourself against sickness and motoring mishaps with **Europ Assistance** (252 High St., Croydon, Surrey CR0 1NF, tel. 081/680–1234). It is also wise to take out insurance to cover loss of luggage (though check to see whether you are already covered through your existing homeowner's policy). Trip cancellation insurance is another wise buy. The **Association of British Insurers** (Aldermary House, 10–15 Queen St., tel. 071/248–4477) will give comprehensive advice on all aspects of vacation insurance.

Tour Operators As a result of the price battle that has raged over transatlantic fares, most tour operators now offer excellent budget packages to the United States. Among those you might consider as you plan your trip are:

Cosmosair plc (Ground Floor, Dale House, Tiviot Dale, Stockport, Cheshire SK1 1TB, tel. 061/480–5799).
Jetsave (Sussex House, London Rd., East Grinstead, West Sussex RH19 1LD, tel. 0342/312033).
Kuoni Travel Ltd. (Kuoni House, Dorking, Surrey RH5 4AZ, tel. 0306/76711).
Poundstretcher (Atlantic House, Hazelwick Ave., Three Bridges, Crawley, West Sussex RH10 1NP, tel. 0293/518022).
Premier Holidays (Premier Travel Center, Westbrook, Milton Rd., Cambridge CB4 1YQ, tel. 0223/355977).
Speedbird (Pacific House, Hazelwick Ave., Three Bridges, Crawley, West Sussex RH10 1NP, tel. 0293/611611).

Airfares Many ticket brokers offer budget flights to San Francisco. Some of these fares can be extremely difficult to come by, however, so be sure to book well in advance. Also check on APEX and other money-saving fares through the airlines or your travel agent. The small ads of daily and Sunday newspapers are another good source of information on low-cost flights.

When to Go

Anytime of the year is the right time to go to San Francisco, acknowledged to be one of the most beautiful cities in the world. The city itself enjoys a temperate marine climate. The fog rolls in during the summer, but it seems less an inconvenience than part of the atmosphere of this never-mundane place. As long as you remember to bring along sweaters and jackets, even in August, you can't miss!

San Francisco is on the tip of a peninsula, surrounded on three sides by the Pacific Ocean and San Francisco Bay. Its climate is quintessentially marine and moderate: It never gets very hot— anything above 80 degrees is reported as a shocking heat wave—or very cold (as far as the thermometer is concerned, anyway).

For all its moderation, however, San Francisco can be tricky. In the summertime, fog often rolls in from the ocean, blocking the sun and filling the air with dampness. At times like this you'll want a coat, jacket, or warm sweater instead of the shorts or lightweight summer clothes that seem so comfortable in most North American cities during July and August. Mark Twain is credited with observing that the coldest winter he ever spent was one summer in San Francisco. He may have been exaggerating, but it's best not to expect a hot summer in this city.

If you travel to the north, east, or south of the city, you will find the summer months much warmer. Shirtsleeves and thin cottons are usually just fine for the Wine Country.

Be prepared for some rain during the winter months, especially December and January. Winds off the ocean can add to the chill factor, so pack some warm clothing to be on the safe side.

Climate The following are average daily maximum and minimum temperatures for San Francisco.

Jan.	55F	13C	May	66F	19C	Sept.	73F	23C
	41	5		48	9		51	11
Feb.	59F	15C	June	69F	21C	Oct.	69F	21C
	42	6		51	11		50	10
Mar.	60F	16C	July	69F	21C	Nov.	64F	18C
	44	7		51	11		44	7
Apr.	62F	17C	Aug.	69F	21C	Dec.	57F	14C
	46	8		53	12		42	6

Current weather information on more than 750 cities around the world—450 of them in the United States—is only a phone call away. Dialing **WeatherTrak** at 900/370-8728 will connect you with a computer, with which you can communicate by touch tone—at a cost of 95¢ per minute. The number plays a taped message that tells you to dial a three-digit code for the destination in which you are interested. The code is either the area code (in the United States) or the first three letters of the foreign city. For a list of all access codes, send a stamped, self-addressed envelope to Cities, 98 Terrace Way, Greensboro, NC 27403. For further information, call 800/247-3282.

Festivals and Seasonal Events

Jan.: The **Shrine East-West All-Star Football Classic,** America's oldest all-star sports event, is played every year in the Stanford University Stadium in Palo Alto, some 25 miles south of San Francisco. (Shrine East-West Game, 1651 19th Ave., 94122, tel. 415/661–0291.)

Jan.–Apr.: Whale-watching can be enjoyed throughout the winter months and well into April, as hundreds of gray whales migrate along the Pacific coast. For information about viewing sites and special excursions, contact the California Office of Tourism (801 K St., Suite 1600, Sacramento 95814, tel. 916/ 322–1397).

Feb.: The **Chinese New Year** celebration in San Francisco lasts for a week, as North America's largest Chinese community marks the change in the calendar. It culminates with the justly famous Golden Dragon Parade. For a complete schedule of events, send a stamped, self-addressed envelope to Chinese New Year, Box 6977, 94101; or contact the Chinese Chamber of Commerce (730 Sacramento St., 94108, tel. 415/982–3000).

Mar.: On the Sunday closest to March 17, San Francisco's **St. Patrick's Day** celebration is marked by a long parade through the downtown area and by snake races. (San Francisco Convention and Visitors Bureau, 201 3rd St., Suite 900, 94103, tel. 415/ 974–6900.)

Apr.: The **Cherry Blossom Festival,** an elaborate presentation of Japanese culture and customs, winds up with a colorful parade through San Francisco's Japantown. A detailed schedule is available after mid-March; send a stamped, self-addressed envelope to Japan Center (1520 Webster St., 94115, tel. 415/922– 6776).

May: The **San Francisco** *Examiner* **Bay to Breakers Race** is crowded and jovial and takes runners across the city on a 7.5-mile route from bayside to oceanside. There are abundant festivities before and after the race; it's a huge San Francisco event that can be enjoyed by participants and spectators. (Examiner Bay to Breakers, 110 5th St., tel. 415/777–7770, for recorded information tel. 415/777–7773.)

May–June: Carnival, held yearly in the city's Mission District, is a Mardi Gras–like revel that includes a parade, a street festival, and a costume contest in which participants indulge their fantasies through masquerade, music, and dance. (San Francisco Convention and Visitors Bureau, 201 3rd St., Suite 900, 94103, tel. 415/974–6900.)

July: The city's **Fourth of July** celebration is held at Crissy Field in the Presidio and features family festivities beginning in midafternoon and a fireworks display at 9 PM. (San Francisco Convention and Visitors Bureau, 201 3rd St., 94103, tel. 415/ 974–6900.)

Sept.: The **San Francisco Blues Festival** is held annually on the Great Meadow at Fort Mason. (San Francisco Convention and Visitors Bureau— 201 3rd St., 94103, tel. 415/974–6900.)

Sept.–Oct.: The **Renaissance Pleasure Faire** is held on weekends in Novato, 20 miles north of San Francisco. Three thousand costumed participants stage an Elizabethan harvest festival and achieve quite a bit of authenticity. (Living History Centre, Box B, Novato 94948, tel. 415/892–0937.)

Oct.: The **Grand National Livestock Exposition, Rodeo, and Horse Show,** held at an immense San Francisco facility appropriately named the Cow Palace, is a world-class annual competition, with thousands of top livestock and horses. (Cow Palace, Box 34206, 94134, tel. 415/469–6065.)

Nov.–Dec.: The **Dickens Christmas Fair,** a re-creation of Dickens's London at holiday time, is presented by actors and craftspeople on weekends during November and December. (Living History Centre, Box B, Novato 94948, tel. 415/892–0937 or 415/620–0433.)

Dec.: The **Pickle Family Circus,** a particularly joyous group that started out as a band of street performers during the early 1970s, performs annually during the holiday season at the Palace of Fine Arts Theater in the Marina District. (Pickle Family Circus, 400 Missouri St., 94107, tel. 415/826–0747.)

What to Pack

Clothing   The most important single rule to bear in mind when packing for a vacation in the San Francisco Bay Area is to prepare for changes in temperature. An hour's drive can take you up or down many degrees, and the variation from daytime to nighttime in a single location is often marked. Take along sweaters, jackets, and clothes for layering as your best insurance for coping with variations in temperature. Include shorts and/or cool cottons unless you are packing only for a midwinter ski trip. Always tuck in a bathing suit. You may not be a beach lover, but the majority of overnight lodgings include a pool, a spa, and a sauna; you'll want the option of using these facilities.

While casual dressing is a hallmark of the California lifestyle, men will need a jacket and tie for many good restaurants in the evening, and women will be more comfortable in something dressier than regulation sightseeing garb.

Considerations of formality aside, bear in mind that San Francisco can be chilly at any time of the year, especially in summer, when the fog is apt to descend and stay. Nothing is more pitiful than the sight of uninformed tourists in shorts, their legs blue with cold. Take along clothes that will keep you warm, even if the season doesn't seem to warrant it.

Miscellaneous   Although you can buy supplies of film, sunburn cream, aspirin, and most other necessities almost anywhere in California (unless you're heading for the wilderness), it is a bother, especially if your time is limited, to have to search for staples. Take along a reasonable supply of the things you know you will be using routinely and save your time for sheer enjoyment.

An extra pair of glasses, contact lenses, or prescription sunglasses is always a good idea; the loss of your only pair can damage a vacation.

It is important to pack any prescription medications you need regularly as well as prescriptions that are occasionally important, such as allergy medications. If you know you are prone to certain medical problems and have good, simple ways of dealing with early manifestations, take along what you might need, even though you may never use it.

Cash Machines

An increasing number of the nation's banks belong to a network of ATMs (automatic teller machines) that dispense cash 24 hours a day in cities throughout the country. There are eight major networks in the United States, the largest of which are Cirrus, owned by MasterCard, and Plus, affiliated with Visa. Some banks belong to more than one network. These cards are not issued automatically; you must ask for them. If your bank doesn't belong to at least one network, you should consider moving your funds, because ATMs are becoming as essential as check cashing. Cards issued by Visa and MasterCard also can be used in the ATMs, but the fees are usually higher than the fees on bank cards and there is a daily interest charge on the "loan" even if monthly bills are paid on time. Each network has a toll-free number you can call to locate machines in a given city. The Cirrus number is 800/424-7787; the Plus number is 800/843-7587. Check with your bank for fees and for the amount of cash you can withdraw in a day.

Traveling with Film

If your camera is new, shoot and develop a few rolls of film before leaving home. Pack some lens tissue and an extra battery for your built-in light meter. Invest about $10 in a skylight filter and screw it onto the front of your lens. It will protect the lens and also reduce haze.

Film doesn't like hot weather. If you're driving in summer, don't store film in the glove compartment or on the shelf under the rear window. Put it behind the front seat on the floor, on the side opposite the exhaust pipe.

On a plane trip, never pack unprocessed film in check-in luggage; if your bags are X-rayed, you can say good-bye to your pictures. Always carry undeveloped film with you through security and ask to have it inspected by hand. (It helps to isolate your film in a plastic bag, ready for quick inspection.) Inspectors at U.S. airports are required by law to honor requests for hand inspection; abroad, you'll have to depend on the kindness of strangers.

The old airport scanning machines—still in use in some Third World countries—use heavy doses of radiation that can turn a family portrait into an early morning fog. The newer models—used in all U.S airports—are safe for anything from 5 to 500 scans, depending on the speed of your film. The effects are cumulative; you can put the same roll of film through several scans without worry. After five scans, though, you're asking for trouble.

If your film gets fogged and you want an explanation, send it to the **National Association of Photographic Manufacturers** (550 Mamaroneck Ave., Harrison, NY 10528). They will try to determine what went wrong. The service is free.

Traveling with Children

The watchword for traveling with children is to plan ahead as much as possible. That way, the trip will be a lot more fun for all of you.

Motels and hotels, with few exceptions, do welcome children. Often they can stay free in the same room with their parents, with nominal charges for cribs and $5–$10 charges for an extra bed. In addition, major hotels usually have lists of baby-sitters so that parents can leave for nonchild-related activities.

If you have children, you won't need to be told that you should have a good supply of things on hand to keep them busy in the car, on the air-plane, on the train, or however you are traveling. If you're traveling by car, you'll have the option of stopping frequently. Just getting the children out of the confines of the car for a little while has an advantage; an even bigger advantage comes when you can stop at a park and the children can run or use a playground.

When you are sightseeing, try to plan some things that will be of special interest to your children. They may tolerate a museum and even show interest in a historic building or two, but put a zoo into the itinerary whenever you can.

Publications *Family Travel Times* is an 8- to 12-page newsletter published 10 times a year by TWYCH (Travel with Your Children, 80 8th Ave., New York, NY 10011, tel. 212/206–0688). Subscription ($35) includes access to back issues and twice-weekly opportunities to call in for specific advice.

Great Vacations with Your Kids: The Complete Guide to Family Vacations in the U.S., by Dorothy Ann Jordon and Marjorie Adoff Cohen (E.P. Dutton, 2 Park Ave., New York, NY 10016; $12.95), details everything from city vacations to adventure vacations to child-care resources.

Places to Go with Children in Northern California, by Elizabeth Pomada (Chronicle Books, 1 Hallidie Plaza, San Francisco, CA 94102, tel. 800/722–6657; $9.95).

Eating Out with Kids in San Francisco, by Carole Terwilliger Meyers (Carousel Press, Box 6061, Albany, CA 94706, tel. 415/527–5849; $9.95).

Kidding Around in San Francisco is a free brochure available from the San Francisco Convention and Visitors Bureau (Box 6977, San Francisco 94101, tel. 415/974–6900).

Home Exchange Exchanging homes is a surprisingly low-cost way to enjoy a vacation in another part of the country. **Vacation Exchange Club, Inc.** (Box 820, Haleiwa, HI 96712, tel. 800/638–3841) specializes in domestic home exchanges. The club publishes three directories a year—in February, April, and August—and updated late listings throughout the year. Annual membership, which includes your listing in one book, a newsletter, and copies of all publications, costs $50. **Loan-a-Home** (2 Park La., 6E Mount Vernon, NY 10552, tel. 914/664–7640) is popular with academics on sabbatical and businesspeople on temporary assignment. There's no annual membership fee or charge for listing your home, however, one directory and a supplement costs $35.

Getting There On domestic flights, children under 2 not occupying a seat travel free. Various discounts apply to children 2 to 12 years of age. Regulations regarding infant travel on airplanes are in the process of being changed. Until they do, however, if you want to be sure your infant is secured in his/her own safety seat, you must buy a separate ticket and bring your own infant car seat. (Check with the airline in advance; certain seats aren't allowed. Or write for the booklet "Child/Infant Safety Seats Acceptable for Use in Aircraft," from the Federal Aviation Administration, APA–200, 800 Independence Ave., SW, Washington, DC 20591, tel. 202/267–3479.) Some airlines allow babies to travel in their own safety seats at no charge if there's a spare seat available on the plane; otherwise safety seats are stored and the child must be held by a parent. If you opt to hold your baby on your lap, do so with the infant outside the seatbelt so he or she won't be crushed in case of a sudden stop.

Also inquire about special children's meals or snacks. See the February 1990 and 1992 issues of *Family Travel Times* for "TWYCH's Airline Guide," which contains a rundown of the children's services offered by 46 airlines.

Hints for Disabled Travelers

California is a national leader in providing the handicapped with access to attractions and facilities. Since 1982 the state building code has required that all construction for public use include access for the disabled. State laws more than a decade old provide special privileges, such as license plates allowing special parking spaces, unlimited parking in time-limited spaces, and free parking in metered spaces. I.D. from states other than California is honored.

People with disabilities should plan ahead for travel; check with providers when you make arrangements for transportation, lodging, and special sightseeing and events. Allow plenty of time to meet bus, train, and plane schedules. Be sure your wheelchair is clearly marked if it is carried with other luggage.

Greyhound-Trailways Lines (tel. 800/752–4841; TDD 800/345–3109) will carry a disabled person and companion for the price of a single fare.

Amtrak (tel. 800/USA–RAIL) advises requesting redcap service, special seats, or wheelchair assistance when you make reservations. Also note that not all stations are equipped to provide these services. All handicapped passengers are entitled to a 25% discount on regular, discounted coach fares. A special children's handicapped fare is also available, offering qualified children ages 2–12 a 50% discount on already discounted children's fares. Check with Amtrak to be sure discounts are not exempt when you plan to travel. For a free copy of *Access Amtrak*, which outlines all services for the elderly and handicapped, write to Amtrak (National Railroad Corp., 400 N. Capitol St. NW, Washington, DC 20001, tel. 800/872–7245).

The **National Park Service** provides a Golden Access Passport free of charge to those who are medically blind or have a permanent disability; the passport covers the entry fee for the holder and anyone accompanying the holder in the same private vehicle as well as a 50% discount on camping and various other user fees. Apply for the passport in person at a national recreation facility that charges an entrance fee; proof of disability is required. For additional information, write to the National Park Service (Box 37127, Washington, DC 20013–7127).

The **Society for the Advancement of Travel for the Handicapped** (26 Court St., Penthouse, Brooklyn, NY 11242, tel. 718/858–5483 in New York; tel. 213/986–4246 in Los Angeles) is a good source of access information for the disabled. Annual membership is $45; for senior travelers and students, $25. Send $1 and a stamped, self-addressed envelope for a list of tour operators who arrange travel for the disabled.

The Information Center for Individuals with Disabilities (Fort Point Place, 1st floor, 27–43 Wormwood St., Boston, MA 02210, tel. 617/727–5540; TDD 617/727–5236) offers useful problem-solving assistance, including lists of travel agencies that specialize in tours for the disabled.

Travel Industry and Disabled Exchange (TIDE, 5435 Donna Ave., Tarzana, CA 91356, tel. 818/368–5648) is an industry-based organization with a $15-per-person annual membership fee. Members receive a quarterly newsletter and information on travel agencies and tours.

Moss Rehabilitation Hospital Travel Information Service (1200 West Tabor Rd., Philadelphia, PA 19141–3009, tel. 215/456–9600; TDD 215/456–9602) provides information on tourist sights, transportation, and accommodations for destinations around the world for a small fee.

Mobility International USA (Box 3551, Eugene, OR 97403, tel. 503/343–1284) is a membership organization with a $20 annual fee offering information on accommodations, organized study, and so forth, around the world.

Publications   *The Itinerary* (Box 2012, Bayonne, NJ 07002, tel. 201/858–3400) is a well-respected bimonthly travel magazine for the disabled. Call for a subscription ($10 for a year, $20 for two); it's not available in stores.

Twin Peaks Press (Box 129, Vancouver, WA 98666, tel. 206/694–2462 or 800/637–2256 for orders only) specializes in books for the disabled. *Travel for the Disabled* ($9.95) offers helpful hints as well as a comprehensive list of guidebooks and facilities geared to the disabled. *Directory of Travel Agencies for the Disabled* ($12.95) lists more than 350 agencies throughout the world. *Wheelchair Vagabond* ($9.95) helps independent travelers plan for extended trips in cars, vans, or campers. Twin Peaks also offers a "Traveling Nurse's Network," which provides registered nurses trained in all medical areas to accompany and assist disabled travelers.

Access to the World: A Travel Guide for the Handicapped, by Louise Weiss, offers tips on travel and accessibility around the world. It is available from Henry Holt & Co. for $12.95 plus $2 shipping (tel. 800/247–3912; the order number is 0805 001417).

A Guide to San Francisco for the Person Who is Disabled is published annually by the Mayor's Council on Disabilities Concerns (Box 1595, 94101, tel. 415/554–6141). Call between 10 AM and 3 PM for information referrals.

All stations in BART (Bay Area Rapid Transit) are equipped with elevators. Call the station agent on the white courtesy telephone. Stations also have accessible rest rooms, phones, and drinking fountains. For information on a Bay Region Transit Discount Card, call BART at tel. 415/464–6000.

Hints for Older Travelers

Many discounts are available to older travelers: Meals, lodging, entry to various attractions, car rentals, tickets for buses and trains, and campsites are among the prime examples.

The age that qualifies you for these senior discounts varies considerably. The American Association of Retired Persons will accept you for membership at age 50, and your membership card will qualify you for many discounts. The state of California will reduce the cost of your campsite, but you must be at least 62.

If you are 50, our advice is to ask about senior discounts even if there is no posted notice. Ask at the time you are making reservations, buying tickets, or being seated in a restaurant. Carry proof of your age, such as a driver's license, and, of course, any membership cards in organizations that provide discounts for seniors. Many discounts are given solely on the basis of age, without membership requirement. A 10% cut on a bus ticket and $2 off a pizza may not strike you as major savings, but they add up, and you can cut the cost of a trip appreciably if you remember to take advantage of these options.

The American Association of Retired Persons (1909 K St. NW, Washington, DC 20049, tel. 202/662–4850) has two programs for independent travelers: (1) the Purchase Privilege Program, through which members can obtain discounts on car rentals, sightseeing, hotels, motels, and resorts; and (2) the AARP Motoring Plan, provided by Amoco, which furnishes emergency aid (road service) and trip-routing information for an annual fee of $33.95 for a single person or married couple. The **AARP Travel Service** also arranges group tours in conjunction with **American Express Vacations** (Box 5014, Atlanta, GA 30302, tel. 800/241–1700 or 800/637–6200 in GA).

Elderhostel (75 Federal St., Boston, MA 02110–1941, tel. 617/426–7788) is an innovative program for people 60 years of age or over (only one member of a traveling couple needs to be 60 to qualify). Participants live in dorms on 1,200 campuses in the United States and around the world. Mornings are devoted to lectures and seminars, afternoons to sightseeing and field trips. The fee includes room, board, tuition, and round-trip transportation.

National Council of Senior Citizens (925 15th St. NW, Washington, DC 20005, tel. 202/347–8800) is a nonprofit advocacy group with 5,000 local clubs across the country. Annual membership is $12 per person or per couple. Members receive a monthly newspaper with travel information and an ID card for reduced-rate hotels and car rentals.

Mature Outlook (6001 N. Clark St., Chicago, IL 60660, tel. 800/336–6330), a subsidiary of Sears Roebuck & Co., is a travel club for people over 50, offering discounts at Holiday Inns and a bimonthly newsletter. Annual membership is $9.95 per person or couple. Instant membership is available at participating Holiday Inns.

September Days Club is run by the moderately priced Days Inns of America (tel. 800/241–5050). The $12 annual membership fee for individuals or couples over 50 entitles them to reduced car-rental rates and reductions of 15%–50% at 95% of the chain's more than 350 motels.

Greyhound Lines (tel. 800/752–4841; TDD 800/345–3109) and **Amtrak** (tel. 800/USA–RAIL) offer special fares for senior citizens.

Golden Age Passport is a free lifetime pass to all parks, monuments, and recreation areas run by the federal government. Permanent U.S. residents 62 years of age and over may pick them up in person at any national park that charges admission. The passport covers the entrance fee for the holder and anyone accompanying the holder in the same private vehicle. It also provides a 50% discount on camping and various other user fees.

Publications *The Senior Citizen's Guide to Budget Travel in the United States and Canada* is available for $4.95, including postage, from Pilot Books (103 Cooper St., Babylon, NY 11702, tel. 516/422–2225).

The Discount Guide for Travelers Over 55, by Caroline and Walter Weintz, lists helpful addresses, package tours, reduced-rate car rentals, etc., in the United States and abroad. To order, send $7.95 plus $1.50 shipping and handling to NAL/Cash Sales (Bergenfield Order Dept., 120 Woodbine St., Bergenfield, NJ 07621, tel. 800/526–0275).

Smoking

Limitations on smoking are becoming increasingly common; if you smoke, be sensitive to restrictions. If you do not smoke, ask for and expect accommodations for nonsmokers on airplanes, in hotels, in restaurants, and in many other public places.

Most hotels and motels have nonsmoking rooms; in larger establishments entire floors are reserved for nonsmokers. Most bed-and-breakfast inns do not allow smoking on the premises.

Most eating places of any size have nonsmoking sections. Many cities and towns in California have ordinances requiring areas for nonsmokers in restaurants and many other public places.

The trend in California, a health-conscious state, is toward more No Smoking signs. Expect to see them in many places.

Further Reading

While there are many novels with a San Francisco setting, they don't come any better than *The Maltese Falcon* by Dashiell Hammett, the founder of the hard-boiled school of detective fiction. First published in 1930, Hammett's books continue to be readily available in new editions, and the details about the fog, the hills, and seedy offices south of Market continue to be accurate.

Other novels are John Gregory Dunne's recent *The Red White and Blue*, Stephen Longstreet's *All or Nothing* and *Our Father's House*, and Alice Adams's *Rich Rewards*. Many of the short stories in Adams's collection, *To See You Again*, have Bay Area settings.

Two books that are filled with interesting background information on the city are Richard H. Dillon's *San Francisco: Adventurers and Visionaries* and *San Francisco: As It Is, As It Was* by Paul C. Johnson and Richard Reinhardt.

For anecdotes, gossip, and the kind of detail that will make you feel almost like a native San Franciscan, get hold of any of the books by the longtime San Francisco *Chronicle* columnist Herb Caen: *Baghdad-by-the-Bay, Only in San Francisco, One Man's San Francisco*, and *San Francisco: City on Golden Hills*.

Arriving and Departing

By Plane

San Francisco International Airport is just south of the city, off U.S. 101. American carriers serving San Francisco are **Alaska Air, American, Continental, Delta, Southwest, TWA, United,** and **USAir.** International carriers include **Air Canada, Canadian Pacific, Japan Air Lines, British Airways, China Airlines, Qantas, Air New Zealand, Mexicana,** and **Pan American.** Many of these same airlines serve the Oakland Airport, which is across the bay but not much farther away from downtown San Francisco (via I-880 and I-80), although traffic on the Bay Bridge may at times make travel time longer.

When booking reservations, keep in mind the distinction between nonstop flights (no stops and no changes), direct flights (no changes of aircraft, but one or more stops), and connecting flights (one or more changes of planes at one or more stops). Connecting flights are often the least expensive, but they are the most time-consuming and the biggest nuisance.

Smoking As of late February 1990, smoking was banned on all scheduled routes within the 48 contiguous states; within the states of Hawaii and Alaska; to and from the U.S. Virgin Islands and Puerto Rico; and on flights of under six hours to and from Hawaii and Alaska. The rule applies to the domestic legs of all foreign routes but does not affect international flights.

On a flight where smoking is permitted, you can request a nonsmoking seat during check-in or when you book your ticket. If the airline tells you there are no seats available in the nonsmoking section on the day of the flight, insist on one: Department of Transportation regulations require U.S. carriers to find seats for all nonsmokers, provided they meet check-in time restrictions.

Luggage Regulations *Carry-on Luggage* New rules have been in effect since January 1988 on U.S. airlines with regard to carry-on luggage. The model for the new rules was agreed to by the airlines in December 1987 and then circulated by the Air Transport Association with the understanding that each airline would present its own version.

Under the model, passengers are limited to two carry-on bags. For a bag you wish to store under the seat, the maximum dimensions are 9″ × 14″ × 22″. For bags that can be hung in a closet or on a luggage rack, the maximum dimensions are 4″ × 23″ × 45″. For bags you wish to store in an overhead bin, the maximum dimensions are 10″ × 14″ × 36″. Your two carryons must each fit one of these sets of dimensions, and any item that exceeds the specified dimensions is generally rejected as a carryon and handled as checked baggage. Keep in mind that an airline can adapt these rules to circumstances; don't be surprised when you are allowed only one carry-on bag on an especially crowded flight.

The rules list eight items that may be carried aboard in addition to the two carryons: a handbag (pocketbook or purse), an overcoat or wrap, an umbrella, a camera, a reasonable amount of reading material, an infant bag, and crutches, a cane, braces, or other prosthetic device upon which the passenger is dependent. Infant/child safety seats can also be brought aboard if parents have purchased a ticket for the child or if there is space in the cabin; check with the airline before you go, however, because regulations concerning infant travel are in the process of being changed.

Note that these regulations are for U.S. airlines only. Foreign airlines generally allow one piece of carry-on luggage in tourist class, in addition to handbags and bags filled with duty-free goods. Passengers in first and business classes are also allowed to carry on one garment bag. It is best to check with your airline in advance to confirm its rules regarding carry-on luggage.

Checked Luggage U.S. airlines allow passengers to check two or three suitcases whose total dimensions (length + width + height) do not exceed 62" and whose weight does not exceed 70 pounds.

Rules governing foreign airlines vary from one airline to another, so check with your travel agent or the airline itself before you go. All airlines allow passengers to check two bags. In general, expect the weight restriction on the two bags to be not more than 70 pounds each, and the size restriction to be 62" total dimensions for each bag.

Lost Luggage Airlines are responsible for lost or damaged property only up to $1,250 per passenger on domestic flights; $9.07 per pound (or $20 per kilo) for checked baggage on international flights; and up to $400 per passenger for unchecked baggage on international flights. When you carry valuables, either take them with you on the airplane or purchase additional insurance for lost luggage. Some airlines will issue additional luggage insurance when you check in, but many do not. Rates are generally $1 for every $100 valuation, with a maximum of $25,000 valuation per passenger. Hand luggage is not included.

Insurance for lost, damaged, or stolen luggage is available through travel agents or from various insurance companies. Two that issue luggage insurance are Tele-Trip, a subsidiary of Mutual of Omaha, and The Travelers Corporation.

Tele-Trip (tel. 800/228–9792) operates sales booths at airports and issues insurance through travel agents. Tele-Trip will insure checked luggage for up to 180 days; rates vary according to the length of the trip.

The Travelers Corporation (Ticket and Travel Dept., 1 Tower Sq., Hartford, CT 06183, tel. 203/277–0111 or 800/243–3174) will insure checked or hand luggage for $500 to $2,000 valuation per person, for a maximum of 180 days. For 1 to 5 days, the rate for a $500 valuation is $10; for 180 days, $85. The two companies offer the same rates on both domestic and international flights. Consult the travel pages of your Sunday newspaper for the names of other companies that insure luggage. Before you travel, itemize the contents of each bag in case you need to file an insurance claim. Be certain to put your home address on each piece of luggage, including carry-on bags. If your luggage is stolen and later recovered, the airline will deliver the luggage to your home free of charge.

From the Airport to Downtown **SFO Airporter** (tel. 415/495–8404) provides bus service between downtown and the airport, making the round of downtown hotels. Buses run every 20 minutes from 5 AM to midnight, from the lower level outside the baggage claim area. The fare is $5 one-way.

For $9, **Supershuttle** will take you from the airport to anywhere within the city limits of San Francisco. At the airport, after picking up your luggage, call 415/871-7800 and a van will pick you up within five minutes. To go to the airport, make reservations (tel. 415/558-8500) 24 hours in advance. The Supershuttle shops at the upper level of the terminal, along with several other bus and van transport services.

Taxis to or from downtown take 20-30 minutes and average $30.

By Train

Amtrak (tel. 800/USA-RAIL) trains (the *Zephyr*, from Chicago via Denver, and the *Coast Starlight*, traveling between San Diego and Seattle) stop at the Oakland Depot; from there buses will take you across the Bay Bridge to the Transbay Terminal at 1st and Mission streets in San Francisco.

By Bus

Greyhound-Trailways serves San Francisco from the Transbay Terminal at 1st and Mission streets (tel. 415/558-6789).

By Car

Route I-80 finishes its westward journey from New York's George Washington Bridge at the Bay Bridge, linking Oakland and San Francisco. U.S. 101, running north-south through the entire state, enters the city across the Golden Gate Bridge and continues south down the peninsula, along the west side of the bay.

Car Rentals

The best approach to renting a car in San Francisco is to wait a day or two. First see how well suited the cable cars are to this city of hills, how well the Muni buses and streetcars get you around every neighborhood, how efficiently BART delivers you practically anywhere on the bay. Unless you're preparing to take excursions into Marin County or the Wine Country, you probably won't need to rent a car.

Major national companies such as **Hertz** (tel. 800/654-3131), **Avis** (tel. 800/331-1212), **National** (tel. 800/328-4567), and **Budget** (tel. 800/527-0770) have locations at the airport and in the Market Street area downtown. Average rates are $35-$45 daily for a subcompact with 75-100 free miles daily and a charge of 30¢ per mile after that.

San Francisco has many good budget rental-car companies: **Alamo** (tel. 800/327-9633), **American International** (tel. 800/527-0202), **Enterprise** (tel. 800/325-8007), and **Apple** (tel. 800/732-7753) are a few. At the other end of the price spectrum, **AutoExotica** (tel. 415/885-1100) rents a full line of Porsches, Lamborghinis, and other luxury cars. The San Francisco Visitor Information Office (tel. 415/391-2000) has a full list of area rental-car companies.

Find out a few essentials *before* you arrive at the rental counter. (Otherwise a sales agent could talk you into additional costs you don't need.) The major added cost in renting cars is usually the so-called collision damage waiver (CDW), generally an $8–$12 daily surcharge. Find out from the rental agency you're planning to use what the waiver will cover. Your own employee or personal insurance may already cover the damage to a rental car. If so, bring along a photocopy of the benefits section of your insurance policy.

More and more companies now hold renters responsible for theft and vandalism if they don't buy the CDW. In response, some credit card and insurance companies are extending their coverage to rental cars. These include **Dreyfus Bank Gold and Silver MasterCards** (tel. 800/847–9700), **Chase Manhattan Bank Visa Cards** (tel. 800/645–7352), and **Access America** (tel. 800/851–2800).

Also remember to ask about weekend and promotional rates when comparing prices, to get a reservation number, and to be sure you understand all the provisions of an agreement before you sign it. You will in many cases have to pay extra for the privilege of picking up a car in one location and dropping it off at another; it's best to inquire about the difference in cost.

Staying in San Francisco

Important Addresses and Numbers

Tourist Information The **San Francisco Convention and Visitors Bureau** maintains a visitors information center on the lower level at Hallidie Plaza (Powell and Market streets), just three blocks from Union Square, near the cable car turnaround and the Powell Street entrance to BART. *Weekdays 9–5, Sat. 9–3, Sun. 10–2. Tel. 415/974–6900. Summary of daily events: tel. 415/391–2001.*

Emergencies **Police** or **ambulance**, telephone 911.

Doctors Two hospitals with 24-hour emergency rooms are **San Francisco General Hospital** (1001 Potrero Ave., tel. 415/821–8200) and the **Medical Center at the University of California, San Francisco** (500 Parnassus Ave. at 3rd Ave., near Golden Gate Park, tel. 415/476–1000).
Access Health Care provides drop-in medical care at two San Francisco locations, daily 8–8. No membership is necessary. *1604 Union St. at Franklin St., tel. 415/775–7766; and 26 California St. at Drumm St., tel. 415/397–2881.*

Pharmacies Several **Walgreen Drug Stores** have 24-hour pharmacies, including stores at 500 Geary Street near Union Square (tel. 415/673–8413) and 3201 Divisadero Street at Lombard Street (tel. 415/931–6417). Also try the Walgreen pharmacy on Powell Street near Market Street. *135 Powell St., tel. 415/391–7222. Open Mon.–Sat. 8 AM–midnight, Sun. 9 AM–8 PM. AE, MC, V.*

Getting Around

Because San Francisco is relatively compact and because it's so very difficult to find parking, we recommend that you do your exploring on foot or by bus as much as possible. You may not need a car at all, except perhaps for exploring the Presidio, Golden Gate Park, Lincoln Park, the Western Shoreline, and for making excursions out of town.

How to Get There from Union Square is a handy free booklet that will tell you how to reach approximately 50 points of interest in the city by public transportation. You can pick it up at the Redwood Empire Association Visitor Information Center (1 Market Plaza, Spear St. Tower, Suite 1001, tel. 415/543–8334) on weekdays 9 AM–4:30 AM.

By BART **Bay Area Rapid Transit** (tel. 415/788–BART) sends air-conditioned aluminum trains at speeds of up to 80 miles an hour across the bay to Oakland, Berkeley, Concord, Richmond, and Fremont. Trains also travel south from San Francisco as far as Daly City. Wall maps in the stations list destinations and fares (85¢–$3). Trains run Mon.–Sat. 6 AM–midnight, Sun. 9 AM–midnight.

A $2.60 excursion ticket buys a three-county tour. You can visit any of the 34 stations for up to four hours as long as you exit and enter at the same station.

By Bus The **San Francisco Municipal Railway System,** or **Muni** (tel. 415/673–MUNI), includes buses and trolleys, surface streetcars, and the new below-surface streetcars, as well as cable cars. There is 24-hour service, and the fare is 85¢ for adults, 15¢ for senior citizens, and 25¢ for children ages 5–17. Exact change is always required. Free transfers are available.

A $6 pass good for unlimited travel all day ($10 for three days) on all routes can be purchased from ticket machines at cable car terminals.

By Cable Car "They turn corners almost at right angles; cross other lines, and for all I know, may run up the sides of houses," wrote Rudyard Kipling in 1889. In June 1984 the 109-year-old system returned to service after a $58.2 million overhaul. Because the cable cars had been declared a National Historic Landmark in 1964, renovation methods and materials had to preserve the historical and traditional qualities of Andrew Hallidie's system. The rehabilitated moving landmark has been designed to withstand another century of use.

The Powell-Mason line (No. 59) and the Powell-Hyde line (No. 60) begin at Powell and Market streets near Union Square and terminate at Fisherman's Wharf. The California Street line (No. 61) runs east and west from Market Street near the Embarcadero to Van Ness Avenue.

Cable cars are popular, crowded, and an experience to ride: Move toward one quickly as it pauses, wedge yourself into any available space, and hold on! The views from many cars are spectacular, and the sensation of moving up and down some of San Francisco's steepest hills in a small, open-air clanging conveyance is not to be missed.

The fare is $2 for adults, $1 for children 5–17. Exact change is required.

By Taxi Rates are high in the city, although most rides are relatively short. It is unfortunately almost impossible to hail a passing cab, especially on weekends. Either phone or use the nearest hotel taxi stand to grab a cab. See the Yellow Pages for numbers of taxi companies.

By Car Driving in San Francisco can be a challenge, what with the hills, the one-way streets, and the traffic. Take it easy, remember to curb your wheels when parking on hills, and use public transportation whenever possible. On certain streets, parking is forbidden during rush hours. Look for the warning signs; illegally parked cars are towed. This is a great city for walking and a terrible city for parking. Downtown parking lots are often full and always expensive. Finding a spot in North Beach at night, for instance, may be impossible.

Guided Tours

In selecting a tour, bear in mind that the size of the vehicle will affect the character of the tour to some degree. Smaller vans can go to spots where the larger buses cannot maneuver or are not permitted, such as the Marina and the Palace of Fine Arts. Drivers of vans are sometimes more amenable to stopping for picture taking.

Unless specifically noted, the costs given for guided tours do not include meals or refreshments.

Orientation Tours **Golden City Tours** offers 14-passenger vans for their six-hour city tours, which include a drive across the Golden Gate Bridge to Sausalito and a 1½-hour stopover at Fisherman's Wharf. (You also have the option of taking a ferry from Sausalito to the Wharf.) Customers are picked up at all major airport hotels. A shorter afternoon tour omits Sausalito. *Tel. 415/692–3044. Tours daily. Make reservations the day before. Cost: $28. Afternoon tour $18.50.*

Golden Gate Tours uses both vans and buses for its 3½-hour city tour, offered mornings and afternoons. You can combine the tour with a bay cruise. Customers are picked up at hotels and motels. Senior citizen and group rates are available. *Tel. 415/ 788–5775. Tours daily. Make reservations the day before. Cost: $20 adults, $10.50 children under 12, $18.50 senior citizens. Cruise combo: $26 adults, $15 children under 12, $24.50 senior citizens.*

Gray Line offers a variety of tours of the city, the Bay Area, and northern California. Their city tour, on buses or double-decker buses, lasts 3½ hours and departs from the Trans-Bay Terminal at 1st and Mission streets five to six times daily. Gray Line also picks up at centrally located hotels. *Tel. 415/558–9400. Tours daily. Make reservations the day before. Cost: $21.50 adults, $10.75 children.*

The Great Pacific Tour uses 13-passenger vans for its daily 3½-hour city tour. Bilingual guides may be requested. They pick up at major San Francisco hotels. Tours are available to Monterey, the Wine Country, and Muir Woods. *Tel. 415/626–4499. Tours daily. Make reservations the day before, or, possibly, the same day. Cost: $25 adults, $22 senior citizens, $18 children 5–11.*

Maxi Tour and Guides puts 13 passengers in the vans for its morning and afternoon 3- to 3½-hour city tours. With sufficient advance notice, driver-guides who speak French, German, Italian, or Spanish can be reserved. A Muir Woods/Sausalito tour and a Wine Country tour are also offered. Picks up at hotels. *Tel. 415/441–6294. Tours daily, except Dec. 25. Make reservations 1 to 2 days ahead; arrangements for foreign-language guides may take longer. Cost: $25 adults, reduced price for children.*

San Francisco Scenic Route. Near Escapes (Box 193005, San Francisco 94119, tel. 415/386–8687) has produced an audio cassette with music and sound effects that will take you in your own car "where the tour buses can't go." It will guide you past Fisherman's Wharf, Chinatown, Golden Gate Park, Twin Peaks, Ghirardelli Square, Mission Dolores, the Civic Center, and other tourist attractions. Another cassette offers a detailed walking tour of Chinatown; both come with route maps. They are available in a few local outlets, or you can get them mail-order for $12 (or $14 with Visa or MasterCard).

Starlane Tours operates 14-passenger vans, 25-passenger microbuses, and 47-passenger motor coaches. (Prices are the same for all.) Starlane picks up at hotels for its three daily city tours, which last 3½ hours and explore past and present and the diverse neighborhoods of San Francisco. Stops are made at Twin Peaks, the Japanese Tea Garden in Golden Gate Park, Cliff House, and Vista Point across the Golden Gate Bridge. A bay cruise or a visit to Alcatraz may be added. Nightclub, Chinatown, and San Francisco By Night tours are available in the evening. Muir Woods, the Wine Country, Marine World, Monterey, and Yosemite are also offered as one-day tours. *Tel. 415/ 982–2223. Tours daily. Make reservations the day before, or, possibly, the same day; for Alcatraz in summer, reserve several days in advance. Cost: $21 adults, $11 children; with bay cruise, $27 and $15; with Alcatraz, $30 and $16.*

Special-Interest Tours

Near Escapes (Box 3005-K, 94119, tel. 415/386–8687) plans unusual activities in the city and around the Bay Area. Recent tours and activities include tours of a Hindu temple in the East Bay, the Lawrence Berkeley Laboratory, the aircraft maintenance facility at the San Francisco Airport, and the quicksilver mines south of San Jose. The Julia Morgan Architectural Tour focuses on the work of one of the most prominent California architects of the early 20th century. Send $1 and a self-addressed, stamped envelope for a schedule for the month you plan to visit San Francisco.

Walking Tours

Castro District. Trevor Hailey leads a 3½-hour tour focusing on the history and development of the city's gay and lesbian community, including restored Victorian homes, shops and cafés, and the NAMES Project, home of the AIDS memorial quilt. Tours depart at 10 AM most days from Castro and Market streets. *Tel. 415/550–8110. Cost: $25, including breakfast or lunch.*

Chinatown with the "Wok Wiz." Cookbook author Shirley Fong-Torres leads a 3½-hour tour of Chinese markets, other businesses, and a fortune cookie factory. *Tel. 415/355–9657. Cost: $30, including lunch. Shorter tours, $15–$22.*

Chinese Cultural Heritage Foundation (tel. 415/986–1822) offers two walking tours of Chinatown. The Heritage Walk leaves Saturday at 2 PM and lasts about two hours. *Cost: $9 adults, $2 children under 12.* The Culinary Walk, a three-hour stroll through the markets and food shops, plus a dim sum lunch, is held every Wednesday at 10:30 AM. *Cost: $18 adults, $9 children.*

City Guides. The Friends of the Library run free walking tours all over the city, lasting 1–1½ hours, slightly longer on weekends. Tours include the Gold Rush City, Historic Market Street, City Hall, North Beach, Coit Tower, Golden Gate Bridge, and the Presidio. *For a monthly schedule, write (and send self-addressed, stamped envelope) to Friends of the Library—City Guides, San Francisco Public Library, Main Branch, Civic Center, San Francisco 94102, tel. 415/558–3981. No reservations. Admission free.*

Dashiell Hammett Tour. Don Herron gives four-hour, three-mile literary walking tours designed around the life of Hammett and his character Sam Spade. Tours depart between May and August at Saturday noon from the main library at 200 Larkin Street. *Tel. 415/564–7021. Cost: $5.*

Golden Gate Park. The Friends of Recreation and Parks (tel. 415/221–1311) offer free, guided 1½- to 2-hour walking tours of the park, May–October.

Heritage Walks. The Foundation for San Francisco's Architectural Heritage, headquartered in the Hass-Lilienthal House at 2007 Franklin Street, sponsors architectural tours of nearby Pacific Heights, with excursions to Russian Hill and the Presidio. *Tel. 415/441–3004. Cost: $3.*

2 Portrait of San Francisco

Living with the Certainty of a Shaky Future

by John Burks

John Burks is a professor of journalism and humanities at San Francisco State University. He has served as editor-in-chief of two of the city's leading magazines, City *and* San Francisco Focus, *was a* Newsweek *correspondent and managing editor of* Rolling Stone, *and currently edits the quarterly* American Kite.

There's never been any question *whether* there will be another earthquake in San Francisco. The question is how soon. Even the kids here grow up understanding that it's just a matter of time, and from grade school on, earthquake safety drills become routine. *At the first rumble, duck under your desk or table or stand in a doorway,* they are instructed. *Get away from windows to avoid broken glass. When the shaking stops, walk—don't run—outdoors, as far away from buildings as possible.*

Sure as there are hurricanes along the Gulf of Mexico and blizzards in Maine, San Francisco's earthquakes are inevitable. Nobody here is surprised when the rolling and tumbling begins—it happens all the time. Just in the six months following the jarring 1989 earthquake, for instance, seismologists reported hundreds of aftershocks, ranging from the scarcely perceptible to those strong enough to bring down buildings weakened by October's jolt.

The Bay Area itself was created in upheaval such as this. Eons ago, a restless geology of shifting plates deep in the earth gave birth to the Sierra Mountains and the Pacific Coast Range. Every spring when the snows melted, the runoff rushed down from the mile-high Sierra peaks westward across what would eventually be known as California. Here, the runoff ran up against the coastal range, and a vast inland lake was formed.

The rampaging waters from the yearly thaw eventually crashed through the quake-shattered Coast Range to meet the Pacific Ocean, creating the gap now spanned by the Golden Gate Bridge. This breakthrough created San Francisco Bay, one of the world's great natural harbors, its fertile delta larger than that of the Mississippi River. What a fabulous setting for the city-to-be—surrounded on three sides by water, set off by dramatic mountainscapes to the north and south, and blessed by cool ocean breezes.

All this and gold, too. The twisting and rolling of so-called terra firma exposed rich veins of gold at and near ground level that otherwise would have remained hidden deep underground. The great upheaval pushed the Mother Lode to the surface and set the scene for the Gold Rush. But before the '49 miners came the Europeans. In the late-15th century, the Spanish writer Garci Ordonez de Montalvo penned a fictional description of a place he called California, a faraway land ruled by Queen Califia, where gold and precious stones were so plentiful the streets were lined with them.

Montalvo's vision of wealth without limit helped fuel the voyages of the great 15th- and 16th-century European explorers in the new world. They never did hit pay dirt here, but the name California stuck nevertheless.

Northern California was eventually settled, and in 1848, the population of San Francisco was 832. The discovery of gold in the California hills brought sudden and unprecedented wealth to this coastal trading outpost and her population exploded; by the turn of the century San Francisco was home to 343,000 people.

En route to its destiny as a premier city of the West, San Francisco was visited by innumerable quakes. Yet while the city's very foundations shook, residents found that each new rattler helped to strengthen San Francisco's self-image of adaptability. Robert Louis Stevenson wrote of the quakes' alarming frequency: "The fear of them grows yearly in a resident; he begins with indifference and ends in sheer panic." The big shaker of 1865 inspired humorist Mark Twain to look at the quakes in a different light by writing an earthquake "almanac" for the following year, which advised:

Oct. 23—Mild, balmy earthquakes.
Oct. 26—About this time expect more earthquakes; but do not look for them . . .
Oct. 27—Universal despondency, indicative of approaching disaster. Abstain from smiling or indulgence in humorous conversation . . .
Oct. 29—Beware!
Oct. 31—Go slow!
Nov. 1—Terrific earthquake. This is the great earthquake month. More stars fall and more worlds are slathered around carelessly and destroyed in November than in any month of the twelve.
Nov. 2—Spasmodic but exhilarating earthquakes, accompanied by occasional showers of rain and churches and things.
Nov. 3—Make your will.
Nov. 4—Sell out.

On the whole, those who settled in San Francisco were more inclined toward Twain's devil-may-care attitude— those who succumbed to Stevenson's panic didn't stick around for long. Certainly the multitude of vices that saturated the metropolis were sufficient to distract many men from their fears; throughout Chinatown and the infamous Barbary Coast opium dens, gin mills, and bordellos operated day and night.

Money flowed. Money tempted. Money corrupted. The city was built on graft, and city hall became synonymous with corruption under the influence of political crooks like Blind Chris Buckley and Boss Ruef. The very building itself was a scandal. Planned for completion in six months at a cost of half a million dollars, the city hall ultimately took 29 years to build at a graft-inflated cost of $8 million, an astronomical sum at the dawning of the 20th century. When the San Andreas Fault set loose the 1906 earthquake, the most devastating ever to hit an American city, city hall was one of the first buildings to come crashing down. Its ruins exposed the shoddiest of building materials, an ironic symbol of the city's crime-ridden past.

The 1906 earthquake and fire has come to define San Francisco both for itself and the outside world. In the immediate aftermath of the catastrophe, San Franciscans wondered whether they ought to believe the preachers and reformers who declared that this terrible devastation had been wrought upon their wicked city by the avenging hand of God. San Franciscans asked themselves whether, somehow, they had earned it.

But the city was quick to prove its character. Fifty years earlier, six separate fires had destroyed most of San Francisco—yet each time it was rebuilt by a citizenry not ready to give up on either the gold or the city that gold had built. Now, in 1906, heroic firefighters dynamited one of the city's main thoroughfares to prevent the inferno from spreading all the way to the Pacific. The mood of San Franciscans was almost eerily calm, their neighborliness both heartwarming and jaunty. "Eat, drink, and be merry," proclaimed signs about town, "for tomorrow we may have to go to Oakland." No sooner had the flames died than rebuilding began—true to San Francisco tradition. Forty thousand construction workers poured into town to assist the proud, amazingly resilient residents.

The 1906 earthquake provided a chance to rethink the hodge-podge, get-rich-quick cityscape that had risen in the heat of Gold Rush frenzy. City fathers imported the revered urban planner Daniel Burnham, architect of the magnificent 1893 Chicago World's Fair, to re-invent San Francisco. "Make no little plans," Burnham intoned. "They have no power to stir men's souls."

The city's new Civic Center, built under Burnham's direction, was raised to celebrate the city's comeback and is regarded as one of America's most stately works of civic architecture. Its city hall stands as a monument to the city's will to prevail—from its colonnaded granite exterior to its exuberant interior, once described by Tom Wolfe as resembling "some Central American opera house. Marble arches, domes, acanthus leaves . . . quirks and galleries and gilt filigrees . . . a veritable angels' choir of gold." The inscription found over the mayor's office seems to sum it all up: "San Francisco, O glorious city of our hearts that has been tried and not found wanting, go thou with like spirit to make the future thine."

In 1915, San Francisco dazzled the world with its Panama–Pacific Exposition, designed to prove not only that it was back, but that it was back bigger and better and badder than ever before. An architectural wonderland, the Expo was built on 70 acres of marshy landfill, which later became the residential neighborhood called the Marina District. When the October 1989 earthquake struck, this neighborhood was badly damaged, and became a focus as the entire nation tuned in to see how San Francisco and her people would fare this time around.

Like the gold that surfaced in the Mother Lode, the 1989 quake once again brought out the best in this region's people. Out at Candlestick Park, 62,000 fans were waiting for the start of the World Series between the San Francisco Giants and the Oakland A's when everything started shaking. They cut loose with big cheer after the temblor subsided. One San Francisco fan quickly hand-lettered a sign and held it aloft: "That was Nothing—Wait Til the Giants Bat." When it became apparent that there would be no ball played that night, the fans departed from the ballpark, just like in a grade school earthquake safety drill, quietly and in good order.

This was what millions of TV viewers across the nation first saw of the local response to this major (7.1) earthquake and, by and large, the combination of good humor and relative calm they observed was an accurate reflection of the prevailing mood around the city. San Franciscans were not about to panic. Minutes after the quake struck, a San Francisco couple spread a lace tablecloth over the hood of their BMW and, sitting in the driveway of their splintered home, toasted passersby with champagne. Simultaneously, across San Francisco Bay, courageous volunteers and rescue workers set to work digging through the pancaked rubble of an Oakland freeway in the search for survivors, heedless that they, too, could easily be crushed in an aftershock. Throughout the Bay Area, hundreds volunteered to fight the fires, clear away the mess, assist survivors, and donate food, money, and clothing.

San Francisco's city seal features the image of a phoenix rising from the flames of catastrophe, celebrating the city's fiery past and promising courage in the face of certain future calamity. The 1989 shake possessed only about one-fortieth the force of the legendary 1906 quake, and all projections point to the inevitability of another Big One, someday, on at least the scale of '06. Often people from other, more stable, parts of the world have trouble understanding how it is possible to live with such a certainty.

The *San Francisco Bay Guardian*, shortly after the 1989 quake, spoke for many Bay Area residents: "We live in earthquake country. Everybody knows that. It's a choice we've all made, a risk we're all more or less willing to accept as part of our lives. We're gambling against fate, and last week our luck ran out. It was inevitable—as the infamous bumper sticker says, Mother Nature bats last."

Former San Francisco Mayor Diane Feinstein explained it this way: "Californians seem undaunted. We [know] we'll never be a match for Mother Nature. But the principal thing that seems to arise from the ash and rubble of a quake is the strong resolve to rebuild and get on with life."

3 Exploring San Francisco

Orientation

by Toni Chapman

*A San Francisco
travel and feature
writer whose
articles have
appeared in major
national and
international
magazines, Toni
Chapman
produces and hosts
a cable television
travel program.
She is a member of
the Society of
American Travel
Writers.*

Few cities in the world cram so much diversity into so little space. San Francisco is a relatively small city, with fewer than 750,000 residents nested on a 46.6-square-mile tip of land between San Francisco Bay and the Pacific Ocean.

San Franciscans cherish the city's colorful past, and many older buildings have been spared from demolition and nostalgically converted into modern offices and shops. For more than a century, the port city has been trafficking the peoples of the world. Today the city is again establishing strong commercial relations with the nations of the Pacific Rim. The unusually large number of residents with ties to other cultures flavors the cuisine, commerce, and charisma of the city. It also encourages a tolerance for deviations in customs and beliefs.

It's no accident that the San Francisco Bay Area has been a center for the environmental movement. An awareness of geographical setting permeates San Francisco life, with ever-present views of the surrounding mountains, ocean, and bay. Much of the city's neighborhood vitality comes from the distinct borders provided by its hills and valleys, and many areas are so named: Nob Hill, Russian Hill, Noe Valley. San Francisco neighborhoods are self-aware, and they retain strong cultural, political, and ethnic identities. Locals know this pluralism is the real life of the city. If you want to experience San Francisco, don't just stay downtown—visit the neighborhoods.

To do so you must navigate a maze of one-way streets and restricted parking zones. Public parking garages or lots tend to be expensive, as are the hotel parking spaces. The famed 40-plus hills can be a problem for drivers who are new to the terrain. People who know the city agree that one of the best ways to see and experience its many moods and neighborhoods is by foot. Those museums on wheels—the cable cars—or the numerous buses or trolleys can take you to or near many of the area's attractions. In the exploring tours that follow, we have often included information on public transportation.

Hills are a daily challenge to visitor and resident alike; good walking shoes are essential. Climate, too, is a consideration in deciding what to wear. There are dramatic temperature changes, especially in summer, when the afternoon fog rolls in. Winds are often a problem, both on the bay and cityside. Year-round, layered clothing are most adaptable to changing conditions; a cap or scarf and sunglasses are useful. Casual city togs are appropriate; shorts and tank tops are for southern California's climate.

Numbers in the margin correspond with points of interest on the Downtown San Francisco map.

Tour 1: Union Square

Since 1850 Union Square has been the heart of San Francisco's downtown. Its name derives from a series of violent pro-Union demonstrations staged in this hilly area just prior to the Civil War. This area is where you will find the city's finest department stores and most elegant boutiques. There are 40 hotels within a three-block walk of the square, and the downtown theater district is nearby.

The square itself is a 2.6-acre oasis planted with palms, box-wood, and seasonal flowers, peopled with a kaleidoscope of characters: office workers sunning and brown-bagging, street musicians, always at least one mime, several vocal and deter-mined preachers, and the ever-increasing parade of panhan-dlers. Smartly dressed women and camera-laden tourists usually hurry past the denizens. Throughout the year, the square hosts numerous public events: fashion shows, free noon-time concerts, ethnic celebrations, and noisy demonstrations. Auto and bus traffic is often gridlocked on the four streets bor-dering the square. Post, Stockton, and Geary are one-way, while Powell runs in both directions until it crosses Geary, where it then becomes a one-way street to Market Street. Un-ion Square covers a convenient but costly four-story under-ground garage. Close to 3,000 cars use it on busy holiday shopping and strolling days.

❶ Any visitor's first stop should be the **San Francisco Visitors In-formation Center** (tel. 415/391–2000) on the lower level of Hallidie Plaza at Powell and Market streets. It is open daily, and the multilingual staff will answer specific questions as well as provide maps, brochures, and information on daily events. The office provides 24-hour recorded information (tel. 415/391–2001).

❷ The **cable car terminus,** also at Powell and Market streets, is the starting point for two of the three operating lines. The Powell-Mason line climbs up Nob Hill, then winds through North Beach to Fisherman's Wharf. The Powell-Hyde car also crosses Nob Hill, but then continues up Russian Hill and down Hyde Street to Victorian Park across from the Buena Vista Cafe and near Ghirardelli Square.

Andrew Hallidie introduced the system in 1873 when he dem-onstrated his first car on Clay Street. In 1964 the tramlike vehi-cles were designated national historic landmarks. Before 1900 there were 600 cable cars spanning a network of 100 miles. To-day there are 39 cars in the three lines, and the network covers just 12 miles. Most of the cars date from the last century, al-though the cars and lines had a complete $58 million overhaul during the early 1980s. There are seats for about 30 passen-gers, with usually that number standing or strap-hanging. If possible, plan your cable car ride for mid-morning or mid-after-noon during the week to avoid crowds. In summertime there are often long lines to board any of the three systems. (*See* Get-ting Around by Cable Car in Chapter 1.)

❸ A two-block stroll north along bustling Powell Street leads to **Union Square** with its fashionable stores, fine hotels, and photogenic flower stalls. At center stage, the **Victory Monu-ment** by Robert Ingersoll Aitken commemorates Commodore George Dewey's victory over the Spanish fleet at Manila in 1898. The 97-foot Corinthian column, topped by a bronze figure symbolizing naval conquest, was dedicated by President Theo-dore Roosevelt in 1903 and withstood the 1906 earthquake.

After the earthquake and fire in 1906, the square was dubbed "Little St. Francis" because of the temporary shelter erected for residents of the St. Francis Hotel. The actor John Barry-more was among the guests pressed into volunteering to stack bricks in the square. His uncle, thespian John Drew, remarked,

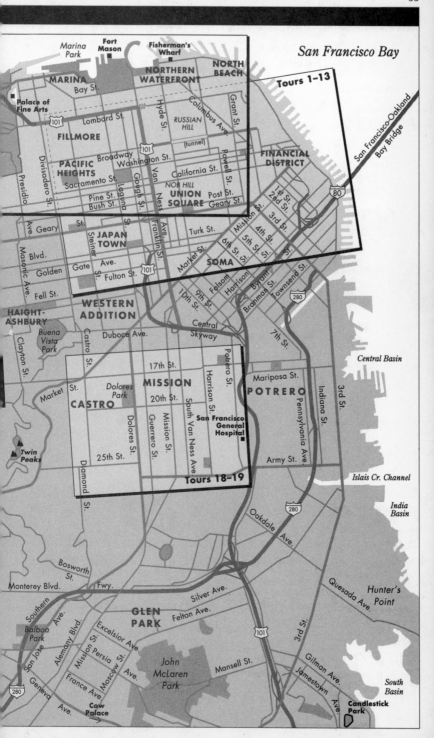

San Francisco Bay

Tours 1–13

Tours 18–19

Downtown San Francisco: Tours 1-13

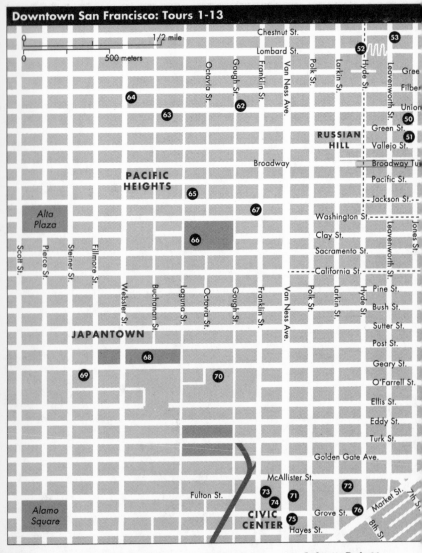

San Francisco Bay

TELEGRAPH HILL

NORTH BEACH

NOB HILL

CHINATOWN

FINANCIAL DISTRICT

UNION SQUARE

SOMA

N

"It took an act of God to get John out of bed and the United States government to get him to work."

❹ The Westin St. Francis Hotel, on the southwest corner of Post and Powell, was built here in 1904 and was gutted by the 1906 disaster. The second-oldest hotel in the city was conceived by Charles Crocker and his associates as an elegant hostelry for their millionaire friends. Swift service and sumptuous surroundings were hallmarks of the property. A sybarite's dream, the hotel's Turkish baths had ocean water piped in. A new, larger, more luxurious residence was opened in 1907 to attract loyal clients from among the world's rich and powerful. Today you can relax over a traditional teatime or opt for champagne and caviar in the dramatic Art Deco Compass Rose lounge in the lobby. Elaborate Chinese screens, secluded seating alcoves, and soothing background music make it an ideal time-out after frantic shopping or sightseeing. For dining, before or after the theater (within walking distance), visit the award-winning Victor's. After a breathtaking ride up 30-plus stories in an outside, glass-walled elevator, guests enter a warm, wood-paneled lobby area with recessed bookshelves housing leather-bound classics. Floor-to-ceiling windows offer spectacular views of the bay and the city. Superb California cuisine is enhanced by a select list of California and French wines.

❺ Both the Geary and Curran theaters are a few blocks west on Geary Street. The **Geary** (415 Geary St., tel. 415/749–2228) is home of the American Conservatory Theatre. Now in its 26th season, A.C.T. is one of North America's leading repertory companies. The 1,300-seat house normally offers a 34-week season to 20,000 subscribers, presenting both classical and contemporary dramas. The theater was closed indefinitely as a result of the October 1989 earthquake, and currently productions are being run at the Stage Door theater (420 Mason St.) and elsewhere until repairs are complete. Its main box office **❻** remains open. The **Curran** (445 Geary St., tel. 415/474–3800) is noted for showcasing traveling companies of Broadway shows.

❼ The **San Francisco Ticket Box Office Service** (STBO, tel. 415/433–STBS) has booths on both the Stockton Street side of Union Square, opposite Maiden Lane, and in Embarcadero One. Open from noon till 7:30 PM, Tuesday through Saturday, it provides day-of-performance tickets (cash or traveler's checks only) to all types of performing arts events at half price, as well as regular full-price box-office services. Telephone reservations are not accepted.

❽ Just a dash up from STBS, the newly renovated **Grand Hyatt San Francisco** (345 Stockton St.) offers exciting city views from its lounge, the Club 36. Stop and examine sculptor Ruth Asawa's fantasy fountain honoring the city's hills, bridges, and unusual architecture plus a wonder world of real and mythical creatures. Ms. Asawa was born in Los Angeles County but has lived in San Francisco since 1949. Children and friends helped Ms. Asawa shape the hundreds of tiny figures created from baker's clay and then assembled on 41 large panels from which molds were made for the bronze casting. The artist's distinctive designs decorate many public areas in the city. You can see her famous mermaid fountain at Ghirardelli Square.

❾ Across the street is the small, deluxe **Campton Place Hotel** (340 Stockton St.). Opened in 1983, it is the ultimate in sumptuous furnishings, quiet elegance, and superior service. The dining room is a palette of peach, ivory, and gray tones; fresh flowers and handsome table appointments create a charming ambience.

⑩ Pop around the corner into **Maiden Lane,** which runs from Stockton to Kearny streets. Known as Morton Street in the raffish Barbary Coast era, this red-light district reported at least one murder a week. But the 1906 fire destroyed the brothels and the street emerged as Maiden Lane. It has since become a chic and pricey mall. The two blocks are closed to vehicles from 11 AM until 4 PM. During the day, take-out snacks can be enjoyed while resting under the gay, umbrella-shaded tables. Masses of daffodils and bright blossoms and balloons bedeck the lane during the annual spring festival. A carnival mood prevails, with zany street musicians, artsy-craftsy people, and throngs of spectators.

⑪ Note **140 Maiden Lane:** This handsome brick structure is the only Frank Lloyd Wright building in San Francisco. With its circular interior ramp and skylights, it is said to have been a model for his designs for the Guggenheim Museum in New York. It now houses the **Circle Gallery,** a showcase of contemporary artists. Be sure to study the unique limited-edition art jewelry designed by internationally acclaimed Erté. *Open Mon.–Sat. 10–6, Sun. 11–5.*

⑫ The **Crocker Galleria** (Post and Kearny Sts., tel. 415/392–0100) is an imaginatively designed three-level complex of fine dining and shopping establishments capped by a dazzling glass dome. One block north of Kearny, Sutter Street is lined by prestigious art galleries, antiques dealers, smart hotels, and noted designer boutiques. Art Deco aficionados will want to linger at the
⑬ striking medical/dental office building at **450 Sutter Street.** Handsome Mayan-inspired designs are used in both exterior and interior surfaces of the 1930 terra-cotta-colored skyscraper.

Time Out Most stores and shops here open at about 9:30–10 AM. Venturing out early and settling down to a leisurely breakfast before the day's traffic and shoppers hit in full force is a nice way to ease into a busy day of sightseeing. **Mama's** (398 Geary St.) has always been a favorite for either light or full-breakfast selections. Or blow the day's meal budget at **Campton Place Hotel.** Wonderful breads and muffins, delicious hash, and out-of-season fruits are lavishly served. *340 Stockton St., tel. 415/781–5155. Reservations advised for brunch. Open weekdays 7–11 AM, Sat. 8–11:30 AM, Sun. brunch 8 AM–2:30 PM.*

Serious shoppers will find the entire Union Square area richly rewarding. Bordering the square itself are leading department and specialty stores. **I. Magnin & Co.,** on the south side of Union Square at Stockton Street, is noted for its designer fashions, magnificent fur salon, and in-house fine jeweler, Laykin & Cie. Just across Stockton Street is the checkerboard-faced **Neiman Marcus,** opened in 1982. Philip Johnson's controversial design replaced an old San Francisco favorite, the City of Paris; all that remains is the great glass dome. **Macy's,** with entrances on Geary, Stockton and O'Farrell streets, has huge selections of clothing for all members of the family, plus extensive furniture and household accessories departments. The men's department—one of the world's largest—occupies its own building across Stockton Street. Opposite is the new **FAO Schwarz** children's store, with its extravagant assortment of life-size stuffed animals, animated displays, and steep prices. **Saks Fifth Avenue,** at the northwest corner of the square at Post and Powell streets, still caters to the upscale shopper. Nearby are the pricey international boutiques of Hermes of Paris, Gucci, Celine of Paris, Alfred Dunhill, Louis Vuitton, and Cartier. (*See* Chapter 4.)

(14) Across Market Street from the cable car turnaround, the rehabilitated corner of 5th Street is now occupied by the gleaming **San Francisco Centre.** Opened in October 1988, this urban mall is anchored by the huge **Nordstrom's** department store. Its glass-topped circular court and spiral escalators lead to over 35 other stores. Foot-weary shoppers can rejuvinate themselves at **Spa Nordstrom** on the fifth floor, or lunch in the **City Centre Grille,** overlooking Market Street.

Tour 2: The Financial District

The heart of San Francisco's financial district is Montgomery Street. It was here in 1848 that Sam Brannan proclaimed the historic gold discovery on the American River. At that time, all the streets below Montgomery between California and Broadway were wharves. At least 100 ships were abandoned by frantic crews and passengers all caught up in the '49 gold fever. Many of the wrecks served as warehouses or were used as foundations for new constructions.

The financial district is roughly bordered by Kearny Street on the west, Washington Street on the north, and Market Street on the southeast. On workdays it is a congested canyon of soaring skyscrapers, gridlock traffic, and bustling pedestrians. In the evenings and on weekends the quiet streets allow walkers to admire the distinctive architecture. Unfortunately, the museums in corporate headquarters are closed then.

(15) The city's most photographed high rise is the 853-foot **Transamerica Pyramid** at 600 Montgomery Street, between Clay and Washington streets at the end of Columbus Avenue. Designed by William Pereira and Associates in 1972, the $34 million controversial symbol has become more acceptable to local purists as it gained San Francisco instant recognition worldwide. There is a public viewing area on the 27th floor (open weekdays 8–4). You can relax in a redwood grove along the east side of the building.

(16) The granite and marble **Bank of America** building dominates the territory bounded by California, Pine, Montgomery, and Kearny streets. The 52-story polished red granite complex is crowned by a chic cocktail and dining restaurant. As in almost all corporate headquarters, the interiors display impressive original art, while outdoor plazas include avant-garde sculptures. A massive abstract black granite sculpture designed by the Japanese artist Masayuki in the mall has been dubbed the "Banker's Heart" by local wags.

Soaring 52 stories above the financial district, the Bank of America's **Carnelian Room** (tel. 415/433–7500) offers elegant and pricey dining with a nighttime view of the city lights. This is an excellent spot for a drink at sunset. By day, the room is the exclusive Banker's Club, open to members or by invitation. For a Chinese dinner with a French touch, try **Tommy Toy's** (655 Montgomery St.). Mr. Toy has re-created the opulent splendor of the 19th-century Empress Dowager's reading room. (The prices reflect the decor.)

⑰ Diagonally across Montgomery Street is the **Wells Fargo Bank History Museum** (420 Montgomery St.). There were no formal banks in San Francisco during the early years of the Gold Rush, and miners often entrusted their gold dust to saloon keepers. In 1852 Wells Fargo opened its first bank in the city, and the company established banking offices in the Mother Lode camps using stagecoaches and pony express riders to service the burgeoning state. (California's population had boomed from 15,000 to 200,000 between 1848 and 1852.) The History Museum displays samples of nuggets and gold dust from major mines, a mural-size map of the Mother Lode, original art by Western artists Charlie Russell and Maynard Dixon, mementos of the poet bandit Black Bart, and letters of credit and old bank drafts. The showpiece is the red, century-old Concord stagecoach, which in the mid-1850s carried 15 passengers from St. Louis to San Francisco in three weeks. *Admission free. Open banking days 9–5.*

⑱ The **Russ Building** (235 Montgomery St.) was called "the skyscraper" when it was built in 1927. The Gothic design was modeled after the Chicago Tribune Tower, and until the 1960s was San Francisco's tallest—at just 31 stories. Prior to the 1906 earthquake and fire, the site was occupied by the Russ House, considered one of the finest hostelries in the city.

⑲ The **Mills Building and Tower** (220 Montgomery St.) was the outstanding prefire building in the financial district. The 10-story all-steel construction had its own electric plant in the basement. The original Burnham and Root design of white marble and brick was erected in 1891–92. Damage from the 1906 fire was slight; its walls were somewhat scorched but were easily refurbished. Two compatible additions east on Bush Street were added in 1914 and 1918 by Willis Polk, and in 1931 a 22-story tower completed the design.

Ralph Stackpole's monumental 1930 granite sculptural groups, *Earth's Fruitfulness* and *Man's Inventive Genius*, flank another imposing structure, the **Pacific Stock Exchange** (which dates
⑳ from 1915), on the south side of Pine Street at Sansome Street. The Stock Exchange Tower around the corner at 155 Sansome Street is a 1930 modern classic by architects Miller and Pfleuger, featuring an Art Deco gold ceiling and black marble-walled entry. *Pacific Stock Exchange, 301 Pine St., 94104, tel. 415/393–4000. Tours by 2-week advance reservation; minimum 8 persons.*

Stroll down Sansome Street and turn right on Sutter Street.
㉑ The **Hallidie Building** (130 Sutter St. between Kearny and Montgomery Sts.) was built as an investment by the University of California Regents in 1918 and named for cable car inventor and university regent Andrew S. Hallidie. It is believed to be the world's first all-glass-curtain-wall structure. Architect Willis Polk's revolutionary design hangs a foot beyond the reinforced concrete of the frame. It dominates the block with its reflecting glass, decorative exterior fire escapes that appear to

be metal balconies, the Venetian Gothic cornice, and horizontal ornamental bands of birds at feeders.

Time Out At lunchtime on weekdays you can rub elbows with power brokers and politicians in venerable **Jack's Restaurant** (615 Sacramento St., tel. 415/986–9854). Opened in 1864 and a survivor of the quake, Jack's is a purveyor of traditional American fare—steaks, chops, seafood, and stews. Reservations are suggested.

For excellent fresh seafood, San Franciscans in the know go to **Sam's Grill** (374 Bush St., tel. 415/421–0594). It's so popular for lunch you must arrive before 11:30 for even a chance at a table. Dinner service stops at 8:30, and Sam's is closed on weekends.

Tour 3: The Embarcadero and Lower Market Street

In one instance, the 1989 Loma Prieta earthquake changed San Francisco for the better: The Embarcadero freeway had to be torn down, making the foot of Market Street clearly visible for the first time in 30 years. The trademark of the port is the ㉒ quaint **Ferry Building** that stands at the Embarcadero. The clock tower is 230 feet high and was modeled by Arthur Page Brown after the campanile of Seville's cathedral. The four great clock faces on the tower, powered by the swinging action of a 14-foot pendulum, stopped at 5:17 on the morning of April 18, 1906, and stayed that way for the following 12 months. The 1896 building survived the quake and is now the headquarters of the Port Authority and the World Trade Center. A waterfront promenade that extends from this point to the Oakland Bay Bridge is great for jogging, watching the sailboats on the bay (if the day is not too windy), or enjoying a picnic. Ferries from here sail to Sausalito, Larkspur, and Tiburon.

Strolling back up Market Street, one's attention is drawn to the ㉓ huge **Embarcadero Center** complex. Frequently called "Rockefeller Center West," its eight buildings include over 100 shops, 40 restaurants, and two hotels, as well as high-rise residential towers and town-house condos. A three-tiered pedestrian mall links the buildings, and much attention has been given to attractive landscaping throughout the development. Louise Nevelson's dramatic 54-foot-high black-steel sculpture, "Sky Tree," stands guard over Building 3.

Time Out **Splendido's** (Embarcadero Center Four, tel. 415/986–3222) is a comfortable Mediterranean inn nestled amid the high rises. Its Italianate California cuisine, featuring fresh grilled meats and unusual marinades, has made this spot an instant classic. Lunch is the most popular meal here, and its always very crowded, so try to reserve ahead.

㉔ The **Hyatt Regency Hotel** (5 Embarcadero) was designed by John Portman and is noted for its spectacular lobby and 20-story hanging garden. Just in front of the hotel is the Justin Herman Plaza. There are arts and crafts shows, street musicians, and mimes here on weekends year-round. Kite-flying is popular here. A huge concrete sculpture, the Vaillancourt Fountain, has had legions of critics since its installation in 1971; most of the time the fountain does not work, and many feel it is an eyesore.

㉕ The venerable **Sheraton-Palace Hotel** was recently restored and has resumed its place among San Francisco's grandest. Opened in 1875, the hotel was one of the city's most elegant lodging facilities. Destroyed by fire following the 1906 earthquake, it was rebuilt in 1909 and reopened on the site at Market and New Montgomery streets. Over $135 million has been spent on renovations, which included the restoration of the sumptuous glass-domed Garden Court and the installation of original mosaic tile floors in Oriental-rug designs. Maxfield Parrish's wall-size painting, *The Pied Piper*, which is currently housed in the de Young Museum, will return to the Pied Piper Room.

㉖ The **Old San Francisco Mint**, at 5th and Mission streets, reopened as a museum in 1973. The century-old brick-and-stone building exhibits a priceless collection of gold coins. Visitors tour the vaults and can strike their own souvenir medal on an 1869 press. *Admission free. Open weekdays 10–4.*

Tour 4: South of Market (SoMa)

The vast tract of downtown land south of Market Street along the waterfront and west to the Mission district is now known by the acronym SoMa (patterned after New York City's south-of-Houston SoHo). Formerly known as South of the Slot because of the cable-car slot that ran up Market Street, the area has a history of housing recent immigrants to the city—beginning with tents set up in 1848 by the gold-rush miners and continuing for decades. Except for a brief flowering of English-inspired elegance during the mid-19th century in the pockets of South Park and Rincon Hill, the area was reserved for newcomers who couldn't yet afford to move to another neighborhood. Industry took over most of the area when the big earthquake collapsed most of the homes into their quicksand bases.

Ten years ago the San Francisco Redevelopment Agency grabbed 87 acres of run-down downtown land, leveled anything that stood on them, and began the largest building program in
㉗ the city's history: **Yerba Buena Center.** Over $1.5 billion will be used to bring new developments onto the site. Much of the project is still in the planning stage, but it will eventually include, along with the already completed hotel and convention center, the new Museum of Modern Art, a performing arts theater, and a rarity for downtown—open space. The neighborhood has already been transformed in unforeseen ways. As soon as the Moscone Convention Center was completed in 1981, the area became a focal point for cultural and architectural urban gentrification.

For years industrial South of Market had been a stomping ground for the gay leather set, and a dozen bars frequented by the group had existed alongside warehouses and small factories. But the increasing visibility of gay culture, joined with redevelopment fervor, gave South of Market a social sanction it hadn't had for a hundred years. As the AIDS crisis bore down particularly on sexually promiscuous gay men, the gay bars began to be replaced by trendier straight ones. Within a few years, South of Market was transformed into SoMa, a center for San Francisco nightclubbing, dining, and gallery hopping.

There are really two SoMas, one during the day and the other at night; one for businesspeople, the other for the (mostly

28 young) leisure class. The **Moscone Convention Center,** on Howard Street between 3rd and 4th streets, remains the centerpiece of the redevelopment area. It is distinguished by a contemporary glass-and-girder lobby at street level (most of the exhibit space is underground) and a monolithic, column-free interior that was the site of the 1983 Democratic convention. In 1989 the center began a $150 million expansion project that will double its size, with planned additions to the roof of the existing facility, and new exhibit space underneath the adjacent park. The work will go on through 1992, though the center will continue to be in use.

Up 4th Street from the Moscone Convention Center you can't **29** miss the new **San Francisco Marriott at Moscone Center** (777 Market St.), the latest architectural curiosity to have the city in an uproar. Its 40-story ziggurat construction topped with reflecting glass pinwheels has elicited gasps from newspaper columnists and passersby alike, earning it comparisons with a juke box, a high-rise parking meter, and a giant rectal thermometer. It takes its civic place in a long line of blooper buildings in The City (the Transamerica pyramid; the old Jack Tar—now the Cathedral Hill—Hotel; and the San Francisco Federal Building) that keep the city talking and passing newer and newer building ordinances. Whether San Franciscans will come to embrace the building—as they have the Transamerica pyramid—is an open question; what's certain is that the hotel's 1,500 rooms already lure many of the city's 500,000 yearly visiting conventioneers. The new Marriott contains the city's largest ballroom, a complete health spa, and seven restaurants.

30 One block away, Air France's deluxe 32-story **Meridien San Francisco** (50 3rd St.) was itself a building of some architectural controversy, placed crosswise at the end of its street.

For daytime activities the rest of SoMa may be considered "under construction," but for nighttime entertainment it's ready to go. The hottest area is around 11th Street, with its mix of nightclubs and restaurants. **The Oasis** (11th and Folsom Sts., tel. 415/621–8119) was the club that started luring straights back to a predominantly gay neighborhood, with its pool-on-the-premises parties and live music. The **DNA Lounge** (375 11th St., tel. 415/626–1409) has a more aggressive new-wave attitude, and at the **Paradise Lounge** (11th and Folsom Sts., tel. 415/861–6906) you can catch such oddball specialty acts as chanteuse Connie Champagne and her Tiny Bubbles.

Slim's (333 11th St., tel. 415/621–3330) is Huey Lewis's new club on the block, and with its focus on "American roots" rock/rhythm-and-blues music it should be around for a while.

Time Out There are several fine restaurants in the area, but for atmosphere none of them can compare with good ol' rockin' and rollin' **Hamburger Mary's.** The decor is funky, the music loud, the clientele polymorphous, and the thick hamburgers served on slices of nine-grain bread and piled high with grilled onions. Probably no place in the city has been able to mix straights and gays in the same place so successfully and keep the feeling of urban adventurousness bordering on party. *1582 Folsom St., tel. 415/626–5767. Open Mon.–Fri. 11 AM–2 AM, Sat.–Sun. 10 AM–2 AM.*

SoMa is where artists live, hang out, and also show their work in several galleries on the cutting edge of San Francisco's art scene. **Artspace** (1286 Folsom St., tel. 415/626–9100) operates more like a museum than a gallery, highlighting new artists in a not-for-sale setting. **New Langton Arts** (1246 Folsom St., tel. 415/626–5416) is one of the city's longest-surviving alternative exhibit and performance spaces. Its focus is mixed-media and performance art, and it offers a provocative series of readings and talks. **Eye Gallery** (1151 Mission St., tel. 415/431–6911) and **San Francisco Camerawork** (70 12th St., tel. 415/621–1001), as their names imply, turn the light on up-and-coming photographers.

The **Ansel Adams Center** (250 4th St., tel. 415/495–7000) showcases both historical and contemporary photography, with a permanent collection of Adams's own work. *Admission: $4 adults, $3 students, $2 youths 12–17 and senior citizens, children under 12 free. Open Tues.–Sun. 11–6.*

A new restaurant row has taken shape down Folsom Street between 7th and 8th streets. **Julie's Supper Club** (1123 Folsom St., tel. 415/861–0707), is the most distinctive, with its pink-and-black '50s decor, curved leatherette bar, and ambience designed for drinking martinis. **Rings** (1131 Folsom St., tel. 415/621–2111) has seasonal cuisine prepared on a mesquite grill; **Eddie Jacks** (1151 Folsom St., tel. 415/626–2388) is internationally nouvelle; **Milano Joe's** (1175 Folsom St., tel. 415/861–2815) is a high-tech palace with northern Italian cooking; and the **Half Shell** (64 Rausch St., tel. 415/552–7677), in little Rausch alley, specializes in seafood. Be sure to take a closer look at **Brain Wash** (1122 Folsom St., tel. 415/431–9274), the very unique combination laundromat and café! Where else can you go to socialize and get your housework done at the same time?

In keeping with SoMa's tradition of being the underside of the city, it now offers you the underside of shopping: discount outlets. On Saturdays, the small alleys between 3rd and 7th streets and between Townsend and Harrison streets are crowded with hungry shoppers looking to save that magic 50%. Start at 3rd Street between Brannan and Townsend streets; there are 20 discount shops at the 660 Center Arcade, offering everything from designer fashions to Icelandic sweaters. A few blocks south, near China Basin, the casual emporium **Esprit** has its huge outlet store, with a café for weary bargain-hunters on the premises. *499 Illinois St., tel. 415/957–2550. Open weekdays 10–8, Sat. 10–7, Sun. 11–5.*

Tour 5: Jackson Square

In the Gay Nineties San Francisco had earned the title of "the Wickedest City in the World." The saloons, dance halls, cheap hotels, and brothels of its Barbary Coast attracted sailors and gold rushers. Most of this red-light district was destroyed in **31** the 1906 fire; what remains is now part of **Jackson Square.** A stroll through this district recalls some of the romance and rowdiness of early San Francisco.

Some of the city's earliest business buildings still stand in the blocks of Jackson Square between Montgomery and Sansome streets. By the end of World War II, most of the 1850 brick structures had fallen on hard times. In 1951, however, things changed. A group of talented, preservation-minded designers and furniture wholesale dealers selected the centrally located, depressed area for their showrooms. By the 1970s, the reclaimed two- and three-story renovated brick buildings were acclaimed nationwide. In 1972 the city officially designated the area—bordered by Columbus Avenue on the west, a line between Broadway and Pacific Avenue on the north, Washington on the south, and Sansome Street on the east—as San Francisco's first historic district. Seventeen buildings were given landmark status.

Jackson Square became the interior design center of the West. Unfortunately, property values soared, forcing many of the fabric and furniture outlets to move to the developing Potrero Hill section. Advertising agencies, attorneys, and antiques dealers now occupy the charming renovations.

The Ghirardelli Chocolate Factory was once housed at **415 Jackson.** In 1857 Domenico Ghirardelli moved both his growing business and his family into this property. It was quite common for the upper floors of these buildings to be used as flats by either the building's owners or its tenants. By 1894 Ghirardelli had moved his expanding chocolate enterprise to Ghirardelli Square.

Another historic building is the former A. P. Hotaling and Company whiskey distillery at **451 Jackson.** This handsome brick building retains the iron shutters installed in 1866 to "fireproof" the house.

Around the corner, south toward Washington, is the much-photographed compound at **722–28 Montgomery Street,** headquarters of Melvin Belli, the "King of Torts," one of the nation's most flamboyant attorneys. Mr. Belli has rejuvenated these nostalgic relics with red plush and gaslight Victorian splendor. Neighbors have emulated this rich period decor.

The **Golden Era Building** at 732 Montgomery Street also dates from the 1850s. It was the home of the most substantial literary periodical published locally during the 1850s and 1860s. Mark Twain and Bret Harte were two of its celebrated contributors.

Time Out Big windows, white walls, and chains of red peppers, garlic, and sausage set the stage for homemade pastas, charcoal-broiled seafood, and select wines, all of which make **Ciao** a special stop for lunch or dinner. *230 Jackson St., tel. 415/982–9500. Dinner reservations advised.*

The mood at **Ernie's** on Montgomery Street near Pacific Avenue is dramatically different. Its sumptuous Barbary Coast elegance, talented young chef, and outstanding wine selection have attracted the rich and famous for over 25 years. *847 Montgomery St., tel. 415/397–5969. Reservations required. Dress: formal.*

Tour 6: Chinatown

A city within a city, this is the largest Chinese community outside of Asia. Approximately 100,000 Chinese live in a 24-block downtown area just south of North Beach (and in the Richmond district's "New Chinatown"). Chinatown has been revitalized by the fairly recent immigration of Southeast Asians, who have added new character and life to the neighborhood. Downtown

Chinatown is officially defined as an area reaching from Bay Street south to California Street and from Sansome Street at the edge of downtown west to Van Ness Avenue; these boundaries actually include much of Russian Hill and Nob Hill.

Visitors usually enter Chinatown through the green-tiled dragon-crowned **Chinatown Gate** at Bush Street and Grant Avenue. To best savor this district, explore it on foot (it's not far from Union Square), even though you may find the bustling, noisy, colorful stretches of Grant and Stockton streets north of Bush difficult to navigate. Parking is extremely hard to find, and traffic is impossible. As in Hong Kong, most families shop daily for fresh meats, vegetables, and bakery products. This street world shines with much good-luck crimson and gold; giant beribboned floral wreaths mark the opening of new bakeries, bazaars, and banks.

San Francisco has pioneered the resurrection of Chinese regional cooking for American palates. Cantonese cuisine, with its familiar staples of chow mein and chop suey (said to be invented in San Francisco by Gold Rush–era Chinese cooks) now exists alongside spicier Szechuan, Hunan, and Mandarin specialties. With almost 100 restaurants squeezed into a 14-block area, Chinatown offers plenty of food. In the windows of markets on Stockton Street and Grant Avenue you can see roast ducks hanging, fresh fish and shellfish swimming in tanks, and strips of Chinese-style barbecued pork shining in pink glaze. The streets are crowded day and night.

The handsome brick **Old St. Mary's Church** at Grant and California streets served as the city's Catholic cathedral until 1891. Granite quarried in China was used in the structure, which was dedicated in 1854. Diagonally across the intersection is **St. Mary's Park,** a tranquil setting for local sculptor Beniamino (Benny) Bufano's heroic stainless-steel and rose-colored granite Sun Yat Sen. The 12-foot statue of the founder of the Republic of China was installed in 1937. Bufano was born in Rome on October 14, 1898, and died in San Francisco on August 16, 1970. His stainless-steel and mosaic statue of St. Francis welcomes guests at San Francisco International Airport.

Shopping surrounds the stroller on **Grant Avenue.** Much of what is offered in the countless curio shops is worthless, and discerning visitors may be dismayed by the gaudy and glittery gimcrackery. In recent years, however, a growing number of large department-store-type operations have opened. Most feature an ever-growing array of products from the People's Republic. You'll find, too, that visiting the Chinese markets, even just window-gazing, is fascinating. Note the dragon-entwined lampposts, the pagoda roofs, and street signs with Chinese calligraphy.

The city's first house was built in 1836 at the corner of Grant Avenue and Clay Street; it was later destroyed in the 1906 earthquake. Turn right here and a short walk will take you to **Portsmouth Square,** the potato patch that became the plaza for Yerba Buena. This is where Montgomery raised the American flag in 1846. Note the bronze galleon atop a nine-foot granite shaft. Designed by Bruce Porter, the sculpture was erected in 1919 in memory of Robert Louis Stevenson, who often visited the site during his 1879–80 residence. In the morning, the park is crowded with people performing solemn t'ai chi rituals.

36 From here you can walk to the **Chinese Cultural Center,** which frequently displays exhibits of Chinese-American artists as well as traveling exhibits of Chinese culture. The center also offers Saturday-afternoon walking tours of historic points in Chinatown. *In the Holiday Inn, 750 Kearny St., tel. 415/986–1822. Admission free. Open Tues.–Sat. 10–4.*

You're now on the edge of North Beach and could easily walk over to the City Lights bookstore or other North Beach sites.

The original Chinatown burned down after the 1906 earthquake; the first building to set the style for the new Chinatown is near Portsmouth Square, at 743 Washington Street. The **37** three-tiered pagoda called the **Old Chinese Telephone Ex-** **38** **change** was built in 1909. Also worth a visit is **Buddha's Universal Church,** 720 Washington Street, a five-story, hand-built temple decorated with murals and tile mosaics. *Open 2nd and 4th Sun. of the month, 1–3.*

Time Out Skip that Big Mac you've been craving; opt instead for dim sum, a variety of pastries filled with meat, fish, and vegetables, the Chinese version of a smorgasbord. Over a dozen Chinese restaurants feature this unusual lunch/brunch adventure from about 11 AM to 3 PM. In most places, stacked food-service carts patrol the premises; customers select from the varied offerings, and the final bill is tabulated by the number of different saucers on the table. Dim sum restaurants tend to be big, crowded, noisy, cheap, and friendly. Suggestions are often offered by nearby strangers as to what is inside the tempting morsels. Two favorites on Pacific Avenue, two blocks north of Washington Street, between Stockton and Powell streets, are **Hong Kong Tea House** (835 Pacific Ave.) and **Tung Fong** (808 Pacific Ave.). Many of the smaller, inexpensive Chinese restaurants and cafés do not accept credit cards; some serve beer and wine.

Waverly Place is noted for ornate painted balconies and Chinese temples. **Tien Hou Temple,** at 125 Waverly Place, was ded- **39** icated to the Queen of the Heavens and Goddess of the Seven Seas by Day Ju, one of the first three Chinese to arrive in San Francisco in 1852.

40 The **Chinese Historical Society** traces the history of Chinese immigrants and their contributions to the state's rail, mining, and fishing industries. *650 Commercial St. (near Sacramento and Montgomery Sts.), tel. 415/391–1188. Admission free. Open Tues.–Sat. 12–4.*

The other main thoroughfare in Chinatown, where locals shop for everyday needs, is **Stockton Street,** which parallels Grant Avenue. This is the real heart of Chinatown. Housewives jostle one another as they pick apart the sidewalk displays of Chinese vegetables. Double-parked trucks unloading crates of chickens or ducks add to the all-day traffic jams. You'll see excellent examples of Chinese architecture along this street. Most note- **41** worthy is the elaborate **Chinese Six Companies** (843 Stockton St.) with its curved roof tiles and elaborate cornices. Folk-art murals grace the walls of an apartment building at Stockton Street and Pacific Avenue. Displays of jade and gold glitter from jewelry windows—the Chinese value these items above all other ornaments. It's an easy ½-hour walk back downtown **42** to Union Square via the **Stockton Street Tunnel,** which runs from Sacramento Street to Sutter Street. Completed in 1914, this was the city's first tunnel to accommodate vehicular and pedestrian traffic.

Tour 7: North Beach and Telegraph Hill

Like neighboring Chinatown, North Beach, centered on Columbus Avenue north of Broadway, is best explored on foot. In the early days there truly was a beach. At the time of the Gold Rush, the bay extended into the hollow between Telegraph and Russian hills. North Beach, less than a square mile, is the most densely populated district in the city and is truly cosmopolitan. Much of the old-world ambience still lingers in this easygoing and polyglot neighborhood. Novelist Herbert Gold, a North Beach resident, calls the area "the longest running, most glorious American bohemian operetta outside Greenwich Village."

Like Chinatown, this is a section of the city where you can eat and eat. Restaurants, cafés, delis, and bakeries abound. Many Italian restaurants specialize in family-style full-course meals at reasonable prices. A local North Beach delicacy is focaccia bread—spongy pizzalike dough slathered with olive oil and chives or tomato sauce. Eaten warm or cold, it is the perfect walking food.

Among the first immigrants to Yerba Buena during the early 1840s were young men from the northern provinces of Italy. By 1848, the village, renamed San Francisco, had become an overnight boomtown with the discovery of gold. Thousands more poured into the burgeoning area, seeking the golden dream. For many the trail ended in San Francisco. The Genoese started the still-active fishing industry, as well as much-needed produce businesses. Later the Sicilians emerged as leaders of the fishing fleets and eventually as proprietors of the seafood restaurants lining Fisherman's Wharf. Meanwhile, their Genoese cousins established banking and manufacturing empires.

43 **Washington Square** may well be the daytime social heart of what was once considered "Little Italy." By mid-morning groups of conservatively dressed elderly Italian men are sunning and sighing at the state of their immediate world. Nearby, laughing Asian and Caucasian playmates race through the grass with Frisbees or colorful kites. Multinational denim-clad mothers exchange shopping tips and ethnic recipes. Elderly Chinese matrons stare impassively at the passing parade. Camera-toting tourists focus their lenses on the adjacent Roman-**44** esque splendor of **Saints Peter and Paul,** often called the Italian Cathedral. Built in 1924, its twin-turreted terra-cotta towers are local landmarks. On the first Sunday of October, the annual Blessing of the Fleet is celebrated with a mass followed by a parade to Fisherman's Wharf. Another popular annual event is the Columbus Day pageant.

The 1906 earthquake and fire devastated this area, and the park provided shelter for hundreds of the homeless. **Fior d'Italia,** facing the cathedral, is San Francisco's oldest Italian restaurant. The original opened in 1886 and continued to operate in a tent after the 1906 earthquake until new quarters were ready. Surrounding streets are packed with savory Italian delicatessens, bakeries, Chinese markets, coffeehouses, and ethnic restaurants. Wonderful aromas fill the air. (Coffee beans roasted at **Graffeo** at 733 Columbus Avenue are shipped to customers all over the United States.) Stop by the **Panelli Brothers** deli (1419 Stockton St.) for a memorable, reasonably priced meat-and-cheese sandwich to go. **Florence Ravioli Factory** (1412 Stockton St.) features garlic sausages, prosciutto, and mortadella, as well as 75 tasty cheeses and sandwiches to go. **Victoria** (1362 Stockton St.) has heavenly cream puffs and eclairs. Around the corner on Columbus Avenue is **Molinari's,** noted for the best salami in town and a mouthwatering array of salads. (There is usually a wait for service.)

45 South of Washington Square and just off Columbus Avenue is the **Church of Saint Francis of Assisi** (610 Vallejo St.). This 1860 Victorian Gothic building stands on the site of the frame parish church that served the Gold Rush Catholic community.

Over the years, North Beach has attracted creative individualists. The Beat Renaissance of the 1950s was born, grew up, flourished, then faltered in this then-predominantly Italian enclave. The Beat gathering places are gone, and few of the original leaders remain. Poet Lawrence Ferlinghetti still holds **46** court at his **City Lights Bookstore** (261 Columbus Ave.). The face of North Beach is changing. The bohemian community has migrated up Grant Avenue above Columbus Avenue. Originally called Calle de la Fundacion, Grant Avenue is the oldest street in the city. Each June a street fair is held on the upper part of the avenue, where a cluster of cafés, boutiques, and galleries attract crowds.

Time Out The richness of North Beach lifestyle is reflected in the neighborhood's numerous cafés. Breakfast at **Caffe Roma** (414 Columbus Ave.) and create your own omelet from a list of 11 ingredients. Skip the main room with its pastel murals of cherubs and settle at one of the umbrella-shaded tables on the patio. Moviemaker Francis Ford Coppola is a regular, and the adjoining Millefiori Inn, a charming bed-and-breakfast, frequently hosts film celebrities.

Across the street is **Caffe Puccini** (411 Columbus Ave.). It could be Italy: Few of the staff speak English. Their *caffe latte* (coffee, chocolate, cinnamon, and steamed milk) and strains of Italian operas recall *Roman Holiday*. A Saturday morning must is around the corner at **Caffe Trieste** (601 Vallejo St.). Get there at about 11; at noon, the Giotta family's weekly musical begins. The program ranges from Italian pop and folk music to favorite family operas. The Trieste opened in 1956 and became headquarters for the area's beatnik poets, artists, and writers. **Caffe Malvina** (1600 Stockton St.) started during the 1950s and was among the first U.S. importers of Italian-made espresso machines.

47 **Telegraph Hill** rises from the east end of Lombard Street to about 300 feet and is capped with the landmark Coit Tower, dedicated as a monument to the city's volunteer firemen. Early during the Gold Rush, an eight-year-old who would become one of the city's most memorable eccentrics, Lillie Hitchcock Coit, arrived on the scene. Legend relates that at age 17, "Miss Lil" deserted a wedding party and chased down the street after her favorite engine, Knickerbocker No. 5, clad in her bridesmaid finery. She was soon made an honorary member of the Knickerbocker Company, and after that always signed herself "Lillie Coit 5" in honor of her favorite fire engine. Lillie died in 1929 at the age of 86, leaving the city about $100,000 of her million-dollar-plus estate to "expend in an appropriate manner . . . to the beauty of San Francisco."

Telegraph Hill residents command some of the best views in the city, as well as the most difficult ascent to their aeries. The Greenwich stairs lead up to Coit Tower from Filbert Street, and there are steps down to Filbert Street on the opposite side of Telegraph Hill. Views are superb en route, but most visitors should either taxi up to the tower or take the Muni bus No. 39 Coit at Washington Square. To catch the bus from Union Square, walk to Stockton and Sutter streets, board the Muni No. 30, and ask for a transfer to use at Washington Square (Columbus Ave. and Union St.) to board the No. 39 Coit. Public parking is very limited at the tower, and on holidays and weekends there are long lines of cars and buses winding up the narrow road.

48 **Coit Tower** stands as a monument not only to Lillie Coit and the city's firemen but also to the influence of the political radical Mexican muralist Diego Rivera. Fresco was Rivera's medium, and it was his style that unified the work of most of the 25 artists who painted the murals in the tower. The murals were commissioned by the U.S. government as a Public Works of Art Project. The artists were paid $38 a week. Some were fresh from art schools; others found no market for art in the dark depression days of the early 1930s. An illustrated brochure for sale in the tiny gift shop explains the various murals dedicated to the workers of California. There is an elevator to the top that provides a panoramic view of both the Bay Bridge and Golden Gate Bridge; directly offshore is the famous Alcatraz and just behind it, Angel Island, a hikers' and campers' paradise. Be sure to carry a camera and binoculars. There are often artists at work in **Pioneer Park,** at the foot of the tower. Small paintings of the scene are frequently offered for sale at modest prices. The impressive bronze statue of Christopher Columbus, *Discoverer of America*, was a gift of the local Italian community.

Walk down the Greenwich Steps east to Montgomery Street, and turn right. At the corner where the Filbert Steps intersect, you'll find the Art Deco masterpiece at 1360 Montgomery Street. (*See* Off the Beaten Track, below.) Its elegant etched-glass gazelle and palms counterpoint the silvered fresco of the heroic bridgeworker—echoed by an actual view of the Bay Bridge in the distance. Descend the Filbert Steps, amid roses, fuchsias, irises, and trumpet flowers, courtesy of Grace Marchant, who labored for nearly 30 years to transform a dump into one of San Francisco's hidden treasures. At the last landing before the final descent to Sansome Street, pause and sit on the bench to breathe in the fragrance of roses as you gaze at the bridge and bay below. A small bronze plaque set into the bench reads: "I have a feeling we're not in Kansas anymore."

At the foot of the hill you will come to the Levi Strauss headquarters, a carefully landscaped $150 million complex that appears so collegial and serene it is affectionately known as LSU (Levi Strauss University). Fountains and grassy knolls complement the stepped-back redbrick buildings and provide a stress-reducing environment perfect for brown-bag lunches.

Time Out You can choose the ingredients for an urban picnic at **Il Fornaio** (in the Plaza, 1265 Battery St., tel. 415/986–0100). The Uno Poco di Tutti deli offers a variety of cold pasta salads and such treats as giant artichokes stuffed with bread crumbs and capers. A bakery will provide you with Italian sweets, or you can eat in the dining room, choosing from the house specialties: meats from the rotisserie or pizzas from the oak-fired ovens. Down Battery Street, the **Fog City Diner** has attracted the city's young professionals since it opened in 1985. The menu is basically down-home American; regular diners recommend the crab cakes. Make reservations, even for a late lunch. The prices are moderate and the atmosphere is comfortable. *1300 Battery St., tel. 415/982–2000. Open Sun.–Thurs. 11:30 AM–11 PM, Fri.–Sat. 11:30 AM–midnight.*

Tour 8: Russian Hill

Just nine blocks or so from downtown, Russian Hill has long been home to old San Francisco families and, during the 1890s, to a group of bohemian artists and writers that included Charles Norris, George Sterling, and Maynard Dixon. An old legend says that during San Francisco's early days the steep hill (294 feet high) was the site of a cemetery for Russian seal hunters and traders. Now the hills are covered with an astounding array of housing: simple studios, sumptuous pied-à-terres, Victorian flats, and costly boxlike condos.

At Union Square, board the Powell-Mason cable car and hop off at Vallejo and Mason streets. This will put you at an ideal spot from which to photograph Alcatraz Island and the bay. Slowly
49 start climbing the Vallejo Steps up to attractive **Ina Coolbrith Park.** An Oakland librarian and poet, Ina introduced both Jack London and Isadora Duncan to the world of books. For years she entertained literary greats in her Macondray Lane home (near the park). In 1915 she was named poet laureate of California.

A number of buildings in this neighborhood survived the 1906 earthquake and fire and still stand today. The house at 1652 Taylor Street was saved by alert fire fighters who spotted the American flag on the property and managed to quench the flames using seltzer water and wet sand. A number of brown-shingle structures on Vallejo Street designed by Willis Polk, one of the city's most famous architects, also survived. For years, the Polk family resided at 1013 Vallejo Street. Stroll past 1034–1036 Vallejo—both buildings, tucked in between new million-dollar condominium neighbors, were designed by Polk.

At this point, two secluded alleys beckon: To the north, **Russian Hill Place** has a row of Mediterranean-style town houses designed by Polk in 1915. On **Florence Place** to the south, 1920s stucco survivors reign over more contemporary construction.

Follow Vallejo Street west to Jones Street, turn right, and continue on to Green Street. The 1000 block of Green, on one of the three crests of Russian Hill, is one of the most remarkable
50 blocks in San Francisco. The **Feusier House** (1067 Green St.), built in 1857 and now a private residence, is one of two octagonal houses left in the city. On the other side of the street (at 1088) is the **1907 firehouse.** Local art patron Mrs. Ralph K. Da-

vies bought it from the city in 1956. There is a small museum, and the property is often used for charity benefits.

Continue west on Green Street to Hyde Street, where the Hyde-Powell cable car line runs. Turn right and stroll up to Union Street. (If you're tired of walking, stop at the original Swensen's for an ice-cream treat.) At this point you have two options: You can meander down Union Street to Jones Street, **51** turn right and walk a few steps down to magical **Macondray Lane,** a quiet cobbled pedestrian street lined with Edwardian cottages. From a flight of steep wooden stairs that lead down to Taylor Street you'll get some spectacular views of the bay. From Taylor Street it is then a short walk downhill to North Beach.

Your other option is to keep walking north on Hyde Street **52** three blocks to **Lombard Street.** Stretching the length of just one block, San Francisco's "crookedest street" drops down the east face of Russian Hill in eight switchbacks to Leavenworth Street. Few tourists with cars can resist the lure of the scary descent. Pedestrians should be alert while using the steep steps, especially when photographing the smashing views.

At the base of the steps, turn left on Leavenworth Street and then right on Chestnut Street. At 800 Chestnut Street is the **53** **San Francisco Art Institute.** Established in 1871, it occupied the Mark Hopkins home at California and Mason streets from 1893 to 1906. The school carried on in temporary quarters until 1926, when the present Spanish Colonial building was erected on the top of Russian Hill. Be sure to see the impressive seven-sectioned fresco painted in 1931 by the Mexican master Diego Rivera. There are also frequent exhibitions of student efforts.

From here you can walk back to Hyde Street and take the cable car back downtown or walk a few blocks north to the wharf. Hardy walkers will probably prefer to walk down to Columbus Avenue and then west on North Point or Beach streets to Ghirardelli Square, the Cannery, and Aquatic Park.

Tour 9: Nob Hill

If you don't mind climbing uphill, Nob Hill is within walking distance of Union Square. Once called the Hill of Golden Promise, it became Nob Hill during the 1870s when "the Big Four"— Charles Crocker, Leland Stanford, Mark Hopkins, and Collis Huntington—built their hilltop estates. It is still home to many of the city's elite as well as four of San Francisco's finest hotels.

In 1882 Robert Louis Stevenson called Nob Hill "the hill of palaces." But the 1906 earthquake and fire destroyed all the palatial mansions. The shell of one survived. The Flood brownstone (1000 California St.) was built by the Comstock silver baron in 1886 at a reputed cost of $1,500,000. In 1909 the property was **54** purchased by the prestigious **Pacific Union Club.** The 45-room exclusive club remains the bastion of the wealthy and powerful. Adjacent is a charming small park noted for its frequent art shows.

55 Neighboring **Grace Cathedral** (1051 Taylor St.) is the seat of the Episcopal Church in San Francisco. The soaring Gothic structure took 53 years to build. The gilded bronze doors at the east entrance were taken from casts of Ghiberti's *Gates of Paradise* on the baptistery in Florence. The superb rose window is illuminated at night. There are often organ recitals on Sundays at 5 PM, as well as special programs during the holiday seasons.

56 The huge **Masonic Auditorium** (1111 California St.) is also the site of frequent musical events, including "Todays Artists," a concert series that highlights young classical musicians.

57 What sets the **Fairmont Hotel** (California and Mason Sts.) apart from other luxury hotels is its legendary history. Since its dazzling opening in 1907, the opulent marble palace has hosted presidents, royalty, and local nabobs. The lobby sports as much plush red-velvet upholstery as anyone could ever want to see. The eight-room $4,000-a-day penthouse suite was used frequently in the TV series "Hotel," and the stunning Nob Hill Spa and Fitness Club is on the premises.

58 The stately **Mark Hopkins Hotel,** across California Street, is remembered fondly by thousands of World War II veterans who jammed the Top of the Mark lounge before leaving for overseas
59 duty. At California and Powell streets stands the posh **Stanford Court Hotel,** a world-class establishment known for service and personal attention. The structure is a remodeled 1909 apartment house.

60 The **Huntington** (1075 California St.) is impeccably British in protecting the privacy of its celebrated guests.

61 The **Cable Car Museum** (Washington and Mason Sts.) exhibits photographs, scale models, and other memorabilia from the cable car system's 115-year history. A new 17-minute film is shown continually. *Tel. 415/474–1887. Admission free. Open daily 10–5.*

Tour 10: Union Street

Union Street west of Van Ness Avenue was the first shopping street in San Francisco to renovate its gingerbread Victorians into trendy boutiques, galleries, and restaurants. Known colloquially as Cow Hollow because it was once a rural settlement with small farms, pastures, and resident dairy herds, the area is now known for great shopping, dining, and drinking.

To get to Union Street, take either Muni bus No. 45 from Sutter Street or bus No. 41 from North Beach's Washington Square. Get off at Gough Street and begin walking west. Note the his-
62 toric **Octagon House** (2645 Gough St. at Union St.). It is one of the two remaining examples in the city of this mid–19th-century architectural form. The second landmark octagon is a private residence on Russian Hill. These two curious houses are all that is left locally of a national fad for eight-sided buildings that swept the country during the 1850s, inspired by a book written by a New York phrenologist, Orson S. Fowler. Eight-sided homes were thought to be good luck.

In 1953 the National Society of the Colony Dames of America purchased the Octagon House (built in 1861) for one dollar from the Pacific Gas & Electric Company. One condition stated that the structure had to be moved from its original site across the street at 2648 Gough Street. Today it serves as a museum and center for the society's activities. The house is a treasure trove of American antique furniture and accessories from the 18th and 19th centuries. *Admission free. Open 2nd Sun. and 2nd and 4th Thurs. of each month noon–3.*

Union Street is a favorite browsing ground. Here are some local favorites: The wild yet elegant contemporary art furniture at **Arte Forma** (1775 Union St.) includes multicolored leather sofas and eerie rice-paper lamps by Noguchi. **Images of the North** (1782 Union St.) specializes in superb Inuit art from Alaska and Canada.

Laura Ashley (1827 Union St.) brings a touch of Edwardian elegance to the street. Down the way, the epoch switches to Victorian, where naughty-but-nice romantic lingerie lies behind the quaint doors of **Victoria's Secret** (2245 Union St.)

If you like country furnishings, be sure to view the pre-1935 American quilt collection at **Yankee Doodle Dandy** (1974 Union St.). Delight a youngster with a charming stuffed animal made of vintage quilt bits.

Time Out On the 1900 block are two special eating spots. Try **Bepples** (1934 Union St.) for a fabulous pie-and-coffee break. **Perry's** (1944 Union St.) has long had a reputation as *the* singles bar and the crowds still flock here to see and be seen. It's also a popular all-day drop-in restaurant, and it serves a tasty hamburger.

63 The so-called **Wedding Houses** at 1980 Union Street were built during the late-1870s or 1880s. The romantic history of No. 1980 recounts that its builder, a dairy farmer named James Cudworth, sold the property to a father as wedding presents for his two daughters. In 1963 this property and the adjoining buildings were tastefully transformed from modest residences into charming flower-decked shops and cafés. Join some of San Francisco's young, rich, and trendy at **Prego** (2000 Union St.) and check out the latest in food and finery.

Meander west to Webster Street, make a right, and continue
64 down to the old **Vedanta Temple** (2963 Webster St.) at the corner of Filbert Street. This 1905 architectural cocktail may be the most unusual structure in San Francisco: It's a pastiche of Colonial, Queen Anne, Moorish, and Hindu opulence. Vedanta is the highest of the six Hindu systems of religious philosophy. One of its basic tenets is that all religions are paths to one goal.

If you care to check out still more fashionable shops, return to Union Street and continue on to Fillmore Street. Stroll north down Fillmore to Greenwich Street, where a number of small, fascinating shops have recently opened their doors. Two of the city's top dealers of Oriental art have settled here. On the corner is one of the city's most popular moderately priced restaurants, the casual, always-crowded **Balboa Café.**

Tour 11: Pacific Heights

Pacific Heights forms an east–west ridge along the city's northern flank from Van Ness Avenue to the Presidio and from California Street to the bay. Some of the city's most expensive and dramatic real estate, including mansions and town houses priced at $1 million and up, are located here. Grand old Victorians, expensively face-lifted, grace tree-lined streets, although here and there glossy, glass-walled condo high rises obstruct the view.

Old money and some new, trade and diplomatic personnel, personalities in the limelight, and those who prefer absolute media

anonymity occupy the city's most prestigious residential enclave. Receptions at the Gorden Getty mansion can block
Broadway traffic while irate demonstrators picket the Soviet
Consulate on Green Street. Rolls-Royces, Mercedes, and security systems are commonplace.

Few visitors see anything other than the pleasing facades of
Queen Anne charmers, English Tudor imports, and Baroque
bastions, but strolling can still be a jackpot. The area encompasses a variety of great and small private homes. Many of the
structures stand close together but extend in a vertical direction for two or more stories. A distinguishing feature of some of
the grand residences is an ornate gate.

A good place to begin a tour of the neighborhood is at the corner
of Webster Street and Pacific Avenue, deep in the heart of the
Heights. You can get here from Union Square by taking Muni
bus No. 3 from Sutter and Stockton to Jackson and Fillmore
streets. Turn right and walk one block east to Webster Street.

North on Webster Street, at 2550, is the massive Georgian
brick mansion built in 1896 for William B. Bourn, who had in-
herited a Mother Lode gold mine. The architect, Willis Polk,
was responsible for many of the most traditional and impressive commercial and private homes built from the prequake
days until the early 1920s. (Be sure to see his 1917 Hallidie
Building, 130 Sutter Street; *see* Tour 2: The Financial District,
above.) Polk also designed Bourn's palatial Peninsula estate,
Filoli (*see* The San Francisco Peninsula in Chapter 9).

Neighbors include a consulate and, on the northwest corner,
two classic showplaces. **2222 Broadway** is the three-story Italian Renaissance palace built by Comstock mine heir James
Flood. Broadway uptown, unlike its North Beach stretch, is
big league socially. The former Flood residence was given to a
religious order. Ten years later, the Convent of the Sacred
Heart purchased the Baroque brick Grant house (2220 Broadway) and both serve as school quarters today. A second top-
drawer school, the Hamlin (2120 Broadway), occupies another
Flood property.

Go east on Broadway and at the next corner turn right onto Buchanan Street and continue south to 2090 Jackson Street. The
(65) massive red sandstone **Whittier Mansion** was one of the most
elegant 19th-century houses in the state, built so solidly that
only a chimney toppled over during the 1906 earthquake. Next
door at 2099 Pacific Avenue, is the North Baker Library of the
California Historical Society. The library houses a fine collection of local historical documents but is only open to research-
ers, and has no public displays.

Proceed east another block to Laguna Street. The Italianate
Victorians on the east side of the 1800 block of Laguna Street
cost only $2,000–$2,600 when they were built during the 1870s.
This block is one of the most photographed rows of Victorians
in the city.

(66) One block south, at Washington Street, is **Lafayette Park,** a
four-block-square oasis for sunbathers and dog-and-Frisbee
teams. During the 1860s a tenacious squatter, Sam Holladay,
built himself a big house of wood shipped round the Horn, in the
center of the park. Holladay even instructed city gardeners as

if the land were his own, and defied all attempts to remove him. The house was finally torn down in 1936.

The most imposing residence is the formal French **Spreckels Palace** (2080 Washington St.). Sugar heir Adolph Spreckels's wife was so pleased that she commissioned architect George Applegarth to design the city's European museum, the California Palace of the Legion of Honor in Lincoln Park.

Continue south on Gough Street (pronounced "Goff"), which runs along the east side of the park. A number of Queen Anne Victorians here have been lovingly restored. Two blocks south and one east, at the corner of California and Franklin, is an impressive twin-turreted Queen Anne–style Victorian built for a Gold Rush mining and lumber baron. North on Franklin Street, at 1735, stands a stately brick Georgian, built during the early 1900s for a coffee merchant.

❻ At 2007 Franklin is the handsome **Haas-Lilienthal Victorian.** Built in 1886, at an original cost of $20,000, this grand Queen Anne survived the 1906 earthquake and fire, and is the only fully furnished Victorian open to the public. The carefully kept rooms offer an intriguing glimpse into turn-of-the-century taste and lifestyle. A small display of photographs on the bottom floor proves that this elaborate house was modest compared with some of the giants that fell to the fire. It is operated by the Foundation for San Francisco's Architectural Heritage, and tours are given by docent volunteers. *Tel. 415/441–3004. Admission: $4 adults, $2 senior citizens and children under 12. Open Wed. noon–4, Sun. 11–4:30.*

By the mid-1970s, dozens of San Francisco's shabby gingerbreads were sporting psychedelic-colored facades, and the trend continues. Renovated treasures are found not only in the Haight-Ashbury district but increasingly in the Western Addition as well as in the working-class Mission area.

Tour 12: Japantown

Japanese-Americans began gravitating to the neighborhood known as the Western Addition prior to the 1906 earthquake. Early immigrants arrived about 1860, and they named San Francisco Soko. After the 1906 fire had destroyed wooden homes in other parts of the stricken city, many survivors settled in the Western Addition. By the 1930s the pioneers had opened shops, markets, meeting halls, and restaurants and established Shinto and Buddhist temples. Japantown was virtually disbanded during World War II when many of its residents, including second- and third-generation Americans, were "relocated" in camps.

Today **Japantown,** or "Nihonmachi," is centered on the slopes of Pacific Heights, north of Geary Boulevard, between Fillmore and Laguna streets. The Nihonmachi Cherry Blossom Festival is celebrated two weekends every April with a calendar of ethnic events. Walking in Nihonmachi is more than just a shopping and culinary treat; it is a cultural, sensory experience.

To reach Japantown from Union Square, take the Muni bus No. 38-Geary or No. 2, 3, or 4 on Sutter Street, westbound to Laguna. Remember to have exact change—fare is 85¢; free transfers are good for one direction and one change of vehicles.

We recommend visiting Japantown and the Western Addition during the day. Though the hotel, restaurant, and Kabuki movie complex are relatively safe in the evenings, it is often difficult to avoid long waits at isolated bus stops or to find a cruising cab when you want to get back to the hotel. The proximity of the often-hostile street gangs in the Western Addition could cause unpleasant incidents.

The buildings around the traffic-free **Japan Center Mall** between Sutter and Post streets are of the shoji screen school of architecture, and Ruth Asawa's origami fountain sits in the middle. (*See* Tour 1: Union Square, above, for more information on Ms. Asawa.)

❻❽ The mall faces the three-block-long, five-acre **Japan Center.** In 1968 the multimillion-dollar development created by noted American architect Minoru Yamasaki opened with a three-day folk festival. The three-block cluster includes an 800-car public garage and shops and showrooms selling Japanese products: electronic products, cameras, tapes and records, porcelains, pearls, and paintings.

The center is dominated by its Peace Plaza and Pagoda located between the East and Kinetsu buildings. Designed by Professor Yoshiro Taniguchi of Tokyo, an authority on ancient Japanese buildings, the plaza is landscaped with traditional Japanese-style gardens and reflecting pools. A graceful *yagura* (wooden drum tower) spans the entrance to the plaza and the copper-roofed *Heiwa Dori* (Peace Walkway) at the north end connects the East and Kinetsu buildings. The five-tiered, 100-foot Peace Pagoda overlooks the plaza, where seasonal festivals are held. The pagoda draws on the tradition of miniature round pagodas dedicated to eternal peace by Empress Koken in Nara more than 1,200 years ago. It was designed by the Japanese architect Yoshiro Taniguchi "to convey the friendship and goodwill of the Japanese to the people of the United States." A cultural bridge modeled after Florence's Ponte Vecchio spans Webster Street.

Soko Hardware (1698 Post St.) has been run by the Ashizawa merchant family since 1925. They specialize in beautifully crafted Japanese tools for gardening and carpentry. Visitors interested in Japanese cuisine might purchase seeds of Japanese vegetables to plant at home. They also have those long-sleeved, back-fastening Japanese aprons.

Nichi Bei Bussan (1715 Buchanan St.), in business since 1907, has a collector's choice of quilts covered with fabulous Japanese designs. They are stocked in twin and regular sizes; king-size quilts can be special-ordered. Prices start at about $75. Charming baby's *chan-chan-ko* (tiny printed Japanese-style vests) are popular gifts. Refrigerator door magnets in sushi motifs make super stocking stuffers.

Kinokuniya, on the second floor of the West Building, may have the finest selection of English-language books on Japanese subjects in the United States. There are books on food, ikebana (the art of flower arranging), handsomely bound editions of Japanese philosophy, religion, literature, and art, plus a large selection of elegant art calendars.

Also on the second floor is **Shige Antiques,** where collectors of art-to-wear search for antique hand-painted silk-embroidered kimonos and the all-important waist sash—the obi. The methods of tying the obi indicate the wearer's age, marital status, and even the special events being attended, such as weddings and funerals. The Arita porcelains, silk calligraphy scrolls, tea-ceremony utensils, and treasured lacquerware boxes at Shige will dazzle aficionados.

Asakichi, on the first floor of the West Building, specializes in antique blue-and-white Imari porcelains and handsome *tansu* (chests).

The shops in the East Building are a paradise for souvenir shoppers. Colorful flying-fish kites and delicate floral-patterned cocktail napkins are popular choices.

Some 40 restaurants in the neighborhood feature a choice of Japanese, Chinese, or Korean food. Most are found in the mall, a few are on side streets, and the rest are in the center itself, concentrated on the "street of restaurants" in the West Building. Following the practice in Japan, plastic replicas of the various dishes are on view.

If touring has about done you in, we suggest a brief respite at the **Kabuki Hot Springs** (1750 Geary Blvd.). Open daily, the communal bath is open for men only on Monday, Tuesday, Thursday, and Saturday, and for women only on Wednesday, Friday, and Sunday. The spa offers a number of steam, sauna, and massage packages. One, the Shogun, includes an hour of shiatsu massage. This method concentrates on pressure points in the body and is guaranteed to get you back on the track.

Time Out At a sushi bar, sample the bite-size portions of lightly seasoned rice and seaweed topped with various kinds of seafood, usually raw. Try to manage the chopsticks, dip (don't drench) your portion into the soy sauce, and experience this typical Japanese favorite. Tea, sake, or excellent Japanese beer accompanies these morsels. One warning—the final bill is calculated by portion, and it is not unusual to run up a $20 tab per person. **Isobune,** in the Kentetsu Mall in Japan Center (tel. 415/563–1030), is unusual. The sushi chef prepares a variety of sushi, placing each small portion on a small wooden boat that floats on a "river" of water that circles the counter. The customer then fishes out a sampling.

An inexpensive and popular snack are *ramen* (noodle dishes). The noodles are either boiled and served in a broth or prepared toss-fried with bits of greens and meat added for flavor. **Mifune,** also in the Kintetsu Mall, serves both hot and cold noodles as well as either the fat strands of *udon* noodles or the buckwheat *soba.*

---

⑥⑨ Across Geary Boulevard at Fillmore Street is the famous **Fillmore** auditorium (1805 Geary Blvd., tel. 415/922–3455). During the mid-'60s, Bill Graham, farm equipment salesman turned impresario, started staging concerts and events in an old ballroom and roller-skating rink. His success led to the opening of the Fillmore East in New York. Both venues closed during the 1970s, but Graham went on to present shows in a wide range of locales, including Wolfgang's, and the Shoreline Amphitheater. Before his death in 1991 Graham had again started staging shows at the Fillmore. If you see a long line of strange-haired people snaking down Geary Boulevard, you can be sure they're waiting to see hip entertainment at the Fillmore.

Walk back east on Geary Boulevard to Gough Street. This enclave of expensive high-rise residential towers is known as Cathedral Hill. The dramatic **St. Mary's Cathedral** was dedicated in 1971 at a cost of $7 million. The impressive Catholic cathedral seats 2,500 people around the central altar. Above the altar is a spectacular cascade made of 7,000 aluminum ribs. Four magnificent stained-glass windows in the dome represent the four elements: the blue north window, water; the light-colored south window, the sun; the red west window, fire; and the green east window, earth. Designed by a team of local architects and Pier Nervi of Rome, the Italian travertine church is approached through spacious plazas.

Tour 13: Civic Center

San Francisco's Civic Center stands as one of the country's great city, state, and federal building complexes with handsome adjoining cultural institutions. It's the realization of the theories of turn-of-the-century proponents of the "City Beautiful." In recent years, it's also become the focal point for fine dining in San Francisco.

Facing Polk Street, between Grove and McAllister streets, **City Hall** is a Baroque masterpiece of granite and marble, modeled after the Capitol in Washington. Its dome is even higher than the Washington version, and it dominates the area. In front of the building are formal gardens with fountains, walkways, and seasonal flower beds. Brooks Exhibit Hall was constructed under this plaza in 1958 to add space for the frequent trade shows and other events based in the Civic Auditorium on Grove Street.

San Francisco's increasing numbers of homeless people are often seen in the city's green spaces. Visitors and residents should be aware of possible danger in strolling in park areas and deserted business sectors after dark.

Across the plaza from City Hall on Larkin Street is the main branch of the **San Francisco Public Library.** (A new library is being built around the corner; when the library is completed, this site will become the new Asian Art Museum.) History buffs should visit the San Francisco History Room and Archives on the third floor. Historic photographs, maps, and other memorabilia are carefully documented for the layman or research scholar. *Tel. 415/557-4567. Open Tues., Fri. 12-6; Wed. 1-6; Thurs., Sat. 10-6.*

On the west side of City Hall, across Van Ness Avenue, are the Museum of Modern Art, the Opera House, and Davies Symphony Hall. The northernmost of the three is the Veterans' Building, whose third and fourth floors house the **Museum of Modern Art.** (A new MOMA is under construction as part of the downtown Yerba Buena development.) The museum's permanent collection was significantly enhanced in 1991 by the $40 million Haas bequest, which features Matisse's masterpiece, *Woman in a Hat,* as well as works by Derain, Manet, Monet, and Picasso. Traveling exhibitions bring important national and international paintings, photographs, graphics, and sculpture to the Bay Area. The Museum Store has a select offering of books,

posters, cards, and crafts. The Museum Cafe serves light
snacks as well as wine and beer. *At McAllister St. and Van
Ness Ave., tel. 415/863–8800. Admission: $4 adults, $2 senior
citizens and students 13 and over with ID; free 1st Tues. of the
month. Open Tues., Wed., Fri. 10–5; Thurs. 10–9, Sat., Sun.
11–5. Closed major holidays.*

74 South of the Veteran's Building is the opulent **War Memorial
Opera House,** which opened in 1932. Lotfi Mansouri has taken
over as head of the San Francisco Opera, the largest opera company west of New York. Its regular season of world-class productions runs from September through December.

South of Grove Street, still on Van Ness Avenue, is the $27.5
million home of the San Francisco Symphony, the modern
75 3,000-plus-seat **Louise M. Davies Symphony Hall,** made of glass
and granite. *Grove St. and Van Ness Ave., tel. 415/552–8338.
Cost: $3 adults, $2 senior citizens and students. Tours of Davies Hall Wed. 1:30, 2:30, Sat. 12:30, 1:30. Tours of Davies Hall
and the adjacent Performing Arts Center every ½ hour Mon.
10–2:30.*

The San Francisco Opera Shop, up the street from Davies Hall,
carries books, T-shirts, posters, and gift items associated with
the performing arts. *199 Grove St., tel. 415/565–6414. Open
weekdays 11–6, Sat. noon–6, Sun. noon–6 when there are mat-
inees. (It frequently stays open till 8:30 during performances
of the Opera and Symphony.)*

East of the Civic Center at Market and Fulton streets, the
76 **United Nations Plaza** is the site of a bustling farmers' market on
Wednesday and Sunday.

Time Out There are at least 40 restaurants within walking distance of the
Civic Center. **Max's,** at 601 Van Ness Avenue in Opera Plaza, an
upscale condo complex, serves such old-time favorites as lox
and bagels and roast beef sandwiches as well as chicken Oriental salad, tortilla snacks, and tasty desserts. Don't be in a hurry: Service tends to be slow, especially on show nights (opera or
symphony). Celebrity chef Jeremiah Tower's **Stars** (170 Redwood Alley, near Grove St. and Van Ness Ave.) offers exotic
versions of California cuisine in an atmospheric room reminiscent of a Parisian bistro. For a quick pizza or a grilled chicken
breast sandwich, dash across to **Spuntino** (524 Van Ness Ave.).
Open until midnight on Friday and Saturday, this is an excellent spot for an after-theater cappuccino. No reservations or
credit cards.

Tour 14: The Northern Waterfront

*Numbers in the margin correspond with points of interest on
the Northern Waterfront map.*

For the sight, sound, and smell of the sea, hop the Powell-Hyde
cable car from Union Square to the end of the line. From the
cable car turnaround, Aquatic Park and the National Maritime
Museum are immediately to the west; Fort Mason, with its several interesting museums, is just a bit farther west. If you're
interested in exploring the more commercial attractions,
Ghirardelli Square is behind you and Fisherman's Wharf to the

east. We recommend casual clothes, good walking shoes, and a jacket or sweater for mid-afternoon breezes or foggy mists.

Or you could begin your day with one of the early-morning boat tours that depart from the Northern Waterfront piers. On a clear day (almost always), the morning light casts a warm glow on the colorful homes on Russian Hill, the weather-aged fishing boats cluttered at Fisherman's Wharf, rosy Ghirardelli Square and its fairy-tale clock tower, and the swelling seas beyond the entrance to the bay.

San Francisco is famous for the arts and crafts that flourish on the streets. Each day over 200 of the city's innovative jewelers, painters, potters, photographers, and leather workers offer their wares for sale. You'll find them at Fisherman's Wharf, Union Square, Embarcadero Plaza, and Cliff House. Be wary: Some of the items are from Mexican or other foreign factories, and some may be overpriced. If you can't live without the item, try to bargain.

1 The **National Maritime Museum** (Aquatic Park, at the foot of Polk St.) exhibits ship models, photographs, maps, and other artifacts chronicling the development of San Francisco and the West Coast through maritime history. *Tel. 415/556–8177. Admission free. Open daily 10–5, till 6 in summer.*

2 The museum also includes the **Hyde Street Pier** (2 blocks east), where historic vessels are moored. The *Eureka*, a sidewheel ferry, and the *C.A. Thayer*, a three-masted schooner, can be boarded. Built in 1886, she is the last of the Cape Horn fleet. *Tel. 415/556–6435. Admission: $3 adults, children and senior citizens free. Open daily 10–5, 10–6 in summer.*

The *Pampanito*, at Pier 45, is a World War II submarine. An audio tour has been installed. *Tel. 415/929–0202. Admission: $4 adults, $2 students 12–18, $1 children 6–11, senior citizens, and active military. Open Sun.–Thurs. 9–6, Fri.–Sat. 9–9, daily 9–9 in summer.*

3 **Fort Mason,** originally a depot for the shipment of supplies to the Pacific during World War II, was converted into a cultural center in 1977. The immense, three-story, yellow-stucco buildings are nondescript. Four minimuseums and an outstanding vegetarian restaurant merit mention, however.

The **Mexican Museum** was the first American showcase to be devoted exclusively to Mexican and Mexican-American art. The museum's goal is to expose the vitality and scope of Mexican art from pre-Hispanic Indian terra-cotta figures and Spanish Colonial religious images to modern Mexican masters. Limited space allows only a fraction of the permanent collection, including a recent 500-piece folk-art collection (a gift from the Nelson A. Rockefeller estate), to be exhibited. The museum recently began mounting major special shows. One of the early, very successful exhibits displayed the work of Frida Kahlo, the Mexican surrealist and wife of Diego Rivera. The permanent collection includes such contemporary greats as Rivera, Tamayo, Orozco, Siqueiros, and sculptor Francisco Zuniga. La Tienda, the museum shop, stocks colorful Mexican folk art, posters, books, and catalogues from museum exhibitions. *Fort Mason, Bldg. D., tel. 415/441–0404. Free admission on the 1st Wed. of the month. Admission: $2 adults, $1 senior*

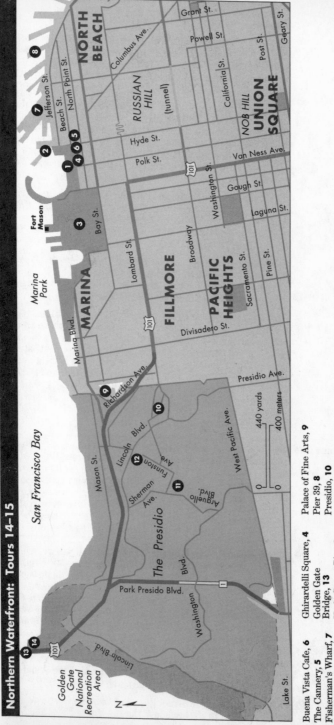

Northern Waterfront: Tours 14–15

NORTH BEACH

Grant St.

Columbus Ave.

Powell St.

Post St.

Geary St.

Jefferson St.

Beach St.

North Point St.

RUSSIAN HILL

California St.

(tunnel)

NOB HILL

UNION SQUARE

Hyde St.

Polk St.

Van Ness Ave.

Washington St.

Gough St.

Fort Mason

Bay St.

Laguna St.

Broadway

Lombard St.

FILLMORE

Pine St.

Sacramento St.

PACIFIC HEIGHTS

Marina Park

MARINA

Divisadero St.

Marina Blvd.

Presidio Ave.

Richardson Ave.

West Pacific Ave.

San Francisco Bay

Lincoln Blvd.

Mason St.

Funston Ave.

440 yards

400 meters

Sherman Ave.

Arguello Blvd.

The Presidio

Park Presido Blvd.

Washington

Blvd.

Golden Gate National Recreation Area

Lincoln Blvd.

Lake St.

N

Buena Vista Cafe, **6**
The Cannery, **5**
Fisherman's Wharf, **7**
Fort Mason, **3**
Fort Point, **14**

Ghirardelli Square, **4**
Golden Gate Bridge, **13**
Hyde Street Pier, **2**
National Maritime Museum, **1**
Officers' Club, **11**

Palace of Fine Arts, **9**
Pier 39, **8**
Presidio, **10**
Presidio Army Museum, **12**

citizens and students, children under 10 free. Open Wed.–Sun. noon–5.

The **Museo Italo Americano** has permanent exhibits of works of 19th- and 20th-century Italian-American artists. Shows include paintings, sculpture, etchings, and photographs. The museum presents special exhibits, lectures, and films. *Fort Mason, Bldg. C, tel. 415/673–2200. Admission free.*

The **San Francisco African-American Historical and Cultural Society** maintains the only black museum west of the Rockies. The permanent collection includes exhibits on black California and black Civil War history. Temporary exhibits focus on living California black artists. *Fort Mason, Bldg. C, Room 165, tel. 415/441–0640. Admission: donation. Open Wed.–Sun. noon–5. We suggest you phone to verify schedules.*

The **San Francisco Crafts and Folk Art Museum** features American folk art, tribal art, and contemporary crafts. *Fort Mason, Bldg. A, tel. 415/775–0990. Admission: $1 adults, 50¢ senior citizens and children; admission free Sat. 10–noon. Open Tues.–Sun. 11–5, Sat. 10–5.*

Several theater companies are housed at Fort Mason. Of particular note is the **Magic Theatre** (Fort Mason, Bldg. D, tel. 415/441–8822), known for producing the works of such contemporary playwrights as Sam Shepard and Michael McClure.

The **SS *Jeremiah O'Brien*** is a World War II Liberty Ship freighter. The ship is staffed by volunteers, and there are special "steaming weekends," when the steam engine is in operation, the coal stove galley is open, and the "Slop Chest" store is set up. This is usually the third weekend of the month, but call to verify. *Fort Mason, Pier 3 East, Marina Blvd. and Buchanan St., tel. 415/441–3101. Admission: $2 adults, $1 children and senior citizens, $5 per family. Admission on steaming weekends: $3 adults, $1 children and senior citizens, $6 per family. Open weekdays 9–3, weekends 9–4.*

Time Out   The San Francisco Zen Center operates a famous and beautiful restaurant at Fort Mason. **Greens** (Fort Mason, Bldg. A, tel. 415/771–6222) has won international acclaim for its innovative vegetarian menu. The room is decorated with contemporary art and offers some of the finest views (from down close to the water) across the bay to the Golden Gate Bridge. Reservations are essential, but you can stop by the bakery during the day and pick up some of their famous bread and pastries.

❹ Spend some time strolling through **Ghirardelli Square,** which is across Beach Street from the National Maritime Museum. This charming complex of 19th-century brick factory buildings has been transformed into specialty shops, cafés, restaurants, and galleries. Until the early 1960s, the Ghirardelli Chocolate Company's aromatic production perfumed the Northern Waterfront. Two unusual shops deserve mention: **Light Opera** specializes in exquisite Russian lacquer boxes. (**Gump's** on Post Street also shows these sophisticated treasures, priced from about $50 to $20,000.) **Xanadu Gallery** displays museum-quality tribal art from Asia, Africa, Oceania, and the Americas. Their array of antique and ethnic jewelry is peerless.

❺ Just east of the Hyde Street Pier, **The Cannery** is a three-story structure built in 1894 to house the Del Monte Fruit and Vegetable Cannery. Now shops, art galleries, and unusual restaurants ring the courtyard. Just across the street, additional shopping and snacking choices are offered at the flag-festooned **Anchorage** mall.

6 The mellow **Buena Vista Cafe** (2765 Hyde St.) claims to be the birthplace of Irish Coffee stateside; local columnist Stan Delaplane is credited with importing the Gaelic concoction. The BV opens at 9 AM, serving a great breakfast. It is always crowded; try for a table overlooking nostalgic Victorian Park with its cable-car turntable.

A bit farther down at Taylor and Jefferson streets is **7** **Fisherman's Wharf.** Numerous seafood restaurants are located here, as well as sidewalk crab pots and counters that offer takeaway shrimp and crab cocktails. Ships creak at their moorings; sea gulls cry out for a handout. By mid-afternoon, the fishing fleet is back to port. T-shirts and sweats, gold chains galore, redwood furniture, acres of artwork—some original—beckon visitors. Wax museums, fast-food favorites, amusing street artists, and the animated robots at Lazer Maze provide diversions for all ages.

Time Out A great family spot on the wharf is **Bobby Rubino's** (245 Jefferson St.). Barbecued ribs, shrimp, chicken, and burgers—there is something tasty for everyone. A favorite with couples is crowded, noisy **Houlihan's** at the Anchorage mall. It is noted for fancy drinks, fantastic bay views, tasty pizza and pastas, plus nightly music and dancing.

Today's tourists daily have the opportunity of enjoying exhilarating cruising on the bay. Among the cruises of the **Red and White Fleet,** berthed at Pier 41, are frequent 45-minute swings under the Golden Gate Bridge and the Northern Waterfront. Advanced reservations are strongly recommended for the very popular Alcatraz Island tour, which enables passengers to take a self-guided tour through the prison and grounds. *Reservations for individuals from Ticketron, Box 26430, 94126, tel. 415/546–2896. Cost: $5; $7.50 with audio tour.*

The **Blue and Gold Fleet,** berthed at Pier 39, provides its passengers with validated parking across the street. The 1¼-hour tour sails under both the Bay and Golden Gate bridges. Dinner-dance cruises run April–mid-December. *Tel. 415/781–7877. Reservations not necessary. Bay Cruise: $14 adults, $7 senior citizens and children 5–18, under 5 free. Summertime dinner-dance cruise: $35 per person (group rates available). Daily departures.*

8 **Pier 39** is the newest of San Francisco's waterfront malls. Dozens of shops with fascinating but often useless merchandise will prove tempting. The myriad eateries confuse some parents seeking only a traditional soda-and-burger stop. Ongoing free entertainment, accessible validated parking, as well as nearby public transportation ensure crowds most days.

Tour 15: The Marina and the Presidio

9 San Francisco's rosy and Rococo **Palace of Fine Arts** is at the very end of the Marina, near the intersection of Baker and Beach streets. The palace is the sole survivor of the 32 tinted plaster structures built for the 1915 Panama-Pacific Exposition. Bernard Maybeck designed the Roman Classic beauty, and legions of sentimental citizens and a huge private donation saved the palace. It was reconstructed in concrete at a cost of $7 million and reopened in 1967. The massive columns, great rotunda, and swan-filled lagoon will be familiar from fashion layouts as well as many recent films. Recently, travelers on package tours from Japan have been using it as a backdrop for wedding-party photos, with the brides wearing Western-style finery.

The interior houses a fascinating hands-on museum, the **Exploratorium.** It has been called the best science museum in the world. The curious of all ages flock here to try to use and understand some of the 600 exhibits. Be sure to include the pitch-black, crawl-through Tactile Dome in your visit. *Tel. 415/ 563–7337. Prices and hours subject to change, so call ahead. Admission: $6 adults, $2 children under 17. For the Tactile Dome, reservations required, and a $6 charge includes museum admission.*

If you have a car, now is the time to use it for a drive through the **Presidio.** (If not, Muni bus No. 38 from Union Square will take you to Park Presidio; from there use a free transfer to bus No. 28 into the Presidio.) A military post for over 200 years, this headquarters of the U.S. Sixth Army may soon become a public park. De Anza and a band of Spanish settlers claimed the area in 1776. It became a Mexican garrison in 1822 when Mexico gained its independence from Spain. U.S. troops forcibly occupied it in 1846.

The more than 1,500 acres of rolling hills, majestic woods, and attractive redbrick army barracks present an air of serenity in the middle of the city. There are two beaches, a golf course, and picnic sites. The **Officers' Club,** a long, low adobe, was the Spanish commandante's headquarters, built about 1776, and is the oldest standing building in the city. The **Presidio Army Museum** is housed in the former hospital and focuses on the role played by the military in San Francisco's development. *On the corner of Lincoln Blvd. and Funston Ave., tel. 415/561–4115. Admission free. Open Tues.–Sun. 10–4.*

Muni bus No. 28 will take you to the **Golden Gate Bridge** toll plaza. San Francisco celebrated the 50th birthday of the orange suspension bridge in 1987. Nearly 2 miles long, connecting San Francisco with Marin County, its Art Deco design is powerful, serene, and tough, made to withstand winds of over 100 miles per hour. Though frequently gusty and misty (walkers should wear warm clothing), the bridge offers unparalleled views of the Bay Area. The east walkway offers a glimpse of the San Francisco skyline as well as the islands of the bay. On a sunny day sailboats dot the water, and brave windsurfers test the often treacherous tides beneath the bridge. The view west confronts you with the wild hills of the Marin headlands, the curving coast south to Lands End, and the majestic Pacific Ocean. There's a vista point on the Marin side, where you can contemplate the city and its spectacular setting.

Fort Point was constructed during the years 1853–1861 to protect San Francisco from sea attack during the Civil War. It was designed to mount 126 cannons with a range of up to 2 miles. Standing under the shadow of the Golden Gate Bridge, the national historic site is now a museum filled with military memorabilia. Guided group tours are offered by National Park Rangers, and there are cannon demonstrations. There is a superb view of the bay from the top floor. *Tel. 415/556–1693. Admission free. Open daily 10–5.*

From here, hardy walkers may elect to stroll about 3½ miles (with bay views) along the **Golden Gate Promenade** to Aquatic Park and the Hyde Street cable car terminus.

Tour 16: Golden Gate Park

Numbers in the margin correspond with points of interest on the Golden Gate Park map.

It was a Scotsman, John McLaren, who became manager of Golden Gate Park in 1887 and transformed the brush and sand into the green civilized wilderness we enjoy today. Here you can attend a polo game or a Sunday band concert and rent a bike, boat, or roller skates. On Sundays, some park roads are closed to cars and come alive with joggers, bicyclists, skaters, museum goers, and picnickers. There are tennis courts, baseball diamonds, soccer fields, and a buffalo paddock, and miles of trails for horseback riding in this 1,000-acre park.

Because it is so large, the best way for most visitors to see it is by car. Muni buses provide service, though on weekends there may be a long wait. On Market Street, board a west-bound No. 5-Fulton or No. 21-Hayes bus and continue to Arguello and Fulton streets. Walk south about 500 feet to John F. Kennedy Drive.

From May through October, free guided walking tours of the park are offered every weekend by the Friends of Recreation and Parks (tel. 415/221–1311).

❶ The oldest building in the park and perhaps San Francisco's most elaborate Victorian is the **Conservatory,** a copy of London's famous Kew Gardens. The ornate greenhouse was originally brought around the Horn for the estate of James Lick in San Jose. The Conservatory was purchased from the Lick estate with public subscription funds and erected in the park. In addition to a tropical garden, there are seasonal displays of flowers and plants and a permanent exhibit of rare orchids.

❷ The eastern section of the park has three museums. The **M.H. de Young Memorial Museum** was completely reorganized in 1989. It now features American art, with collections of painting, sculpture, textiles, and decorative arts from Colonial times through the 20th century. Fifteen new galleries highlight the work of American masters including Copley, Eakins, Bingham, and Sargent. Don't miss the room of landscapes, dominated by Frederic Church's moody, almost psychedelic *Rainy Season in the Tropics*. There is a wonderful gallery of American still-life and trompe l'oeil art and a small selection of classic Shaker furniture. The de Young has also retained its dramatic collection of tribal art from Africa, Oceania, and the Americas, which includes pottery, basketry, sculpture, and ritual clothing and accessories. In addition to its permanent collections, the museum hosts selected traveling shows—often blockbuster events for which there are long lines and additional admission charges.

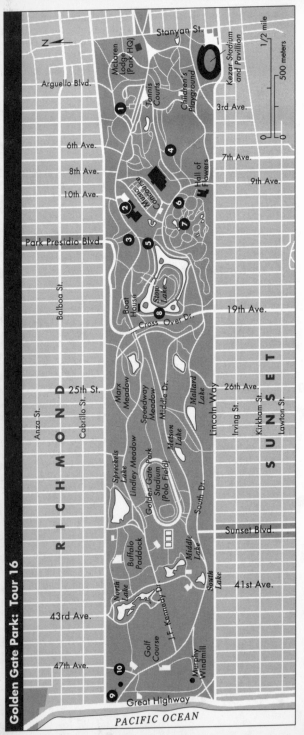

Golden Gate Park: Tour 16

N

Stanyan St.

McLaren Lodge (Park HQ)

Arguello Blvd.

Tennis Courts

Children's Playground

Kezar Stadium and Pavillion

3rd Ave.

1

6th Ave.

4

7th Ave.

8th Ave.

Hall of Flowers

9th Ave.

10th Ave.

Music Concourse

2

6

7

Park Presidia Blvd.

3

5

Boat House

Stow Lake

8

Cross Over Dr.

19th Ave.

Balboa St.

Marx Meadow

Speedway Meadow

Middle Dr.

Metson Lake

Mallard Lake

Lincoln Way

26th Ave.

Irving St.

Kirkham St.

Lawton St.

R I C H M O N D

25th St.

Cabrillo St.

Anza St.

Spreckels Lake

Lindley Meadow

Golden Gate Park Stadium (Polo Field)

South Dr.

Sunset Blvd.

S U N S E T

Buffalo Paddock

J.F. Kennedy Dr.

Middle Lake

South Lake

41st Ave.

North Lake

43rd Ave.

Golf Course

Murphy Windmill

47th Ave.

10

9

Great Highway

PACIFIC OCEAN

1/2 mile

500 meters

Asian Art Museum, **3**

California Academy of Science, **5**

Conservatory, **1**

Dutch Windmill, **9**

Japanese Tea Garden, **4**

M.H. de Young Memorial Museum, **2**

Queen Wilhelmina Tulip Garden, **10**

Shakespeare Garden, **6**

Stow Lake, **8**

Strybing Arboretum, **7**

The museum has an outstanding shop with a wide selection of art objects. The **Cafe de Young,** which has outdoor seating in the Oakes Garden, serves a complete menu of light refreshments until 4 PM. *Tel. 415/863–3330 for 24-hour information. Admission: $4 adults, $2 senior citizens and youths 12–17, under 12 free. Free 1st Wed. and Sat. morning of the month. Note: One admission charge admits you to the de Young, Asian Art, and Legion of Honor museums on the same day. Open Wed.– Sun. 10–5.*

❸ The **Asian Art Museum** is located in galleries that adjoin the de Young. This world-famous Avery Brundage collection consists of more than 10,000 sculptures, paintings, and ceramics that illustrate major periods of Asian art. Very special are the Magnin Jade Room and the Leventritt collection of blue and white porcelains. On the second floor are treasures from Iran, Turkey, Syria, India, Tibet, Nepal, Pakistan, Korea, Japan, Afghanistan, and Southeast Asia. Both the de Young and Asian Art museums have daily docent tours. *Tel. 415/668–8921. Admission collected when entering the de Young. Open Wed.–Sun. 10–5.*

Time Out The **Japanese Tea Garden,** next to the Asian Art Museum, is
❹ ideal for resting after museum touring. This charming four-acre village was created for the 1894 Mid-Winter Exposition. Small ponds, streams, and flowering shrubs create a serene landscape. The cherry blossoms in spring are exquisite. The Tea House (tea, of course, and cookies are served) is popular and busy. *Tel. 415/752–1171. Admission: $2 adults, $1 senior residents of San Francisco and children 6–12. Free 1st Wed. of each month. Open daily 8:30–6:30.*

❺ The **California Academy of Sciences** is directly opposite the de Young Museum. It is one of the five top natural history museums in the country and has both an aquarium and a planetarium. Throngs of visitors enjoy its Steinhart Aquarium, with its dramatic 100,000-gallon Fish Roundabout, home to 14,000 creatures, and a living coral reef with colorful fish, giant clams, tropical sharks, and a rainbow of hard and soft corals. There is an additional charge for Morrison Planetarium shows ($2.50 adults, $1.25 senior citizens and students, tel. 415/750–7138 for daily schedule). The Space and Earth Hall has an "earthquake floor" that enables visitors to ride a simulated California earthquake. The Wattis Hall of Man presents lifelike habitat scenes that range from the icy terrain of the arctic Inuit to the lush highlands of New Guinea. Newly renovated is the Wild California Hall, with a 10,000-gallon aquarium tank showing underwater life at the Farallones (islands off the coast of northern California), life-size elephant seal models, and video information on the wildlife of the state. A stuffed great white shark, caught off the waters of Half Moon Bay, was added in 1989. The genuine 13½-foot, 1,500-pound "Jaws" is suspended in a tank. If you dare, you can look right into its gaping mouth. The innovative Life through Time Hall tells the story of evolution from the beginnings of the universe through the age of dinosaurs to the age of mammals. A cafeteria is open daily until one hour before the museum closes. The Academy Store offers a wide selection of books, posters, toys, and cultural artifacts. *Tel. 415/ 750–7145. Admission: $6 adults, $3 senior citizens and stu-*

dents 12–17, $1 children 6–11. Free 1st Wed. of each month.
Open daily July 4–Labor Day 10–7, Labor Day–July 3 10–5.

⑥ A short stroll from the Academy of Sciences will take you to the free **Shakespeare Garden.** Two hundred flowers mentioned by the Bard, as well as bronze-engraved panels with floral quotations, are set throughout the garden.

⑦ **Strybing Arboretum** specializes in plants from areas with climates similar to that of the Bay Area, such as the west coast of Australia, South Africa, and the Mediterranean. There are many gardens inside the grounds, with 6,000 plants and tree varieties blooming seasonally. *9th Ave. at Lincoln Way, tel. 415/661–0668. Admission free. Open weekdays 8–4:30, weekends and holidays 10–5. Tours leave the bookstore weekdays at 1:30 PM, weekends at 10:30 AM and 1:30 PM.*

⑧ The western half of Golden Gate Park offers miles of wooded greenery and open spaces for all types of spectator and participant sports. Rent a paddleboat or stroll around **Stow Lake.** The **Chinese Pavilion,** a gift from the city of Taipei, was shipped in 6,000 pieces and assembled on the shore of Strawberry Hill Island in Stow Lake in 1981. At the very western end of the park, where Kennedy Drive meets the Great Highway, is the beauti- **⑨ ⑩** fully restored 1902 **Dutch Windmill** and the photogenic **Queen Wilhelmina Tulip Garden.**

Tour 17: Lincoln Park and the Western Shoreline

No other American city provides such close-up viewing of the power and fury of the surf attacking the shore. From Land's End in Lincoln Park you can look across the Golden Gate (the name was originally given to the opening of San Francisco Bay long before the bridge was built) to the Marin Headlands. From Cliff House south to the San Francisco Zoo, the Great Highway and Ocean Beach run along the western edge of the city.

The wind is often strong along the shoreline, summer fog can blanket the ocean beaches, and the water is cold and usually too rough for swimming. Carry a sweater or jacket and bring binoculars.

At the northwest corner of the San Francisco Peninsula is **Lincoln Park.** At one time all the city's cemeteries were here, segregated by nationality. Today there is an 18-hole golf course with large and well-formed Monterey cypresses lining the fairways. There are scenic walks throughout the 275-acre park, with particularly good views from **Land's End** (the parking lot is at the end of El Camino del Mar). The trails out to Land's End, however, are for skilled hikers only: There are frequent landslides, and danger lurks along the steep cliffs.

Also in Lincoln Park is the **California Palace of the Legion of Honor.** The building itself—modeled after the 18th-century Parisian original—is architecturally interesting and spectacularly situated on cliffs overlooking the ocean and the Golden Gate Bridge. Rodin's famous *Thinker* towers over the entry court and presages one of the finest Rodin collections in the world. This museum was redesigned in 1989 to present eight centuries of European art, combining painting, sculpture, and the decorative arts. Its holdings include works by Fra Angelico, Titian, El Greco, and Rembrandt, as well as four galleries of

French Rococo furniture, porcelain, and paintings. The museum also features Impressionist paintings by Manet, Monet, Renoir, and Degas and houses the Achenbach Foundation for Graphic Arts, a collection of over 100,000 prints and drawings. *Legion of Honor Dr., tel. 415/863-3330. Daily docent tours. Admission: $4 adults, $2 senior citizens and youths 12-17, under 12 free. Free 1st Wed. and Sat. morning of each month. Open Wed.–Sun. 10-5. Note: One admission charge admits you to the de Young, Asian Art, and Legion of Honor museums on the same day.*

Cliff House (1066 Point Lobos Ave.), where the road turns south along the western shore, has existed in several incarnations. The original, built in 1863, and several later structures were destroyed by fire. The present building has restaurants, a pub, and a gift shop. The lower dining room overlooks **Seal Rocks** (the barking marine mammals sunning themselves are actually sea lions).

An adjacent (free) attraction is the **Musée Mécanique,** a collection of antique mechanical contrivances, including peep shows and nickelodeons. The museum carries on the tradition of arcade amusement at the Cliff House. *Tel. 415/386-1170. Open weekdays 11-7, weekends 10-7.*

Two flights below Cliff House is a fine observation deck and the Golden Gate National Recreation Area **Visitors Center** (tel. 415/556-8642; open weekdays 10-4:30, weekends 10-5). There are interesting and historic photographs of Cliff House and the glass-roofed **Sutro Baths.** The baths covered three acres just north of Cliff House and comprised six enormous baths, 500 dressing rooms, and several restaurants. The baths were closed in 1952 and burned in 1966. You can explore the ruins on your own (the Visitors Center offers information on these and other trails) or take ranger-led walks on weekends.

Because traffic is often heavy in summer and on weekends, you might want to take the Muni system from the Union Square area out to Cliff House. On weekdays, take the Muni No. 38-Geary Limited to 48th Street and Point Lobos and walk down the hill. (On weekends and during the evenings, the Muni No. 38 is marked 48th Avenue.)

Time Out   Cliff House has several restaurants and a busy bar. The **Upstairs Room** (tel. 415/387-5847) features a light menu with a number of omelet suggestions. The lower dining room, the **Terrace Room** (tel. 415/386-3330), has a fabulous view of Seal Rocks. Reservations are recommended, but you may still have to wait for a table, especially at midday on Sunday.

Below the Cliff House are the **Great Highway** and **Ocean Beach.** Stretching for 3 miles along the western (Pacific) side of the city, this is a beautiful beach for walking, running, or lying in the sun—but not for swimming.

At the Great Highway and Sloat Boulevard is the **San Francisco Zoo.** The zoo was begun in 1889 in Golden Gate Park. At its present home there are 1,000 species of birds and animals, over 130 of which have been designated endangered species. Among the protected are the snow leopard, Bengal tiger, red panda, jaguar, and the Asian elephant. One of the newest attractions is the greater one-horned rhino, next to the African elephants.

Gorilla World, a $2 million exhibit, is the largest and most natural gorilla habitat in a zoo. The circular outer area is carpeted with natural African Kikuyu grass, while trees, shrubs, and waterfalls create communal play areas. The $5 million Primate Discovery Center houses 16 endangered species in atriumlike enclosures. One of the most popular zoo residents is Prince Charles, a rare white tiger and the first of its kind to be exhibited in the West.

There are 33 "storyboxes" throughout the zoo that when turned on with the blue plastic elephant keys ($1.50) recite animal facts and basic zoological concepts in four languages (English, Spanish, Cantonese, and Tagalog).

The children's zoo has a minipopulation of about 300 mammals, birds, and reptiles, plus an insect zoo, a baby animal nursery, and a beautifully restored 1921 Dentzel Carousel. A ride astride one of the 52 hand-carved menagerie animals costs 75¢.

Zoo information, tel. 415/753–7083. Admission: $6 adults, $3 youths 12–15 and senior citizens, under 12 free when accompanied by an adult. Free 1st Wed. of the month. Open daily 10–5. Children's zoo admission: $1, under 3 free. Open daily 11–4.

Tour 18: The Mission District

Numbers in the margin correspond with points of interest on the Mission District and Castro Street map.

During the 19th century the sunny weather of the then-rural Mission District made it a popular locale for resorts, racetracks, and gambling places. At 13th and Mission streets, where freeway traffic now roars overhead, stood Woodward's Gardens, a lush botanical garden with a zoo, playground, and pavilions featuring acrobatic performances.

Mission Street is the commercial center of the district, and all the resident ethnic cultures are reflected in the businesses: Spanish-language theaters, Italian restaurants, Arab-owned clothing stores, Vietnamese markets, and Filipino, Hispanic, and Chinese restaurants and groceries. The majority of Latinos here are from Central America. Most of them settled here during the late 1960s and early 1970s; many of them are now service workers. The Mexican-Americans are a minority of the estimated 50,000 Hispanics in the Mission.

❶ **Mission Dolores,** on palm-lined Dolores Street, is the sixth of the 21 missions founded by Father Junipero Serra. The adobe building was begun in 1782 and was originally known as Mission San Francisco de Assisi. Completed in 1791, its ceiling depicts original Costanoan Indian basket designs, executed in vegetable dyes. There is a small museum, and the mission cemetery contains the graves of more than 5,000 Indians. *Dolores and 16th Sts., tel. 415/621–8203. Admission: $1. Open daily 9–4.*

❷ The nearby **Dolores Park** (Dolores St. between 18th and 20th Sts.) is a great picnic spot that offers dramatic views of the high rises of downtown as a backdrop for the pastel bay-windowed Mission District houses.

Two blocks from Mission Dolores, the area around 16th and Valencia streets is developing its own neighborhood character. A mix of socialists, lesbian-feminists, new wavers, and tradition-

The Mission District and Castro Street : Tours 18–19

Balmy Alley, **6**
Castro Theatre, **8**
Dolores Park, **2**
Galeria de la Raza, **5**
Josephine D. Randall
Junior Museum, **10**
Mission Dolores, **1**

The Names Project, **9**
Precita Eyes and Ears
Art Center, **7**
The Roxie Theater, **3**
The Women's Building
of the Bay Area, **4**

al Hispanics has made it San Francisco's new bohemia. The
❸ **Roxie Theater** (3117 16th St., tel. 415/863–1087) is an aggressive showcase for independent films. Across the street, **Cafe
Picaro** (3120 16th St.) appears to be a leftover from the '60s.
People gather here for political discussions and to work on papers, read books, and play chess while downing strong cappuccino and hearty inexpensive meals.

The cornerstone of the women-owned and -run businesses in
❹ the neighborhood is the **Women's Building of the Bay Area** (3543
18th St., tel. 415/431–1180), which for 10 years has held workshops and conferences of particular interest to women. It
houses offices for many social and political organizations and
sponsors talks and readings by such noted writers as Alice
Walker and Angela Davis. Bulletin boards announce many
women-oriented events in the Bay Area.

Time Out   You can eat better for less money in the Mission District than
anywhere else in the city. Stop in at one of the *taquerias* (taco
parlors), fast-food eateries where the meals are nutritious and
very, very inexpensive. The staples are tacos and burritos—
but they are unlike those served at Americanized fast-food
places. At **La Cumbre** (515 Valencia St., tel. 415/863–8205) and
El Toro (17th and Valencia Sts., tel. 415/431–3351), two of the
neighborhood's most popular taquerias, the tacos are made
with double-corn tortillas piled high with a choice of meat and
beans. And the burritos are large, rolled-flour tortillas stuffed
with meat, rice, and beans. La Cumbre is also well known for
its *carne asada* (charcoal-grilled steak); El Toro for its chicken
simmered in green chili sauce, and *carnitas* (crisp strips of
roast pork).

Colorful, crammed, noisy Mission Street may represent the
commercial artery of the Mission District, but 24th Street is its
heart. Here the area takes on the flavor of another country,
with small open-air groceries selling huge Mexican papayas
and plantains, tiny restaurants serving *sopa de mariscos* (fish
soup), and an abundance of religious shops and Latin bakeries.
The feeling is more rural than on Mission Street and certainly
less Anglo.

❺ **Galeria de la Raza,** at the east end of the street, is an important
showcase for Hispanic art. It shows local and international artists, sometimes mounting events in conjunction with the Mexican Museum at Fort Mason. (A Frieda Kahlo exhibit in 1988
used both venues.) *2855 24th St., tel. 415/826–8009. Open
Tues.–Sat. 1–6.*

Next door to the Gallery is **Studio 24 Galeria Shop,** which sells
folklore handicrafts from Latin America. The studio specializes in figurines from *Dia de los Muertos*, the Latin American
Halloween. The polychrome plaster skeletons—posed as if
singing, dancing, or working—represent deceased family
members come back for a visit, doing the kinds of things they
did in life. The clay groupings can be quite elaborate, using
such settings as cars, couches, and kitchens. The aim is to make
death more familiar and less threatening; don't be surprised to
see a skeleton calmly doing her ironing. Also look for the mar-
velously detailed Peruvian tapestries called *arpedas*, which
also highlight daily life. *2857 24th St., tel. 415/826–8009. Open
Tues.–Sat. noon–6.*

Art in the Mission District is not confined indoors. Keeping alive the tradition of the great muralist Diego Rivera, community artists have transformed the walls of their neighborhood
❻ with paintings. In small **Balmy Alley** (between Treat and Harrison Sts. just off 24th St.), paint changes a funky side street into a dramatic aisle of color and purpose. The murals up and down the alley were begun in 1973 by a group of local children and continued by an affiliation of several dozen artists and community workers to promote peace in Central America. The
❼ **Precita Eyes and Ears Arts Center** gives guided walks of the Mission District's murals. The tour starts with a ½-hour slide presentation, and the walk takes about an hour, visiting over 40 murals in the area. *348 Precita Ave., tel. 415/285–2287. Tours every weekend, 1:30 PM. $3 adults, $1 students under 18. Walks can also be arranged by appointment for groups of 10 or more.*

Bakeries, or *panaderias*, are an essential stop on 24th Street. Don't expect light, buttery, flaky creations. Latin American pastries are strictly down-to-earth—but delicious. Try the Salvadorean specialty, *quesadillas*, which have cheese ground in with the flour and taste like sweet corn muffins; or *cemitas*, cake squares filled with pineapple. You take what looks good, with tongs and a tray provided at the counter. **La Victoria** (2937 24th St.) and **Dominguez** (2951 24th St.) on competing sides of the street are two of the best.

The **St. Francis Candy Store** (2801 24th St.) is a genuine soda fountain and ice-cream parlor that makes its own confections. An anomaly in the neighborhood, it looks like something from a Norman Rockwell painting.

Time Out The Salvadorean restaurants that have opened in the Mission District during the past several years are great eating places. Their fare is a variation of traditional Mexican cooking that offers more stews and sauces. **El Tazumal** (3522 20th St., tel. 415/550–0935), off Mission Street at 20th Street, was one of the pioneers and has excellent, inexpensive lunches and dinners. Try the appetizers called *pupusas* (baked pancakes filled with ground meat or cheese) and the pork *chile verde* (cubes of meat simmered to succulence in a mild green chili/tomatillo sauce).

The Mission District plays fiesta for two important occasions. There is a weekend of festivities around the *cinco de Mayo* (5th of May) holiday, but the neighborhood really erupts into celebration on a sunny weekend in late spring called *carnaval*. This Rio-like three-day extravaganza gets larger each year. Recent festivities closed Harrison Street between 16th and 20th streets, with four stages for live music and dancers, as well as crafts and food booths. A Grand Carnaval Parade along 24th Street caps the celebration.

Tour 19: Castro Street

Starting during the early 1970s, the neighborhood around Castro Street became known for one of the most remarkable urban migrations in American history: the mass arrival of gay men and women in San Francisco, from all over the United States. What had been for decades a sunny, sedate, middle-class neighborhood of mostly Irish and Scandinavian families became a new colony that was either a gay ghetto or, as many thought, Gay Mecca.

Historians are still trying to discover what brought an estimated 100,000 to 250,000 gays into the San Francisco area.
Some point to the libertine tradition rooted in Barbary Coast
piracy, prostitution, and gambling. Others note that as a huge
military embarcation point during World War II, the city was
occupied by tens of thousands of mostly single men. Whatever
the cause, San Francisco became the city of choice for lesbians
and gay men, and Castro Street, nestled at the base of Twin
Peaks and just over Buena Vista hill from Haight Street, became its social, cultural, and political center.

From Powell Street, take the Muni Metro underground (trains
K, L, M, or O) direct to the Castro Street station. You will come
out into Harvey Milk Plaza, named for the man who electrified
the city in 1977 by being voted onto the metropolitan board of
supervisors as an openly gay candidate. The proprietor of a
Castro Street camera store, Harvey Milk proved that the gay
community of San Francisco was a political as well as a social
force. His high visibility accompanied demands by homosexu-
als for thorough inclusion in the city's life—its power structures, not just its disco parties. San Francisco has responded
with a tolerance found nowhere else in the United States: Gay
people sit as municipal judges, police commissioners, and arts
administrators.

Two events, though, have changed the tenor of the community.
On November 27, 1978, barely a year after being elected, Harvey Milk and the liberal mayor George Moscone were assassi-
nated by a disturbed member of the board of supervisors, Dan
White. A few years later gay men began to awaken to a new ter-
ror: AIDS. The gay community has responded to this tragedy
with courage and generosity. The city itself serves as a model
for civic intervention and support during a health crisis. The
Castro has become less flamboyant and a little more sober in
the wake of the crisis; now it's more of a mixed neighborhood,
and more relaxed. It is still, however, the center of gay life. Gay
bars abound, and gay-oriented boutiques line Castro, 18th, and
Market streets.

Across the street from Harvey Milk Plaza is the great neon
8 neighborhood landmark, the **Castro Theatre** marquee. Erected
in 1927, the theater is the grandest of San Francisco's few remaining Art Deco movie palaces. Its elaborate Spanish Baroque interior is well preserved, and a new pipe organ plays
nightly, ending with a traditional chorus of the Jeanette
McDonald standard, "San Francisco." The 1,500-capacity
crowd can be enthusiastic and vocal, talking back to the screen
as loudly as it talks to them. The Castro Theatre is the showcase for many community events, in particular the annual Gay/
Lesbian Film Festival held each June.

Castro Street boasts numerous men's clothing stores. **All
American Boy** (463 Castro St.) is the standard-bearer and set-
ter for casual wear, especially the neighborhood uniform: jeans
and T-shirts. Up the street, **Citizen** (536 Castro St.) counters
with a more colorful selection of designer-inspired clothing.
For athletic wear suitable for sunny days on the street, there's
High Gear (600 Castro St.).

True to its playful name, **Does Your Mother Know** (4079 18th
St.) is a card store like no other, offering specialized greetings
to entertain—and shock. Be prepared; this may be the premier

X-rated card shop in the country. But some cards are just plain funny, with a stellar series featuring local drag queen Doris Fish, a mistress of many disguises.

A Different Light (489 Castro St.) is *not* X-rated. It features books by, for, and about lesbians and gay men. The store hosts numerous book-signings and weekly poetry readings.

Time Out The **Patio Cafe** takes advantage of one of the neighborhood's best features: its great weather. You can brunch in an open-air garden court while you get a California tan. The café is inexpensive and serves a standard American fare of omelets, sandwiches, and traditional dinners. Leisurely breakfasts or brunches are the signature meals, accompanied by the weekend-morning drink of choice: mimosas (champagne and orange juice). There's also a full bar. *531 Castro St., tel. 415/621–4640. Open Mon.–Sat. 8 AM–10:30 PM, Sun. 8:45 AM–10:30 PM.*

❾ Down Market Street **The Names Project** (2363 Market St.) has its offices and public workshop. A gigantic quilt made of over 10,000 hand-sewn and decorated panels has been pieced together by loved ones to serve as a memorial to those who have died of AIDS. People come from all over the country to work in this storefront as a labor of love and grief; others have sent panels here by mail. New additions to the quilt are always on display. The site serves as a dignified in-process tribute to a community's struggle and compassionate involvement.

Just northwest of Castro and Market streets, an outcropping of rock provides one of the best viewing areas in the city. Walk north up Castro Street two blocks to 16th Street and turn left. This is a steep climb, and it gets steeper and a little more rugged, but it's worth the effort. Turn right at Flint Street; the hill to your left is variously known as Red Rock, Museum Hill, and, correctly, Corona Heights. Start climbing up the path by the tennis courts along the spine of the hill; the view downtown is increasingly superb. You don't have to go very high up to have all of northeast San Francisco and the bay before you. In spring you'll be surrounded by California wildflowers, but whenever you climb to the ragged rocks at the top, be sure to carry a jacket with you: The wind loves this spot.

❿ At the base of Corona Heights is the **Josephine D. Randall Junior Museum.** Geared toward children by the Recreation and Parks Department, the museum nevertheless has a variety of workshops and events for both young people and their parents. It includes a Mineral Hall, Animal Room, library, and an excellent woodworking studio. *199 Museum Way, tel. 415/554–9600. Open Tues.–Sat. 10–5 and at night for workshops.*

The Castro neighborhood is allied to three events that are true community holidays. In late September or early October, when San Francisco weather is at its warmest, the annual **Castro Street Fair** takes over several blocks of Castro and Market streets. Huge stages are erected for live music and comedy, alongside booths selling food and baubles. The weather inevitably brings off the men's shirts, and the Castro relives for a moment the permissive spirit of the 1970s.

Each Halloween thousands of revelers (though most are just onlookers) converge on Castro Street from all over the city to watch the perpetual masquerade. Drag queens of all shapes and sizes intentionally reduce the crowd to laughter; the spirit is high and friendly, San Francisco's version of Mardi Gras.

More political is the annual **Lesbian/Gay Pride Celebration and Parade,** by far the city's largest annual event. On the last Sunday in June 250,000 to 500,000 men and women march to the Civic Center to commemorate the birth of the modern gay-rights movement. This is no longer a parochial march; major political figures participate, and it regularly provides the gay community with its most powerful public statement.

Tour 20: Haight-Ashbury

East of Golden Gate Park is the neighborhood known as "the Haight." Once home to large, middle-class families of European immigrants, the Haight began to change during the late 1950s and early 1960s. Families were fleeing to the suburbs; the big old Victorians were deteriorating or being chopped up into cheap housing. Young people found the neighborhood an affordable and exciting community in which to live according to new precepts.

The peak of the Haight as a youth scene came in 1966. It had become the home of many rock bands. The Grateful Dead moved into a big Victorian at 710 Ashbury Street, just a block off Haight Street. Jefferson Airplane had their grand mansion at 2400 Fulton Street. By 1967, 200,000 young people with flowers in their hair were heading for the Haight. The peace and civil rights movements had made "freedom" their generation's password.

Sharing the late-1980s fascination with things of the 1960s, many visitors to San Francisco want to see the setting of the "Summer of Love." Back in 1967, Gray Lines instituted their "Hippie-Hop," advertising it as "the only foreign tour within the continental limits of the United States," piloted by a driver "especially trained in the sociological significance of the Haight." Today's explorers can walk from Union Square to Market Street and hop aboard Muni's No. 7 Haight.

Haight Street has once again emerged as the center of youth culture in San Francisco, though this time it is an amalgam of punkers, neo-hippies, and suburbanites out to spend their cash. The street has become the city's prime shopping district for "vintage" merchandise. Numerous used-clothing emporiums offer their finery; check out **Zebra Zebra** for "endangered clothing" (1388 Haight St.); the **New Government** (1427 Haight St.) for '50s and '60s specialties; as well as **Aardvark's, Held Over,** and **Buffalo Exchange,** all on the 1500 block. **La Rosa** offers previously worn formal wear for rent and sale (1711 Haight St.). The street also boasts several used-book stores and some of the best used-record stores in the city: **Recycled Records** (1377 Haight St.), **Reckless Records** (1401 Haight St.), and **Rough Trade** (1529 Haight St.) focus on classic rock and roll, obscure independent labels, and hard-to-find imports.

While it increases the incidence of panhandlers and the visibility of the homeless, Golden Gate Park also provides the Haight with unique opportunities for recreation and entertainment. You can rent roller skates at **Skates on Haight** (1818 Haight St.) and roll through the park (it's partially closed to traffic for skaters on Sundays); or you can take the more genteel route and rent bicycles at several stops along Stanyan Street, right by the park's entrance.

The Haight's famous political spirit (it was the first neighborhood in the United States to lead a freeway revolt, and it continues to feature regular boycotts against chain stores said to ruin the street's local character) exists alongside some of the finest Victorian-lined streets in the city; over 1000 such houses occupy the Panhandle and Ashbury Heights streets.

Great city views can be had from **Buena Vista Park** at Haight and Lyon streets. One of San Francisco's most attractive bed-and-breakfast inns is the **Spreckels Mansion** at 737 Buena Vista West, several blocks south of Haight Street. The house was built for sugar baron Richard Spreckels in 1887, and later tenants included Jack London and Ambrose Bierce.

Time Out Island cuisine—a mix of Cajun, Southwest, and Caribbean influences—is served at **Cha Cha Cha** (1805 Haight St.), which is informal and inexpensive. The decor is technicolor tropical plastic, and the food is hot and spicy. Try the spicy fried calamari or chili-spiked shrimp. No reservations; expect to wait. *Tel. 415/386–5758. Open daily for lunch and dinner. No credit cards.*

Historic Buildings and Sites

What follows is a list of historical sites that have already been described. For further information see the sections on the specific neighborhoods in this chapter, noted below in parentheses.

Bank of America (The Financial District).
Cannery (The Northern Waterfront).
Chinese Six Companies (Chinatown).
City Hall (Civic Center).
Cliff House (Lincoln Park and the Western Shoreline).
Coit Tower (North Beach).
Conservatory (Golden Gate Park).
Davies Hall (Civic Center).
Embarcadero Center (The Embarcadero and Lower Market Street).
Fairmont Hotel (Nob Hill).
Ferry Building (The Embarcadero and Lower Market Street).
Fort Mason (The Northern Waterfront).
Ghirardelli Square (The Northern Waterfront).
Golden Gate Bridge (The Marina and the Presidio).
Grace Cathedral (Nob Hill).
Hallidie Building (The Financial District).
Hyde Street Pier (The Northern Waterfront).
Jackson Square (Jackson Square).
Land's End (Lincoln Park and the Western Shoreline).
Maiden Lane (Union Square).
Mills Building and Tower (The Financial District).
Mission Dolores (The Mission District).
Old St. Mary's Church (Chinatown).
Pacific Stock Exchange (The Financial District).
Presidio (The Marina and the Presidio).
Russ Building (The Financial District).
St. Francis Hotel (Union Square).

St. Mary's Cathedral (Japantown).
Sheraton-Palace Hotel (The Embarcadero and Lower Market Street).
Sutro Baths (Lincoln Park and the Western Shoreline).
Union Square (Union Square).
Vedanta Society Headquarters (Union Street).
Victory Monument (Union Square).
Wedding Houses (Union Street).
Wright, Frank Lloyd, building (Union Square).

Museums and Galleries

This list of San Francisco's museums includes both museums that were covered in the preceding sections on specific neighborhoods as well as a number that are described here for the first time.

Ansel Adams Center. This new museum showcases both historical and contemporary photography. *250 4th St., tel. 415/495–7000. Admission: $4 adults, $3 students, $2 senior citizens and youths 12–17, children under 12 free. Open Tues.–Sun. 11–6.*
Asian Art Museum (Golden Gate Park).
Cable Car Barn (Nob Hill).
California Academy of Sciences (Golden Gate Park).
California Historical Society (Pacific Heights).
California Palace of the Legion of Honor (Lincoln Park and the Western Shoreline).
Cartoon Art Museum. The focus here is not the juvenile funnies you would expect but the "underground" comics that first emerged in the 1960s. *665 3rd St., tel. 415/546–3922. Admission: $3 adults, $2 students, $1 senior citizens and children under 13. Open Wed.–Fri. 11–5, Sat. 10–5.*
Chevron: A World of Oil. Exhibits and an audiovisual show explore the history of the oil industry. The museum is a five-minute walk from the Market-Powell Street cable car terminus. *555 Market St., lobby level. Admission free. Open weekdays 9–4.*
Chinese Cultural Foundation (Chinatown).
Chinese Historical Society (Chinatown).
de Young Museum, M.H. (Golden Gate Park).
Exploratorium (The Marina and the Presidio).
Fort Point National Historic Site (The Marina and the Presidio).
Haas-Lilienthal House (Pacific Heights).
Jewish Community Museum. Revolving exhibits in this handsome small museum trace important moments in Jewish history. *121 Steuart St., tel. 415/543–8880. Admission: $3 adults, $1 children and senior citizens. Open Sun., Tues.–Fri. 10–4.*
Mexican Museum (The Northern Waterfront).
Mission Dolores (The Mission District).
Museo Italo Americano (The Northern Waterfront).
National Maritime Museum (The Northern Waterfront).
Octagon House (Union Street).
Old San Francisco Mint (The Embarcadero and Lower Market Street).
Palace of Fine Arts (The Marina and the Presidio).
Ripley's Believe It or Not. There are 11 galleries and over 750 exhibits, all either amazing or not. *Fisherman's Wharf. Admission: $6.95 adults, $5.25 senior citizens and children 13–17, $3.75 children 5–12. Open Sun.–Thurs. 10–10, Fri.–Sat. 10–midnight.*
San Francisco Art Institute (Russian Hill).

San Francisco Craft and Folk Art Museum (The Northern Waterfront).

San Francisco Fire Department Museum. Over 100 years of fire-department history are documented with photographs and other memorabilia. *655 Presidio Ave., at Bush St. Take Muni bus No. 38 on Geary St. to Presidio Ave.; walk 2 blocks to Bush St. Admission free. Open Sat. and Sun. 1–4.*

San Francisco Museum of Modern Art (Civic Center).

San Francisco History Room and Archives (Civic Center).

Wax Museum. The museum has almost 300 wax figures of film stars, U.S. presidents, and world celebrities. *145 Jefferson St., Fisherman's Wharf. Admission: $7.95 adults, special discount senior citizens and military, $3.95 children 6–12. Open Sun.–Thurs. 9–10, Fri.–Sat. 9–11.*

Wells Fargo History Museum (The Financial District).

Whittier Mansion (Pacific Heights).

World of Economics. Economics is explained through videotapes, computer games, and electronic displays. *Federal Reserve Bank, 101 Market St. Take Muni bus No. 8 from Market and Powell Sts. to Main and Market Sts. Admission free. Open weekdays 9–4:30.*

Parks and Gardens

Buena Vista Park (Haight-Ashbury).

Coolbrith, Ina, Park (Russian Hill).

Dolores Park (The Mission District).

Dutch Windmill (Golden Gate Park).

Golden Gate Park (Golden Gate Park).

Japanese Tea Garden (Golden Gate Park).

Lafayette Park (Pacific Heights).

Lincoln Park (Lincoln Park and the Western Shoreline).

Pioneer Park (North Beach).

Portsmouth Square (Chinatown).

Queen Wilhelmina Tulip Garden (Golden Gate Park).

St. Mary's Park (Chinatown).

Sigmund Stern Grove. This park encompasses a small valley that forms a kind of natural amphitheater. From mid-June through August, free outdoor Sunday programs feature opera, ballet, jazz, symphony, and ethnic dance. Bring a sweater, in case ocean breezes and fogs roll in. *19th Ave. and Sloat Blvd., in the Sunset District. Take the Muni light rail system (M or K) from Powell and Market Sts. to Sloat Blvd. and West Portal.*

Strybing Arboretum (Golden Gate Park).

Washington Square (North Beach).

San Francisco for Free

This is not a cheap city to live in or visit. Lodging and dining are expensive; museums, shopping, the opera, or a nightclub may set you back a bit. It is possible, however, to do much of your sightseeing very cheaply. Walking is often the best way to get around, and it's not very expensive to use the cable cars and buses. Exploring most of Golden Gate Park is absolutely free, and so is walking across the Golden Gate Bridge.

The Golden Gate National Recreation Area (GGNRA), comprising most of San Francisco's shoreline, Alcatraz and Angel islands, and the headlands of Marin County, is the largest urban park in the world. The Golden Gate Promenade's 3.5-mile footpath runs from Fort Point at the base of the bridge along the shore to Hyde Street Pier. There's also a new 8-mile-long bicycle path along Ocean beach from Cliff House south to Fort Funston, hugging sand dunes and providing constant ocean views. The GGNRA is San Francisco at its natural best.

There are also free organ concerts on Saturday and Sunday at 4 PM in the **Palace of the Legion of Honor** in Lincoln Park (tel. 415/221–4811) and free band concerts on Sunday and holiday afternoons in the **Golden Gate Park band shell,** opposite the de Young Museum (tel. 415/666–7107).

What to See and Do with Children

The attractions described in the above exploring sections offer a great deal of entertainment for children as well as their families. We suggest, for example, visiting the ships at the **Hyde Street Pier** and spending some time at **Pier 39,** where there is a double-decked Venetian carousel. (*See* Tour 14: The Northern Waterfront, above.)

Children will find much to amuse themselves with at **Golden Gate Park,** from the old-fashioned conservatory to the expansive lawns and trails. There is another vintage carousel (1912) at the children's playground. The **Steinhart Aquarium** at the California Academy of Sciences has a "Touching Tide Pool," from which docents will pull starfish and hermit crabs for children or adults to feel. The **Japanese Tea Garden,** although crowded, is well worth exploring; climbing over the high, humpbacked bridges is like moving the neighborhood playground toys into an exotic new (or old) world.

It is also possible to walk across the **Golden Gate Bridge.** The view is thrilling and the wind invigorating, if the children (and adults) are not overwhelmed by the height of the bridge and the nearby automobile traffic. (*See* Tour 15: The Marina and the Presidio, above.)

Many children may enjoy walking along crowded **Grant Avenue** and browsing in the many souvenir shops. Unfortunately, nothing—not even straw finger wrestlers, wooden contraptions to make coins "disappear," shells that open in water to release tissue paper flowers, and other true junk—is as cheap as it once was. (*See* Tour 6: Chinatown, above.)

The **San Francisco Zoo,** with a children's zoo, playground, and carousel, is not far from Ocean Beach. The weather and the currents do not allow swimming, but it's a good place for walking and playing in the surf. (*See* Tour 17: Lincoln Park and the Western Shoreline, above.)

The **Exploratorium** at the Palace of Fine Arts is a preeminent children's museum and is very highly recommended. (*See* Tour 15: The Marina and the Presidio, above.)

Finally, we remind you of the **cable cars.** Try to find time for a ride when the crowds are not too thick (mid-morning or afternoon). It's usually easier to get on at one of the turnarounds at the ends of the lines. (*See* Getting Around by Cable Car in Chapter 1.)

If you're ready to spend a day outside of the city, consider a trip to Vallejo's Marine World Africa USA. (*See* Chapter 9.)

Off the Beaten Track

Dark Passage Do you remember Lauren Bacall's fantastic Art Deco apartment in the 1947 movie *Dark Passage*? Do you remember Humphrey Bogart climbing those unending stairs? In this film, Bogart plays a man who has been convicted of murdering his wife; with the help of Bacall, he escapes from prison and has plastic surgery to disguise himself (and ends up looking like Bogart!). You can take a look at these sites if, after visiting Coit Tower on Telegraph Hill, you turn right, cross the street, and walk down the brick-and-ivy-lined Greenwich Steps, ending up on Montgomery Street. The famous apartment house is number 1360. Just a little ways to the left you can pick up the Filbert Steps or walk down Union Street to Grant Avenue and the North Beach attractions.

Showplace Square A 12-block complex of renovated brick warehouses south of Market Street at the foot of Potrero Hill, Showplace Square is where over 300 furniture wholesalers display some of the most elegant furnishings and accessories in the country. The showrooms are generally closed to the public, but you can tour some of them with Showplace Tours, which is located in the complex's headquarters at the Galleria Design Center. Showplace Square is at the corner of Kansas Street (called Henry Adams St. here, in honor of the developer) and 15th Street and has what is so sorely needed elsewhere in the city—a large parking lot.

Orchids If you are an orchid fancier or if you ever thought you might like to try your hand at growing these exotic flowers, we recommend that you visit **Rod McLellan's Acres of Orchids** in South San Francisco. The McLellan Company runs the largest orchid nursery in the world. Two daily tours (free) lead guests through the large facility and brief them on the propagation of orchids as well as on the history of the company (which led a nationwide fad for gardenias when refrigerated railroad cars made transportation of the delicate blossoms possible).

There is also a large showroom and a gift shop with hundreds of plants from which to choose. Not all orchids are difficult to grow at home, even if you are not Nero Wolfe with a greenhouse and gardener. A cymbidium large enough to produce three sprays of orchids costs about $30–$40. The staff will give you plenty of instructions and pack your plant carefully for transportation home. *1450 El Camino Real, South San Francisco 94080, tel. 415/871–5655. Take I–280 south to the Hickey exit; then go east to El Camino and south (right). Showroom open daily 8–5. Free tours 10:30 and 1:30.*

4 Shopping

by Sheila Gadsden

San Franciscan Sheila Gadsden has worked as an editor and writer for such publications as Woman's Day, Motorland, Travel & Leisure, San Francisco, *and many others.*

San Francisco is a shopper's dream—major department stores, fine fashion, discount outlets, art galleries, and crafts stores are among the many offerings. Most accept at least Visa and MasterCard charge cards, and many also accept American Express, and Diner's Club. A very few accept cash only. Ask about traveler's checks; policies vary. The San Francisco *Chronicle* and *Examiner* advertise sales; for smaller innovative shops, check the San Francisco *Bay Guardian*. Store hours are slightly different everywhere, but a generally trusted rule is to shop between 10 AM and 5 or 6 PM Monday through Saturday (until 8 or 9 PM on Thursday) and from noon until 5 PM on Sunday. Stores on and around Fisherman's Wharf often have longer summer hours.

If you want to cover most of the city, the best shopping route might be to start at Fisherman's Wharf, then continue in order to Union Square and Crocker Galleria, the Embarcadero Center, Jackson Square, Chinatown, North Beach, Chestnut Street, Union Street, Fillmore and Sacramento streets, Japan Center, Haight Street, Civic Center, and South of Market (SoMa).

Major Shopping Districts

Fisherman's Wharf San Francisco's Fisherman's Wharf is host to a number of shopping and sightseeing attractions: **Pier 39, the Anchorage, Ghirardelli Square,** and **The Cannery.** Each offers shops, restaurants, and a festive atmosphere as well as such outdoor entertainment as musicians, mimes, and magicians. Pier 39 includes an amusement area and a double-decked Venetian carousel. One attraction shared by all the centers is the view of the bay and the proximity of the cable car lines, which can take shoppers directly to Union Square.

Union Square San Francisco visitors usually head for shopping at Union Square first. It's centrally located in the downtown area and surrounded by major hotels, from the large luxury properties to smaller bed-and-breakfasts. The square itself is a city park (with a garage underneath). It is flanked by such large stores as **Macy's, Saks Fifth Avenue, I. Magnin,** and **Neiman Marcus. North Beach Leather** and **Gucci** are two smaller upscale stores. Across from the cable car turntable at Powell and Market streets is the **San Francisco Shopping Centre,** with the fashionable **Nordstrom** store in the top five floors of shops. Nearby is **Crocker Galleria,** underneath a glass dome at Post and Kearny streets; 50 shops, restaurants, and services make up this Financial District shopping center, which is topped by two rooftop parks.

Embarcadero Center Five modern towers of shops, restaurants, and offices plus the Hyatt Regency Hotel make up the downtown Embarcadero Center at the end of Market Street. Like most malls, the center is a little sterile and falls short in the character department. What it lacks in charm, however, it makes up for in sheer quantity. The center's 175 stores and services include such nationally known stores as **The Limited, B. Dalton Bookseller,** and **Ann Taylor,** as well as more local or West Coast–based businesses such as the **Nature Company, Filian's European Clothing,** and **Lotus Designer Earrings.** Each tower occupies one block, and parking garages are available.

Downtown San Francisco Shopping

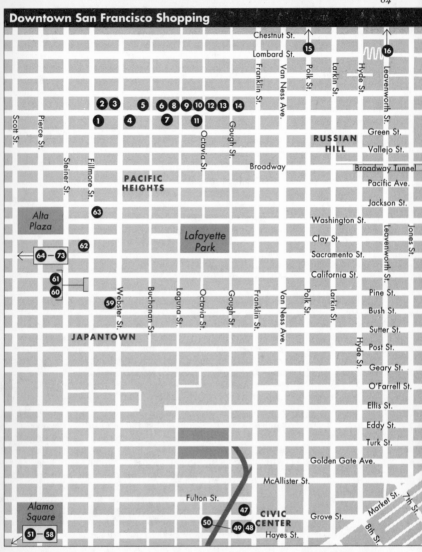

Chestnut St.
Lombard St.
Franklin St.
Van Ness Ave.
Polk St.
Larkin St.
Hyde St.
Leavenworth St.

15   **16**

Green St.

2 **3**   **5**   **6** **8** **9** **10** **12** **13** **14**
1   **4**   **7**   **11**

Octavia St.
Gough St.

RUSSIAN HILL

Vallejo St.

Broadway Tunnel

Broadway

Scott St.
Pierce St.

Pacific Ave.

PACIFIC HEIGHTS

Jackson St.

Steiner St.
Fillmore St.

63

Washington St.

Alta Plaza

Lafayette Park

Clay St.

Leavenworth St.
Jones St.

62

Sacramento St.

64 – **73**

California St.

61
60

Pine St.

Webster St.
Buchanan St.
Laguna St.
Octavia St.
Gough St.
Franklin St.
Van Ness Ave.
Polk St.
Larkin St.

Bush St.

59

Sutter St.

JAPANTOWN

Post St.

Hyde St.

Geary St.

O'Farrell St.

Ellis St.

Eddy St.

Turk St.

Golden Gate Ave.

McAllister St.

Fulton St.

47 **CIVIC CENTER**

Alamo Square

50

Grove St.

Market St.
7th St.

51 – **58**

49 **48**
Hayes St.

8th St.

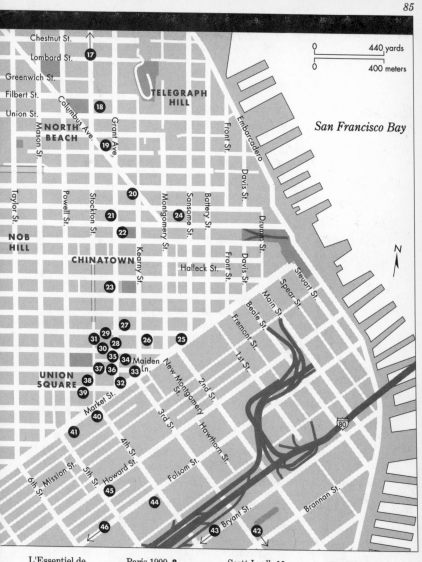

Chestnut St.
Lombard St.
Greenwich St.
Filbert St.
Union St.

NORTH BEACH
Columbus Ave.
Grant Ave.
Stockton St.
Powell St.
Mason St.
Taylor St.

TELEGRAPH HILL

San Francisco Bay

Front St.
Embarcadero
Davis St.
Drumm St.
Front St.
Battery St.
Sansome St.
Montgomery St.
Kearny St.

NOB HILL

CHINATOWN

Halleck St.

Steuart St.
Spear St.
Main St.
Beale St.
Fremont St.
1st St.
2nd St.
New Montgomery St.
Hawthorn St.
3rd St.

UNION SQUARE

Maiden Ln.

Market St.

Mission St.
6th St.
5th St.
4th St.
Howard St.
Folsom St.
Brannan St.
Bryant St.

80

N

0   440 yards
0   400 meters

L'Essentiel de Provence, **13**
Ma-Shi'-Ko Folk Craft, **59**
Macy's, **38**
Malm Luggage, **26**
My Favorite Clothing and Shoe Store, **27**
Nordstom, **41**
North Beach Leather, **37**
O'Desso, **49**
Old and New Estates, **1**

Paris 1900, **8**
Patronik Designs, **7**
Peluche, **67**
Polo/Ralph Lauren, **26**
Rainbeau Bodywear Factory Store, **44**
Regina Linens, **67**
Revival of the Fittest, **57**
The Ritz, **52**
Santa Fe, **70**
Scheuer Linen, **31**

Scott Lyall, **61**
The Sharper Image, **25**
Sheridan-Flynn, **68**
Shreve & Co., **28**
Six Sixty Center, **42**
Smile: A Gallery, **12**
Spellbound, **56**
Sy Aal, **10**
Telegraph Hill Antiques, **18**
Virginia Breier, **73**
Vorpal Gallery, **47**
Walker McIntyre, **71**

The Way We Wore, **62**
Whittler's Mother, **17**
Wholesale Jewelers Exchange, **39**
Yankee Doodle Dandy, **6**
Yerba Buena Square, **45**
Yountville, **63**
Z Gallerie, **4**

Jackson Square Jackson Square is where a dozen or so of San Francisco's finest retail antiques dealers are located. If your passion is 19th-century English furniture, for example, there's a good chance that something here will suit. Knowledgeable store owners and staffs can direct you to other places in the city for your special interests. The shops are along Jackson Street in the Financial District, so a visit there will put you very close to the Embarcadero Center and Chinatown.

Chinatown The intersection of Grant Avenue and Bush Street marks "the Gateway" to Chinatown; here shoppers and tourists are introduced to 24 blocks of shops, restaurants, markets, and temples. There are daily "sales" on gems of all sorts—especially jade and pearls—alongside stalls of bok choy and gingerroot. Chinese silks and toy trinkets are also commonplace in the shops, as are selections of colorful pottery, baskets, and large figures of soapstone, ivory, and jade, including netsukes (carved figures).

North Beach The once largely Italian enclave of North Beach gets smaller each year as Chinatown spreads northward. It has been called the city's answer to New York City's Greenwich Village, although it's much smaller. Many of the businesses here tend to be small clothing stores, antiques shops, or such eccentric specialty shops as **Quantity Postcard** (1441 Grant Ave., tel. 415/986–8866), which has an inventory of 15,000 different postcards. If you get tired of poking around in the bookstores, a number of cafés dot the streets and there are lots of Italian restaurants.

The Marina District Chestnut Street caters to the shopping needs of Marina District residents. It offers more of a neighborhood feeling than do other well-touristed shopping areas. Banks and well-known stores, including **Waldenbooks, The Gap,** and **Lucca Delicatessen Goods,** are interspersed with such unique gift shops as the **Red Rose Gallery,** which specializes in "tools for personal growth," including body scents, exotic clothing, and audiotapes for rejuvenating the mind. Shops start at Fillmore Street and end at Broderick Street.

Union Street Out-of-towners sometimes confuse Union Street—a popular stretch of shops and restaurants five blocks south of the Golden Gate National Recreation Area—with downtown's Union Square. (*See* above.) Nestled at the foot of a hill between the neighborhoods of Pacific Heights and Cow Hollow, Union Street shines with contemporary fashion and custom jewelry. Union Street's feel is largely new and upscale, although there are a few antiques shops and some long-term storekeepers. Shopping here is not limited to wearing apparel, but includes a good bookstore, **Solar Light Books, Union Street Graphics** for posters, and several galleries for crafts, photographs, sculpture, and serigraphs.

Pacific Heights When Pacific Heights residents look for practical services, they look toward Fillmore and Sacramento streets. Both streets feel more like neighborhood streets than upscale shopping areas, and that is exactly their appeal to tourists and natives—easygoing and personal with good bookstores, fine clothing shops, gift shops, thrift stores, and furniture and art galleries. **Sue Fisher King Co.** is an eclectic collection of home accessories at 3067 Sacramento Street, and **The Way We Wore** on Fillmore Street offers unusual vintage clothing, including an extensive collection of hats. The Fillmore Street shopping area runs from Post Street to Pacific Avenue. Most shops on the western end of Sacramento Street are between Lyon and Maple streets.

Japantown Unlike Chinatown, North Beach, or the Mission, the 5-acre **Japan Center** (between Geary and Post Sts.) is contained under one roof. It is actually a mall of stores filled with antique kimonos, beautiful tansu chests, and both new and old porcelains. The center always feels a little empty, but the good shops here are well worth a visit. Japan Center occupies the three-block area between Laguna and Fillmore streets, and between Geary and Post streets.

The Haight **Haight Street** is always an attraction for visitors, if only to see the sign at Haight and Ashbury streets—the geographic center of flower power during the 1960s. These days, instead of tie-dye shirts you'll find good-quality clothing from the 1940s and 1950s, fun jewelry, art from Mexico, and reproductions of Art Deco accessories.

Civic Center The shops and galleries that have sprung up around the Civic Center reflect the cultural offerings of Davies Symphony Hall, Herbst Auditorium, the Opera House, and the Museum of Modern Art. The area is a little sparse compared with other tightly packed shopping streets in the city, but it is well worth a visit. **The San Francisco Opera Shop** at Van Ness Avenue and Grove Street is packed with recordings, books, and posters covering a wide range of music; and the tree-lined block of Hayes Street between Gough and Franklin streets includes art galleries, crafts shops, and pleasant cafés. This area includes Hayes and Grove streets from Polk Street and extends just past Octavia Street.

South of Market South of Market—or SoMa—is where you'll find discount outlets in warehouses next to hip new restaurants and art galleries. At first glance the area doesn't appear to offer very much. But that's only because the streets aren't as spanking-new as some of the more crowded avenues to the north. Venture past the plain doors and down a few alleyways, and you'll see that there's much more than meets the eye.

Department Stores

Emporium (835 Market St., tel. 415/764–2222). This full-service department store carries a complete line of clothing and home furnishings. The prices are reasonable compared with those you'll find at many downtown department stores.

Macy's (Stockton and O'Farrell Sts., tel. 415/397–3333). Designer fashions, an extensive array of shoes, household wares, furniture, food, and even a post office and foreign currency exchange.

Nordstrom (865 Market St., tel. 415/243–8500). Opened in October 1988, this large new downtown store is known for providing excellent service to customers. The building's stunning interior design features spiral escalators circling a four-story atrium. Designer fashions, shoes, accessories, and cosmetics.

Three other large stores that offer high-quality merchandise are **I. Magnin, Neiman Marcus,** and **Saks Fifth Avenue** (all are on Union Square).

Specialty Stores

Antique Furniture City of Shanghai (519–521 Grant Ave., tel. 415/982–5520). In business since 1949, this Chinatown store imports unusual collector's items, early dynasty antiques, rare porcelain, Coromandel Coast furniture, silk, jade, and custom-tailored clothing. Hollywood moviemakers rent pieces here to make their sets look more authentic.

Fumiki (1894 Union St., tel. 415/922–0573). This store offers a fine selection of Asian arts, including antiques, art, fine jewelry, Chinese silk paintings, and Korean and Japanese furniture. Two specialties here are obis (sashes worn with kimonos) and antique Japanese baskets. Other good sources for Japanese antiques are **Genji,** and **Asakichi,** both in Japan Center.

Glen Smith Galleries (2021 Fillmore St., tel. 415/931–3081). The specialties here are 18th- and 19th-century furniture, porcelain, glass, and decorative arts. The gallery is open Tuesday to Saturday from 10 to 5 or by appointment; it is closed noon to 1 PM.

Hunt Antiques (405 Jackson St., tel. 415/989–9531). Fine 17th- to 19th-century period English furniture as well as porcelains, Staffordshire pottery, prints, clocks, and paintings in a gracious country house setting can be found here. This is only one of a dozen or so shops in the Jackson Square area. Others, such as **Foster-Gwin Antiques, Carpets of the Inner Circle,** and the **Antiques Gallery,** are also fine bets.

Telegraph Hill Antiques (580 Union St., tel. 415/982–7055). A very mixed but fine selection is available in this little North Beach shop: fine china and porcelain, crystal, cut glass, Oriental objects, Victoriana, bronzes, and paintings. Open weekdays to 5:30 or by appointment.

Walker McIntyre (3615 Sacramento St., tel. 415/563–0203). This shop specializes in pieces from the Georgian period, but it also offers 19th-century Japanese Imari cloisonné, lamps custom-made from antique vases, and Oriental rugs. Other very fine antiques stores on this street include **Hawley Bragg, Robert Hering,** and **Claire Thomson.**

Antique Jewelry J. M. Lang (323 Sutter St., tel. 415/982–2213). This is another good source for both jewelry and small antique objects, particularly fine glass, amber, and silver.

Old and New Estates (2181-A Union St., tel. 415/346–7525). This shop offers both antique and modern jewelry, crystal, and silver. It is generally open on weekdays from 11 to 6, but the hours do vary, so it's best to call first.

Paris 1925 (1954 Union St., tel. 415/567–1925) specializes in estate jewelry and vintage watches.

Art Galleries There are quite a few galleries around the city. The three mentioned here are only a select sample from the Hayes Valley area near the Civic Center.

Images (372 Hayes St., tel. 415/626–2284) specializes in oil paintings and watercolors by northern California realist and impressionist artists. Crafts and jewelry are also on display. Open Tuesday through Saturday.

O'Desso (384 Hayes St., tel. 415/626–5210) is an imaginative collection of paintings, collages, furniture made by artists, crafts, and jewelry. Open Wednesday through Sunday.

Vorpal Gallery (393 Grove St., tel. 415/397–9200). A premier gallery that focuses on postmodern painting, drawing, and sculpture, Vorpal's also has an excellent collection of graphic arts.

Books **City Lights** (261 Columbus Ave., tel. 415/362–8193). The city's most famous bookstore—and possibly the most comfortable bookstore for browsing—this was a major center for poetry readings during the 1960s. City Lights publishes books as well. The store is particularly well stocked in poetry, contemporary literature and music, and translations of third-world literature. There is also an interesting selection of books on nature, the outdoors, and travel. Open daily 10 AM to midnight.

A Clean Well-lighted Place for Books (601 Van Ness Ave., tel. 415/441–6670). You'll find "a large selection of paperbacks and hardbacks in all fields for all ages," particularly books on opera and San Francisco history.

Kinokuniya Bookstores (1581 Webster St., tel. 415/567–7625). This Japan Center store offers all sorts of books and periodicals in Japanese and English, but a major attraction is the collection of beautifully produced graphics and art books. Closed first Tuesday of every month.

Other excellent bookstores in the city include **Solar Light Books** (general needs), **The Sierra Club Bookstore** (California and the West), and **William Stout Architectural Books** (for interiors, exteriors, graphics, and landscape design).

Fabrics **Britex** (146 Geary St., tel. 415/392–2910). This is one of the city's largest collections of fabrics and notions: There are four floors of colors and patterns.

Edward's Unusual Fabrics (80 Geary St., tel. 415/397–5625). This store offers another fine selection of fabrics, especially good silks.

Far East Fashion (953 Grant Ave., tel. 415/362–8171 or 362–0986). Along with City of Shanghai, this store has one of Chinatown's better selections of Chinese embossed silks and lace.

Fine Gifts and **Biordi** (412 Columbus Ave., tel. 415/392–8096). In the heart of
Specialty Items North Beach, this small colorful store sells Majolica dinnerware and other imported Italian handicrafts and ceramics.

Gump's (250 Post St., tel. 415/982–1616). Featured at this famous store are jewelry, china, home accessories, stationery, imported goods, and art.

Whittler's Mother (Pier 39, the Embarcadero, tel. 415/433–3010). Handcrafted wood reigns here, including carousel animals—both small and full-size—created and painted on the premises.

Other good specialty stores are **Yone** in North Beach (for beads), the **Sharper Image** downtown (gadgets), and **Waterford Wedgwood** on Union Square (crystal and china).

Clothing for **Dottie Doolittle** (3680 Sacramento St., tel. 415/563–3244). This
Children store offers domestic and imported clothing sized from infant to 14 years, as well as baby furniture.

Sheridan-Flynn (3462 Sacramento St., tel. 415/921–5961). This store is an infant clothier that is nationally known for its layettes, carriages, and strollers. It carries a full line of clothing for babies and toddlers, up to size 7.

Yountville (2416 Fillmore St., tel. 415/922–5050). California and European designs are the draw here, from infant to 8 years.

Clothing for Men and Women **Brava Strada** (3247 Sacramento St., tel. 415/567–5757). Featured here are designer knitwear, accessories; Italian and other European leather goods; and one-of-a-kind jewelry from American and European artists. Also on Sacramento Street is **Button Down,** carrying "updated traditional" clothing and accessories.

everri uomo (2122 Union St., tel. 415/922–2613). The focus here is on contemporary Italian fashion for men, including suits, jackets, ties, and shirts.

JLC (2124 Union St., tel. 415/346–0343). This is an award-winning store that features women's clothing, accessories, and lingerie by local and national designers.

Justine (3263 Sacramento St., tel. 415/921–8548). Women's clothes by French designers Dorothee Bis, George Rech, and Ventilo are the draw here, as well as shoes by Charles Kammer.

Kilkenny Shop (Ghirardelli Sq., 900 North Point St., tel. 415/771–8984). Irish handwoven shawls, and throws, dresses, tweed hats, and other accessories are sold here.

Krazy Kaps (Pier 39, tel. 415/296–8930). Here you'll find silly hats as well as top hats, Stetsons, and Greek fishermen's caps—a good assortment for personal use and gift giving.

Peluche (3366 Sacramento St., tel. 415/346–6361). This shop specializes in one-of-a-kind, hand-knit sweaters, mostly from Italy, and European fashions for women.

Polo/Ralph Lauren (Crocker Galleria, Post and Kearny Sts., tel. 415/567–7656). This store offers designer apparel and accessories as well as home furnishings.

Scott Lyall (2029 Fillmore St., tel. 415/567–5225). From casual sportswear to suits and high fashion threads made with Italian fabrics, this store offers men a little of everything at reasonable prices.

Sy Aal (1864 Union St., tel. 415/929–1864). Offering "men's fashion with a woman's point of view," Sy Aal carries a full line of fine clothing, including hand-knits, and specializes in ties.

Other good places for women's clothing stores are Union Square; Crocker Galleria, which has such nationally known shops as **Casual Corner;** and the Embarcadero Center, whose selection includes **Ann Taylor, The Limited,** and **Daisy 9 to 5.**

Handicrafts and Folk Art **Cottonwood** (3461 Sacramento St., tel. 415/346–6020). Fine handcrafted home furnishings and decorative objects, including flatware, dinnerware, leather boxes, sculpture, and baskets abound in this store.

F. Dorian (388 Hayes St., tel. 415/861–3191). Cards, jewelry, and other crafts from Mexico, Japan, Italy, Peru, Indonesia, Philippines, and Sri Lanka as well as items from local craftspeople are the specialties here.

Folk Art International Gallery (Ghirardelli Sq., 900 North Point St., tel. 415/441–6100). This gallery features an extensive contemporary folk-art collection from Mexico, China, Ecuador, France, Sri Lanka, Peru, Haiti, and other countries—masks, boxes, sculpture, baskets, toys, and textiles. The adjoining gallery, **Xanadu** (tel. 415/441–5211), offers artifacts and tribal art from Asia, Africa, Oceania, and the Americas.

Japonesque (Crocker Galleria, Post and Kearny Sts., tel. 415/398–8577). Here you'll find handcrafted wooden boxes, sculpture, paintings, and handmade glass from Japan and the United States.

Ma-Shi'-Ko Folk Craft (1581 Webster St., Japan Center, tel. 415/346–0748). This store carries handcrafted pottery from Japan, including Mashiko, the style that has been in production longer than any other. There are also masks and other hand-crafted goods, all from Japan.

Santa Fe (3571 Sacramento St., tel. 415/346–0180). This is where you'll find old Navajo rugs, ranch furniture, old silver and turquoise jewelry, Indian pots and baskets, and cowboy relics.

Seven Seas (1909 Union St., tel. 415/921–7090). Kimonos, textiles, masks, jewelry, carved wood, and artifacts from Indonesia, Thailand, Peru, and Japan.

Smile: A Gallery (1750 Union St., tel. 415/771–1909). A whimsical, colorful collection of folk art, jewelry, and mobiles, including extraordinarily lifelike images of people, created by an artist in Marin.

Virginia Breier (3091 Sacramento St., tel. 415/929–7173; 900 North Point St., tel. 415/474–5036). A colorful gallery of contemporary and ethnic crafts from Mexico, Indonesia, Korea, Japan, Brazil, and the United States, especially the West Coast; includes decorative and functional items, antiques.

Yankee Doodle Dandy (1974 Union St., tel. 415/346–0346). A large selection of American antique quilts, carvings, handmade stuffed animals, woven throws.

Other shops to look at are **Oggetti** on Union Street, which carries Italian marbleized papers and gifts, **Designs in Motion** at Pier 39, **Images of the North** on Union Street, **Artifacts** on Fillmore Street, and **Xoxo** on Hayes Street.

Jewelry **Dai Fook Jewelry** (848 Grant Ave., tel. 415/391–2828). One of many good jewelry stores in Chinatown, this one has good jade, diamonds, and other gems. Two other good jewelry stores in Chinatown are **Empress** and **Jade Empire,** both on Grant Avenue.

Patronik Designs (1949 Union St., tel. 415/922–9716). Innovative contemporary and custom jewelry. Other good stores on Union are **Union Street Goldsmith** and **David Clay.**

Shreve & Co. (Post St. and Grant Ave., tel. 415/421–2600). One of the city's most elegant jewelers, and the oldest retail store in San Francisco, is located near Union Square.

Wholesale Jewelers Exchange (121 O'Farrell St., tel. 415/788–2365). This is a source for fine gems and finished jewelry at less than retail prices.

Leather **The Coach Store** (164 Grant Ave., tel. 415/392–1772). A branch of the nationally known purveyor of classically designed leather goods, the inventory here includes purses, briefcases, silk scarves, and belts and wallets of all sizes, colors, and weights.

Malm Luggage (Crocker Galleria, Post and Kearny Sts., tel. 415/391–5222). Fine luggage, leather goods, and accessories.

North Beach Leather (190 Geary St., tel. 415/362–8300). One of the best sources for high-quality leather garments—skirts, jackets, pants, dresses, accessories. With its sculpted walls, the store itself is a work of art. The original store is still in business at Fisherman's Wharf (1365 Columbus Ave., tel. 415/441–3208).

Linens **Claire's Antique Linens & Gifts** (3313 Sacramento St., tel. 415/931–3195). Nationally known for Victorian and Edwardian tablecloths and bedspreads. (The store is true to its name; only about 1% of the items are new.) It also sells crystal and china. Everything is available in a wide range of prices.

Regina Linens (3369 Sacramento St., tel. 415/563–8158). Imported handmade linens for bed and tabletop. Also children's clothing—newborn to toddler.

Scheuer Linen (318 Stockton St., tel. 415/392–2813). Luxurious linens for the bed, the bath, and the dining table abound here, including European linens and special designs.

Miscellaneous **Aerial** (The Cannery, 2801 Leavenworth St., tel. 415/474–1566). Here you'll find an eclectic mix of goods—soaps, art supplies, handcrafted leather boxes, clothes, pewter flasks, sunglasses, compasses, and lots of unusual but functional objects.

H. P. Corwith, Ltd. (1833 Union St., tel. 415/567–7252). A unique selection of kitsch, including pop art, jewelry, and "food art" is served up here.

Z Gallerie (2071 Union St., tel. 415/346–9000). Home furnishings in black—butterfly chairs, dinnerware, desks, chairs, lamps, and a variety of high-tech accessories—are the specialties here; also posters, both black-and-white and color. There are other stores in the San Francisco Shopping Centre on Market Street and on Haight Street.

Toiletries **The Body Shop** (2072 Union St., tel. 415/922–4076). These are some of the best concoctions around for the face and body—locally produced soaps, lotions, creams, perfumes, and body oils.

Crabtree & Evelyn (Crocker Galleria, Post and Kearny Sts., tel. 415/392–6111). English and French soaps, shampoos, lotions, creams, shaving supplies, and grooming implements; also jams, assorted condiments, and specialty gifts. Also located at the Embarcadero Center and Ghirardelli Square.

L'essentiel de Provence (1728 Union St., tel. 415/928–4483). Herbs from France can be found here—as well as scented soaps, oils, lotions, and candles.

Toys and Gadgets **FAO Schwarz Fifth Avenue** (88 Stockton St., tel. 415/394–8700). The San Francisco branch of an American tradition, this store features a little of everything from games and stuffed toys to motorized cars and trains.

Forma (1715 Haight St., tel. 415/751–0545) is one of the most imaginative shops in the city, with items ranging from design accessories by artists to 1950s-style lava lamps and toy animals inspired by Japanese monster movies.

Heffalump (1694 Union St., tel. 415/928–4300). This store features toys for most ages, including a beautiful selection of moderate to expensive rocking horses.

Kids Only (1415 Haight St., tel. 415/552–5445). A children's emporium, this store has a little bit of everything.

The Sharper Image (532 Market St., tel. 415/398–6472). This paradise for gadget lovers features everything from five-language translators and super–shock-absorbent tennis racquets to state-of-the-art speaker systems and walkman-size computers. Also at Ghirardelli Square.

Vintage Fashion **Buffalo Exchange** (1555 Haight St., tel. 415/431–7733). One of five stores in the Bay Area and in Arizona, the Haight Street store sells both new and recycled clothing and will also trade items. Also at 1800 Polk St.

Held Over (1599 Haight St., tel. 415/552–3733). An extensive collection of clothing from the 1940s, 1950s, and 1960s.

Spellbound (1670 Haight St., tel. 415/863–4930). Fine fashions from decades past—including bugle-beaded dresses, silk scarves, and suits—are offered here. Some of the inventory comes from estate sales.

The Way We Wore (2238 Fillmore St., tel. 415/346–1386). Fashions from the 1920s through the early 1950s are featured here, including an extensive selection of hats. The men's store is a few blocks away at 1838 Divisadero Street (tel. 415/771–7223).

Vintage Furniture and Accessories

Revival of the Fittest (1701 Haight St., tel. 415/751–8857). Telephones, dishes, assorted collectibles, as well as vintage and reproduction jewelry, clocks, lamps, vases, and furniture can be found here.

The Ritz (1157 Masonic Ave., tel. 415/431–0503). This is a colorful antiques store that offers vintage everything—including jewelry, collectibles, and clocks.

Outlets

A number of clothing factory outlets in San Francisco offer goods at quite reasonable prices. Here are a few of the more popular ones. Outlet maps are available at some of these locations for a nominal fee.

Coat Factory Outlet Store (1350 Folsom St., tel. 415/864–5050). Features discounted coats, jackets, and furs.

Clothing Clearance Center (695 Bryant St., tel. 415/495–7879). You'll find men's casual and business clothing here, as well as women's suits, coats, hats, and shoes.

My Favorite Clothing and Shoe Store (271 Sutter St., tel. 415/397–8464). Four floors of women's clothes and accessories, including an extensive selection of shoes.

Rainbeau Bodywear Factory Store (300 4th St., tel. 415/777–9786). Excellent-quality exercise gear and dancewear in a wide variety of colors, sizes, and styles.

Six Sixty Center (660 3rd St. at Townsend St., tel. 415/227–0464). There are nearly two dozen outlet stores here, offering apparel, accessories, and shoes for men, women, and children. Open Monday–Saturday.

Yerba Buena Square (899 Howard St. at Fifth St., tel. 415/974–5136). The Burlington Coat Factory, with a full range of clothing, is the anchor in this center for apparel, shoes, and toys. It is only two blocks from Market Street, and most of the shops are open daily.

5 Sports, Fitness, Beaches

by Casey Tefertiller

A sportswriter for the San Francisco Examiner, *Casey Tefertiller has been covering local sports for Fodor's for several years.*

One great attraction of the Bay Area is the abundance of activities. Joggers, bicyclists, and aficionados of virtually all sports can find their favorite pastimes within driving distance, and often within walking distance, from downtown hotels. Golden Gate Park has numerous paths for runners and cyclists. Lake Merced in San Francisco and Lake Merritt in Oakland are among the most popular areas for joggers.

For information on running races, tennis tournaments, bicycle races, and other participant sports, check the monthly issues of *City Sports* magazine, available free at sporting goods stores, tennis centers, and other recreational sites. The most important running event of the year is the *Examiner* Bay-to-Breakers race on the third Sunday in May. For information on this race and other running events, call 415/777–2424.

Bicycling

Two bike routes are maintained by the San Francisco Recreation and Park Department (tel. 415/666–7201). One route goes through Golden Gate Park to Lake Merced; the other goes from the south end of the city to the Golden Gate Bridge and beyond. Many shops along Stanyon Street rent bikes.

Boating and Sailing

Stow Lake (tel. 415/752–0347) in Golden Gate Park has rowboat, pedalboat, and electric boat rentals. The lake is open daily for boating, but call for seasonal hours. San Francisco Bay offers year-round sailing, but tricky currents make the bay hazardous for inexperienced navigators. Boat rentals and charters are available throughout the Bay Area and are listed under "boat rentals" in the Yellow Pages. A selected charter is **A Day on the Bay** (tel. 415/922–0227). Local sailing information can be obtained at **The Eagle Cafe** on Pier 39.

Fishing

Numerous fishing boats leave from San Francisco, Sausalito, Berkeley, Emeryville, and Point San Pablo. They go for salmon outside the bay or striped bass and giant sturgeon within the bay. Temporary licenses are available on the charters. In San Francisco, lines can be cast from San Francisco Municipal Pier, Fisherman's Wharf, or Aquatic Park. Trout fishing is available at Lake Merced. Licenses can be bought at sporting goods stores. The cost of fishing licenses ranges from $5 for one day to $21.50 for a complete state license. For charters, reservations are suggested. Some selected sportfishing charters are listed. Mailing addresses are given, but you're more likely to get a response if you call.

Capt. Ron's Pacific Charters (Fisherman's Wharf. Write to 561 Prentiss St., 94110, tel. 415/285–2000).
Capt. Fred Morini (Fisherman's Wharf. Write to 138 Harvard Dr., Larkspur 94939, tel. 415/924–5575).
Muny Sport Fishing (3098 Polk St., 94109, across from Ghirardelli Sq., tel. 415/871–4445). Leaves daily from Fisherman's Wharf.
Wacky Jacky (Fisherman's Wharf. Write Jacky Douglas at 473 Bella Vista Way, 94127, tel. 415/586–9800).

Fitness

Physical fitness activities continue to be popular, but most clubs are private and visitors could have trouble finding a workout location. **Sheraton Hotels** have arrangements with neighboring clubs, and the **Burlingame Hyatt**, near the airport, has a workout facility. **24-hour Nautilus** (1335 Sutter, tel. 415/776–2200) is open to the public for a $10 drop-in fee. **Sante West**

Fitness (3727 Buchanan, tel. 415/563–6222) offers aerobics, low- impact, stretching, and other classes for a $9 drop-in fee.

Golf   San Francisco has four public golf courses, and visitors should call for tee times: **Harding Park,** an 18-hole, par-72 course (at Lake Merced Blvd. and Skyline Blvd., tel. 415/664–4690); **Lincoln Park,** 18 holes, par 69 (34th and Clement Sts., tel. 415/221–9911); **Golden Gate Park,** a "pitch and putt" 9-holer (47th and Fulton Sts., tel. 415/751–8987); **Glen Eagles Golf Course,** a full-size 9-holer in McLaren Park (2100 Sunnydale Ave., tel. 415/587–2425). Another municipal course, **Sharp Park,** is south of the city in Pacifica (tel. 415/355–8546).

Horseback Riding   Western-style horseback riding is available throughout the Bay Area. **Skywood Stables** in Half Moon Bay (10790 Skyline Blvd., tel. 415/726–5188) offers rentals and an overnight camping trip. Two other stables in Half Moon Bay have rentals for beach rides: **Friendly Acres** (2150 N. Cabrillo Hwy., tel. 415/726–8550) and **Sea Horse Ranch** (1828 N. Cabrillo Hwy., tel. 415/726–2362). Other selected stables include **Sonoma Cattle Co.** (tel. 707/996–8566), which offers rides through Jack London State Park and Sugar Loaf Ridge in Sonoma County and, in Marin County, **Five Brooks** (tel. 415/663–1570) and **Miwok Livery** in Mill Valley (tel. 415/383–8048).

Ice Skating   Even sunny California has ice skating. The **San Francisco Ice Rink** (1557 48th Ave., tel. 415/664–1406) is just three blocks south of Golden Gate Park. Also in the Bay Area are **Berkeley Iceland** (2727 Milvia, four blocks from the Ashby BART station, tel. 415/843–8800) and **Belmont Iceland** (815 Old County Rd., tel. 415/592–0532).

Racquetball   The San Francisco Recreation and Park Department maintains a racquetball facility at the **Mission Recreation Center** (2450 Harrison St., tel. 415/695–5012).

Swimming   The San Francisco Recreation and Park Department manages one outdoor swimming pool and eight indoor pools throughout the city. Popular choices are the **Sava Pool** at 19th and Wawona streets and **Mission Pool,** an outdoor facility at 19th and Linda streets.

Tennis   The San Francisco Recreation and Park Department maintains 130 free tennis courts throughout the city. The largest set of free courts is at **Dolores Park,** 18th and Dolores streets, with six courts available on a first-come, first-served basis. There are 21 public courts in **Golden Gate Park;** reservations and fee information can be obtained by calling 415/753–7101.

Windsurfing   Windsurfing is becoming increasingly popular in the Bay Area, with participants taking advantage of the brisk bay breezes to improve their skills. **San Francisco School of Windsurfing** (40A Loyola Terr., tel. 415/750–0412) offers rentals, lessons for beginners on mild Lake Merced, and lessons for more advanced surfers at Candlestick Point. For adventurous types, **Airtime of San Francisco** (3620 Wawona, tel. 415/SKY–1177) offers hang gliding lessons, para-gliding lessons, and rentals off the Marin coastline.

Spectator Sports

For the sports fan, the Bay Area offers a vast selection of events—from yacht races to rodeo to baseball.

Auto Racing	**Sears Point International Raceway** (tel. 707/938–8448), in Sonoma at Highways 37 and 121, offers a variety of motor sports events. The track is also the home of the Bondurant High Performance Driving School. There are motor-sports events at various locations around the Bay Area. Check local papers for details.
Baseball	The **San Francisco Giants** play ball at Candlestick Park (tel. 415/467–8000) and the **Oakland A's** play at the Oakland Coliseum (tel. 415/638–0500). These games rarely sell out, and game-day tickets are usually available at the stadiums. Premium seats, however, often do sell out in advance. City shuttle buses marked Ballpark Special run from numerous bus stops. Remember that Candlestick Park is often windy and cold, so take along extra layers of clothing to deal with changing weather. The Oakland Coliseum can be reached by taking BART trains to the Coliseum stop.
Basketball	The **Golden State Warriors** play NBA basketball at the Oakland Coliseum Arena from October through April. Tickets are available through Ticketron (tel. 415/392–7469). Again, BART trains to the Coliseum stop are the easiest method of travel.
College Sports	Major college football, basketball, and baseball are played at the University of California in Berkeley, at Stanford University on the peninsula in Palo Alto, and at San Jose State. Stanford won the College World Series in the not-so-distant past, and home baseball games at sunny Sunken Diamond often sell out.
Football	The **San Francisco 49ers** play at Candlestick Park, but the games are almost always sold out far in advance, so call first (tel. 415/468–2249).
Horse Racing	Depending on the season, there is racing at **Golden Gate Fields** in Albany, at **Bay Meadows** in San Mateo, or on the Northern California fair circuit. Check local papers for post time and place.
Rodeo and Horse Shows	San Francisco relives its western heritage each October with the **Grand National Rodeo and Livestock Show** at the Cow Palace (tel. 415/469–6000) just south of the city limits in Daly City. The 15-Third bus will take you there. In August the Cow Palace hosts the **San Francisco Equestrian Festival,** featuring such events as dressage and vaulting.
Tennis	The **Civic Auditorium** (999 Grove St.) is the site of the *Volvo Tennis/San Francisco* tournament in early February (tel. 415/239–4800). The *Virginia Slims women's tennis tour* visits the Oakland Coliseum Arena in October.
Yacht Racing	There are frequent yacht races on the bay. The local papers will give you details, or you can be an uninformed but appreciative spectator from the Golden Gate Bridge or other vantage points around town.

Beaches

San Francisco's beaches are perfect for romantic sunset strolls, but don't make the mistake of expecting to find Waikiki-by-the-Metropolis. The water is cold, and the beach areas are often foggy and usually jammed on sunny days. They can be satisfactory for afternoon sunning, but treacherous currents make most areas dangerous for swimming. During stormy months, beachcombers can stroll along the sand and discover a variety of ocean treasures: glossy agates and jade pebbles, sea-sculptured roots and branches, and—rarely—glass floats.

Baker Beach   Baker Beach is not recommended for swimming: Watch for larger-than-usual waves. In recent years, the north end of the beach has become popular with nude sunbathers. This is not legal, but such laws are seldom enforced. The beach is in the southwest corner of the Presidio and begins at the end of Gibson Road, which turns off Bowley Street. Weather is typical for the bay shoreline: summer fog, usually breezy, and occasionally warm. Picnic tables, grills, day-camp areas, and trails are available. The mile-long shoreline is ideal for jogging, fishing, and building sand castles.

China Beach   From April to October, China Beach, south of Baker Beach, offers a lifeguard, gentler water, changing rooms, and showers. It is also listed on maps as Phelan Beach.

Half Moon Bay   The San Mateo County coast has several beaches and some nice ocean views, most notably at Half Moon Bay State Beach. A drive south on Highway 1 is scenic and will provide access to this and other county beaches. You can take Highway 92 east over the mountains to I-280 for a faster but still scenic route back to the city.

Marin Beaches   The Marin headlands beaches are not safe for swimming. The cliffs are steep and unstable, making falls a constant danger. The Marin coast, however, offers two beaches for picnics and sunning: Muir and Stinson beaches. Swimming is recommended only at Stinson Beach, and only from late May to mid-September, when lifeguard services are provided. If possible, visit these areas during the week; both beaches are crowded on weekends.

Ocean Beach   South of Cliff House, Ocean Beach stretches along the western (ocean) side of San Francisco. It has a wide beach with scenic views and is perfect for walking, running, or lying in the sun—but not for swimming.

6 Dining

Introduction

by Jacqueline Killeen

Jacqueline Killeen has been writing about San Francisco restaurants for over 20 years. She is a restaurant critic for San Francisco Focus *magazine.*

San Francisco probably has more restaurants per capita than any city in the United States, including New York. Practically every ethnic cuisine is represented. That makes selecting some seventy restaurants to list here from the vast number available a very difficult task indeed. We have chosen several restaurants to represent each popular style of dining in various price ranges, in most cases because of the superiority of the food, but in some instances because of the view or ambience.

Because we have covered those areas of town most frequented by visitors, this meant leaving out some great places in outlying districts such as Sunset and Richmond. The Richmond District restaurants we *have* recommended were chosen because they offer a type of experience not available elsewhere.

All listed restaurants serve dinner; they are open for lunch unless otherwise specified; restaurants are not open for breakfast unless the morning meal is specifically mentioned.

Parking accommodations are mentioned only when a restaurant has made special arrangements; otherwise you're on your own. There is usually a charge for valet parking. Validated parking is not necessarily free and unlimited; often there is a nominal charge and a restriction on the length of time.

Restaurants do change their policies about hours, credit cards, and the like. It is always best to make inquiries in advance.

The most highly recommended restaurants in each price category are indicated by a star ★.

The price ranges listed below are for an average three-course meal. A significant trend among more expensive restaurants is the bar menu, which provides light snacks—hot dogs, chili, pizza, and appetizers—in the bar for a cost that is often less than $10 for two.

Category	Cost*
Very Expensive	Over $40
Expensive	$25–$40
Moderate	$15–$25
Inexpensive	under $15

per person, excluding drinks, service, and 6.5% sales tax

The following credit card abbreviations are used: AE, American Express; DC, Diners Club; MC, MasterCard; V, Visa. Many restaurants accept cards other than those listed here, and some will accept personal checks if you carry a major credit card.

American

Before the 1980s, it was hard to find a decent "American" restaurant in the Bay Area. In recent years, however, the list has been growing and becoming more diversified, with categories for Creole-Cajun, California cuisine, Southwestern, barbecue, and the all-American diner.

Civic Center
★

Stars. This is the culinary temple of Jeremiah Tower, the superchef who claims to have invented California cuisine. Stars is a must stop on every traveling gourmet's itinerary, but it's also where many of the local movers and shakers hang out as well as a popular place for post-theater dining—open till the wee hours. The dining room has a clublike ambience, and the food ranges from grills to ragouts to sautées—some daringly creative and some classical. Bar menu. *150 Redwood Alley, tel. 415/861–7827. Reservations accepted up to 2 weeks in advance, some tables reserved for walk-ins. Dress: informal. AE, DC, MC, V. No lunch weekends. Closed Memorial Day. Valet parking at night. Expensive.*

Embarcadero
★

Fog City Diner. This is where the diner and grazing crazes began in San Francisco, and the popularity of this spot knows no end. The long, narrow dining room emulates a luxurious railroad car with dark wood paneling, huge windows, and comfortable booths. The cooking is innovative, drawing its inspiration from regional cooking throughout the United States. The sharable "small plates" are a fun way to go. *1300 Battery St., tel. 415/982–2000. Reservations advised several weeks in advance for peak hours. Dress: informal. DC, MC, V. Closed Thanksgiving and Christmas. Moderate.*

MacArthur Park. Year after year San Franciscans acclaim this as their favorite spot for ribs, but the oakwood smoker and mesquite grill also turn out a wide variety of all-American fare, from steaks, hamburgers, and chili to seafood. Takeout is also available at this handsomely renovated pre-earthquake warehouse. *607 Front St., tel. 415/398–5700. Reservations advised. Dress: informal. AE, DC, MC, V. No lunch weekends. Closed Christmas. Valet parking at night. Moderate.*

Financial District

Cypress Club. Fans of John Cunin have flocked here since 1990 when Masa's long-time maître'd opened his own place, which he calls a "San Francisco brasserie." This categorizes the contemporary American cooking somewhat, but the decor defies description. It could be interpreted as anything from a pun on an ancient temple to a futuristic space war. *500 Jackson St., tel. 415/296–8555. Reservations advised. Dress: informal. AE, DC, MC, V. Valet parking at night. Expensive.*

Nob Hill

Fournou's Ovens. There are two lovely dining areas in the elegant Stanford Court Hotel. This is a multilevel room with tiers of tables; the focus of the room is the giant open hearth where many specialties—notably the rack of lamb—are roasted. The restaurant has moved away from its well-known Continental fare to more contemporary American cuisine. Some people opt for the flower-filled greenhouses that flank the hotel and offer views of the cable cars clanking up and down the hill. Wherever you sit, you'll find excellent food and attentive service. *905 California St., tel. 415/989–1910. Reservations advised. Jacket required. AE, DC, MC, V. No lunch weekends. Valet parking. Expensive.*

The Restaurant of the Ritz-Carlton. The less formal of the Ritz's two dining establishments, this is a fine choice for a power breakfast or for lunch on a sunny day when tables are set outside in a large courtyard. The cooking of chef Gary Danko is California contemporary—a vibrant mix of Mediterranean fare with some Asian overtones. At noon, there's even a burger with brie or gorgonzola. *Ritz-Carlton Hotel, Stockton St. at*

Downtown San Francisco Dining

Jefferson St.

Beach St.

North St.

Columbus Ave.

Francisco St.

Chestnut St.

Lombard St.

Greenwich St.

Filbert St.

Union St.

Green St.

Vallejo St.

Broadway Tunnel

Broadway

Pacific St.

Jackson St.

Washington St.

Clay St.

Sacramento St.

California St.

Pine St.

Bush St.

Sutter St.

Post St.

Geary St.

O'Farrell St.

Ellis St.

Eddy St.

Turk St.

Golden Gate Ave.

McAllister St.

Fulton St.

Grove St.

Hayes St.

Fell St.

Oak St.

Page St.

Haight St.

Market St.

Mission St.

Howard St.

Octavia St.

Gough St.

Franklin St.

Van Ness Ave.

Polk St.

Larkin St.

Hyde St.

Leavenworth St.

Jones St.

Taylor St.

Laguna St.

7th St.

8th St.

9th St.

10th St.

11th St.

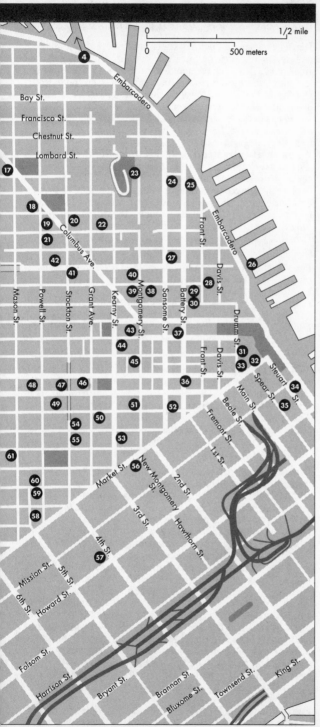

Masa's, **49**

Maykedeh, **22**

Miss Pearl's Jam House, **76**

Monsoon, **77**

North India, **8**

Old Swiss House, **4**

Pacific Heights Bar & Grill, **66**

Palio d´ Asti, **44**

Perry's, **11**

Postrio, **62**

Restaraunt at the Ritz-Carlton, **47**

Ristorante Parma, **5**

Rodin, **9**

S. Asimakopoulos Cafe, **82**

Sam's Grill, **51**

Sanppo, **69**

Scott's Seafood Grill and Bar, **7**

Splendido's, **31**

Square One, **28**

Stars, **78**

Tadich Grill, **36**

Ton Kiang, **71, 72**

Trader Vic's, **63**

Undici, **81**

Washington Square Bar & Grill, **18**

The Waterfront, **26**

Wu Kong, **35**

Yamato, **46**

Yank Sing, **37**

Zuni Cafe Grill, **80**

California St., tel. 415/296–7465. Dress: informal. Reservations advised. AE, DC, MC, V. Valet Parking. Expensive.

North Beach   **Bix.** The owners of Fog City Diner have re-created a '40s supper club in a historic building that was an assay office in Gold Rush days. The place resembles a theater, with a bustling bar and dining tables downstairs and banquettes on the balcony. Opt for the lower level; the acoustics upstairs are dreadful. The menu offers contemporary renditions of 1940s fare; there's piano music in the evenings. *56 Gold St., tel. 415/433–6300. Reservations advised. Dress: informal. AE, DC, MC, V. No lunch Sat. Moderate.*

Washington Square Bar & Grill. You're apt to rub elbows with the city's top columnists and writers in this no-frills saloon. Recently the restaurant broke with North Beach Italian tradition to offer lighter cooking, though pastas and seafood still dominate the menu. Basic bar fare, such as hamburgers and steaks, is also available. Pianist at night; open late. *1707 Powell St., tel. 415/982–8123. Reservations advised. Dress: informal. AE, DC, MC, V. Closed most major holidays. Validated parking at garage around the corner on Filbert St. Moderate.*

Pacific Heights   **Perry's.** The West Coast equivalent of P.J. Clarke's in Manhattan, this popular watering hole and meeting place for the button-down singles set serves good, honest saloon food—London broil, corned beef hash, one of the best hamburgers in town, and a great breakfast. Breakfast is served on weekends. *1944 Union St., tel. 415/922–9022. Reservations accepted. Dress: informal. AE, MC, V. Closed Thanksgiving, Christmas. Moderate.*

South of Market   **Asta.** Named after Nick and Nora's dog in "The Thin Man" series, this new spot is a time capsule of the '30s, with flicks of the famous sleuths on VCRs in the bar. The food, however, is in tune with the 1990s, with bright, creative versions of all-time American favorites and down-home desserts. *Rincon Center, 101 Spear St., 415/495–2782. Reservations accepted. Dress: informal. AE, MC, V. No lunch Sat., no dinner Mon., closed Sun. Validated parking at Rincon Center garage. Moderate.*

Union Square   **Brasserie Savoy.** Although this lively new eatery takes its cues from Parisian brasseries, the end result is cooking (primarily seafood) with a very sophisticated American accent and an ambience that recalls old San Francisco. A signature is the seafood extravaganza, a pedestaled platter of assorted shellfish heaped on ice. Oyster bar and late-supper menu. *580 Geary St., tel. 415/474–8686. Reservations advised. Dress: informal. AE, DC, MC, V. No lunch weekends. Valet parking. Moderate.*

Campton Place. This elegant, ultrasophisticated small hotel put new American cooking on the local culinary map. Although opening chef Bradley Ogden is now at his own place, the Lark Creek Inn, in Marin County, his successor at Campton Place, Jan Birnbaum, carries on Ogden's innovative traditions with great aplomb and has added his own touches from breakfast and Sunday brunch (one of the best in town) through the dinner hours. A bar menu offers some samplings of appetizers, plus a caviar extravaganza. *340 Stockton St., tel. 415/781–5155. Reservations suggested, 2 weeks in advance on weekends. Jacket required at dinner, tie requested. AE, DC, MC, V. Valet parking. Very Expensive.*

★ **Postrio.** Superchef Wolfgang Puck's San Francisco restaurant debut in 1989 caused the biggest culinary commotion locally since Berkeley chef Alice Waters reinvented the pizza, but Puck claims to have done that in Los Angeles. Postrio has an open kitchen (another trend started by Puck) and a stunning three-level bar and dining area, highlighted by palm trees and museum-quality contemporary paintings. The food is Puckish Californian with Mediterranean and Asian overtones, emphasizing pastas, grilled seafood, and house-baked breads. A substantial breakfast and bar menu are served here, too. *545 Post St., tel. 415/776–7825. Reservations advised. Dress: informal. AE, DC, MC, V. Valet parking. Expensive.*

Caribbean

Tenderloin **Miss Pearl's Jam House.** Since its opening in 1989, this Caribbean hot spot in a Tenderloin motel has been jammed with a younger-than-Yuppie crowd at night. But by day it's quiet and lovely, with lunch served out by the pool. The chef draws his inspiration from many West Indian islands, and the intense flavor of the food more than compensates for its lack of authenticity. *601 Eddy St., tel. 415/775–5267. Reservations suggested. Dress: informal. DC, MC, V. No lunch Sat. Closed Mon. Moderate.*

Chinese

For nearly a century, Chinese restaurants in San Francisco were confined to Chinatown and the cooking was largely an Americanized version of peasant-style Cantonese. The past few decades, however, have seen an influx of restaurants representing the wide spectrum of Chinese cuisine: the subtly seasoned fare of Canton, the hot and spicy cooking of Hunan and Szechuan, the northern style of Peking, where meat and dumplings replace seafood and rice as staples, and, most recently, some more esoteric cooking, such as Hakka and Chao Chow. These restaurants are now scattered throughout the city, leaving Chinatown for the most part to the tourists.

Civic Center **Monsoon.** This brilliant new restaurant combines the cuisines of China and Southeast Asia, most notably Thailand. The concept of a pan-Asian menu is common in many of China's coastal cities, and was adapted here by Monsoon founder Bruce Cost, one of the foremost authorities on Asian food in the United States. The subtle surroundings are highlighted by contemporary Asian ceramics. *Opera Plaza, 601 Van Ness Ave., tel. 415/441–3232. Reservations advised. Dress: informal. MC, V. No lunch. Expensive.*

Embarcadero **Harbor Village.** Classic Cantonese cooking, dim sum lunches,
★ and fresh seafood from the restaurant's own tanks are the hallmarks of this 400-seat branch of a Hong Kong establishment, which sent five of its master chefs to San Francisco to supervise the kitchen. The setting is opulent, with Chinese antiques and teak furnishings. *4 Embarcadero Center, tel. 415/781–8833. Reservations not accepted for lunch on weekends. Dress: informal. AE, MC, V. Free validated parking in Embarcadero Center Garage. Moderate.*

Financial District **Yank Sing.** This teahouse has grown by leaps and branches with the popularity of dim sum. The Battery Street location seats 300 and the older, smaller Stevenson Street site has recently been rebuilt in high-tech style. *427 Battery St., tel. 415/*

362–1640. 49 Stevenson St., tel. 415/495–4510. Reservations advised. Dress: informal. Battery-AE, MC, V. Stevenson-MC, V. No dinner. Closed weekends. Inexpensive.

North Beach **Fortune.** The Chao Chow tradition of the southern coast of China is well represented in this small restaurant on the edge of Chinatown. Among the complexly seasoned dishes for which Chao Chow cooking is most noted are braised duck with a garlicky vinegar sauce and an eggy oyster cake. *675 Broadway, tel. 415/421–8130. No reservations at lunch. Dress: informal. MC, V. Inexpensive.*

Hunan. Henry Chung's first café on Kearny Street had only six tables, but his Hunanese cooking merited six stars from critics nationwide. He has now opened this larger place on Sansome Street; it's equally plain but has 250 seats. Smoked dishes are a specialty, and Henry guarantees no MSG. *924 Sansome St., tel. 415/956–7727. Reservations advised. Dress: informal. AE, DC, MC, V. Inexpensive.*

Northern **The Mandarin.** Owner Cecilia Chiang introduced San Francis-
Waterfront cans to the full spectrum of Chinese cooking in 1961, when she
★ opened the original Mandarin in a tiny Post Street locale. Now she holds court in a magnificent setting fit for imperial fare, decorated with paintings and embroideries from her family's palatial homes in Peking. This is one of the world's great restaurants, and its finest offerings, such as Mandarin duck, beggar's chicken cooked in clay, and the Mongolian fire pot, must be ordered a day in advance. Bay view from some tables. *Ghiradelli Sq., tel. 415/673–8812. Reservations advised. Dress: informal. AE, DC, MC, V. Closed Thanksgiving, Christmas. Validated parking in Ghiradelli Sq. garage. Moderate–Expensive.*

Richmond **Hong Kong Flower Lounge.** Many Chinaphiles swear that this outpost of a famous Asian restaurant chain serves the best Cantonese food in town. The seafood is spectacular, as is the dim sum. *5322 Geary Blvd., tel. 415/668–8998. Reservations advised. Dress: informal. AE, MC, V. Moderate.*

Ton Kiang. The Hakka cuisine of south China, rarely found in this country, relies on a natural, lightly seasoned style of cooking. Salt-baked chicken is the great specialty, but the meat and seafood dishes cooked in wine-fermented rice are also recommended. Ton Kiang introduced Hakka cooking to San Francisco in a little spot on Broadway, but has moved to two larger locations on Geary Boulevard. *3148 Geary Blvd., tel. 415/752–4440. 5827 Geary Blvd., tel. 415/386–8530. Dress: informal. Reservations advised. MC, V. Inexpensive.*

South of Market **Wu Kong.** Tucked away in the splashy Art Deco Rincon Center, Wu Kong features the cuisine of Shanghai and Canton. Specialties include dim sum; braised yellow fish; and the incredible vegetable goose, one of the Asian city's famous mock dishes, created from paper-thin layers of dried bean-curd sheets and mushrooms. *101 Spear St., tel. 415/957–9300. Reservations advised. Dress: informal. AE, DC, MC, V. Validated parking at Rincon Center garage. Moderate.*

Continental and Mediterranean

Neither pure French nor pure Italian but a mixture of these and other European cuisines, this category includes some of

San Francisco's classic establishments along with some of its brightest new spots.

Civic Center   **Zuni Cafe Grill.** Zuni's Italian-Mediterranean menu and its un-
★   pretentious atmosphere pack in the crowds from early morning to late evening. A balcony dining area overlooks the large bar, where both shellfish and drinks are dispensed. A second dining room houses the giant pizza oven and grill. Even the hamburgers have an Italian accent: They're served on herbed focaccia buns. *1658 Market St., tel. 415/552–2522. Dress: informal. Reservations advised. AE, MC, V. Closed Mon., Thanksgiving, Christmas. Moderate.*

Embarcadero   **Splendido's.** Mediterranean cooking is the focus at this handsome new restaurant. Diners here are transported to the coast of southern France or northern Italy by the pleasant decor. Among the many winners are the shellfish soup, warm goat cheese and ratatouille salad, *pissaladiere* (the pizza of Provence), and pan-roasted quail with white truffle pasta. Desserts are truly *splendido. Bar menu. Embarcadero Four, tel 415/986–3222. Reservations advised. Dress: informal. AE, DC, MC, V. No lunch Sat. Closed Sun. Validated parking at Embarcadero Center garage. Moderate.*

Financial District   **Garden Court, Palace Hotel.** After a massive, two-year, multi-million-dollar renovation, the Garden Court of the Sheraton Palace has reemerged as the ultimate old San Francisco experience. From breakfast through lunch, teatime, and the early dinner hours, light splashes through the $7 million stained-glass ceiling against the towering Ionic columns and crystal chandeliers. The classic European menu highlights many famous dishes devised by Palace chefs during the early years of this century. *Market and New Montgomery Sts., tel. 415/546–5000. Reservations advised. Jacket required at dinner. AE, DC, MC, V. Expensive.*

Jack's. Little has changed in over 100 years at this bankers' and brokers' favorite. The menu is extensive, but regulars opt for the simple fare—steaks, chops, seafood, and stews. The dining room has an old-fashioned, no-nonsense aura, and private upstairs rooms are available for top-secret meetings. *615 Sacramento St., tel. 415/986–9854. Reservations advised. Jacket and tie required. AE. No lunch weekends. Closed major holidays. Moderate.*

North Beach   **Des Alpes.** Basque dinners are offered here, with soup, salad, *two* entrees, ice cream, and coffee included in the budget price. This haven for trenchermen is a pleasant spot, with wood-paneled walls and checkered oilcloth on the tables. Service is family style. *732 Broadway, tel. 415/788–9900. Reservations advised on weekends. Dress: informal. MC, V. No lunch. Closed Mon. Inexpensive.*

Julius Castle. This turreted landmark building clings to the cliffs of Telegraph Hill and commands sweeping vistas of the bay. The food is traditional French and Italian, with an emphasis on pastas, seafood, and veal. The view and the site compensate for the lack of imagination in the cuisine. *1541 Montgomery St., tel. 415/362–3042. Reservations required. Jacket required. AE, DC, MC, V. No lunch. Closed Thanksgiving, Christmas. Valet parking. Expensive.*

Northern Waterfront   **Old Swiss House.** The food here is not as Swiss as the atmosphere—Alpine-costumed waitresses and flower-bedecked windows with magnificent bay views. But you will find a few Swiss specialties lurking in the predominantly French menu and the service runs like a fine-tuned clock. *Pier 39, tel. 415/434-0432. Reservations advised. Dress: informal. AE, DC, MC, V. Validated parking in evening at Pier 39 garage. Moderate-Expensive.*

Union Square **Bardelli's.** Founded in 1906 as Charles' Oyster House, this turn-of-the-century showplace boasts high vaulted ceilings, massive marble columns, and stained glass. The menu mixes French, Italian, and American fare with such local specialties as chicken Jerusalem (sauced with mushrooms and baby artichokes) and superb fresh seafood. *243 O'Farrell St., tel. 415/ 982-0243. Reservations accepted. Dress: informal. AE, DC, MC, V. No lunch Sat. Closed Sun. Validated parking at Downtown Center garage. Moderate.*

French

French cooking has gone in and out of vogue in San Francisco since the extravagant days of the Bonanza Kings. A renaissance of the classic haute cuisine occurred during the 1960s, but recently a number of these restaurants closed. Meanwhile, nouvelle cuisine went in and out of fashion, and the big draw now is the bistro or brasserie.

Civic Center **California Culinary Academy.** This historic theater houses one of the most highly regarded professional cooking schools in the United States. Watch the student chefs at work on the double-tiered stage while you dine on classic French cooking. Prix-fixe meals and bountiful buffets are served in the main dining room; heart-healthy à la carte lunches are served at Cyril's on the balcony level, and there's a grill on the first floor. *625 Polk St., tel. 415/771-3500. Reservations advised (2-4 weeks for Fri.-night buffet). Jacket requested. AE, DC, MC, V. Closed weekends and major holidays. Moderate-Expensive.*

Financial District **Le Central.** This is the quintessential bistro: noisy and crowded, with nothing subtle about the cooking. But the garlicky pâtés, leeks vinaigrette, cassoulet, and grilled blood sausage with crisp french fries keep the crowds coming. *453 Bush St., tel. 415/ 391-2233. Reservations advised. Dress: informal. AE, MC, V. Closed Sun. and major holidays. Moderate.*

Marina **Rodin.** The nouvelle cuisine is as artful as the Rodin sculptures that decorate this little jewel of a neighborhood restaurant. And the service is ever-so-caring. Dinners are both prix fixe and à la carte. *1779 Lombard St., tel. 415/563-8566. Reservations advised. Dress: informal. DC, MC, V. No lunch. Closed Sun. and major holidays. Nominal charge for parking in motel next door. Expensive.*

Midtown **La Folie.** This pretty storefront café showcases the nouvelle cuisine of Roland Passot, a former sous chef at Illinois' famous Le Français. Much of the food is edible art—whimsical presentations that recall palm trees or peacocks; even a soup garnish that looks like a giant ladybug. The fun spirit of the place lets you forgive the sometimes lackadaisical, though well-intentioned, service. *2316 Polk St., tel. 415/776-5577. Reservations advised. Dress: informal. AE, DC, MC, V. No lunch. Closed Sun. Expensive.*

Nob Hill **The Dining Room of the Ritz-Carlton.** Cesar Ritz would surely approve of the elegant dinner house in this new outpost of his namesake hotel chain. The chef here, Yves Garnier, earned a Michelin star during his tenure at La Coupole in Monaco, and has brought to San Francisco a French cooking style that is classic, yet contemporary in its simplicity. *Ritz-Carlton Hotel, Stockton St. at California St., tel. 415/296-7465. Reservations advised. Jacket required. AE, DC, MC, V. Valet parking. Very expensive.*

North Beach **Amelio's.** A former speakeasy, this historic restaurant evokes turn-of-the-century San Francisco. Once known for its Italian food, the place was revitalized when the brilliant young French chef Jacky Robert became a partner. Robert's food looks as beautiful as it tastes. *1630 Powell St., tel. 415/397-4339. Reservations advised. Jacket required, tie requested. AE, DC, MC, V. Closed Sun., Mon., Christmas, New Year's Day. Very Expensive.*

★ **Ernie's.** This famous old-timer recently had a face-lift, and Alain Rondelli, one of France's most promising young chefs, is now in charge of the kitchen, preparing innovative light versions of French classics (and, at long last, has begun serving lunch). Even so, Ernie's is still steeped with the aura of Gay Nineties San Francisco. *847 Montgomery St., tel. 415/397-5969. Reservations advised. Jacket and tie required. AE, DC, MC, V. Closed major holidays. Valet parking. Very Expensive.*

Pacific Heights ★ **Le Castel.** Trends come and go, but Le Castel has adhered to classic French cooking—with a light touch. You'll even find such rarities as calf's brains and bone marrow. The restaurant is housed in a former Victorian residence that was remodeled with a Moorish touch to the interior. *3235 Sacramento St., tel. 415/921-7115. Reservations advised. Jacket required. AE, DC, MC, V. No lunch. Closed Mon. and most major holidays. Valet parking. Expensive.*

L'Escargot. This intimate, candle-lit café offers traditional three-course dinners at very affordable prices. The rack of lamb and the garlicky snails are among the best in town. *1809 Union St., tel. 415/567-0222. Reservations advised. Dress: informal. AE, DC, MC, V. No lunch. Closed Mon., Christmas, New Year's Day. Moderate.*

South of Market **Bistro Roti.** Tables in the rear of this new waterfront café look out over the bay and bridge, while those at the front surround a boisterous bar. A giant rotisserie and grill turn out succulent chops and roasts, but don't overlook that bistro classic—French onion soup. *155 Steuart St., tel. 415/495-6500. Reservations advised. Dress: informal. AE, MC, V. Weekend brunch. Moderate.*

Union Square ★ **Masa's.** Chef Julian Serrano carries on the tradition of the late Masa Kobayashi. In fact, some Masa regulars even say the cooking is better. The artistry of the presentation is as important as the food itself in this pretty, flower-filled dining spot in the Vintage Court Hotel. *648 Bush St., tel. 415/989-7154. Reservations should be made precisely 21 days in advance. Jacket required. AE, DC, MC, V. No lunch. Closed Sun., Mon., 1st week in July, last week in Dec., 1st week in Jan. Valet parking. Very Expensive.*

★ **Fleur de Lys.** The creative cooking of chef/partner Hubert Keller is drawing rave reviews to this romantic spot that some now consider the best French restaurant in town. The menu changes constantly, but such dishes as lobster soup with lemongrass are a signature. The intimate dining room, like a sheikh's tent, is encased with hundreds of yards of paisley. *777 Sutter St., tel. 415/673–7779. Reservations on weekends advised 2 weeks in advance. Jacket and tie required. AE, DC, MC, V. No lunch. Closed Sun., Thanksgiving, Christmas, New Year's Day. Valet parking. Expensive–Very Expensive.*

Greek and Middle Eastern

The foods of Greece and the Middle East have much in common: a preponderance of lamb and eggplant dishes, a widespread use of phyllo pastry, and an abundance of pilaf.

North Beach   **Maykadeh.** Here you'll find authentic Persian cooking in a setting so elegant that the modest check comes as a great surprise. Lamb dishes with rice are the specialties. *470 Green St., tel. 415/362–8286. Reservations advised. Dress: informal. MC, V. Valet parking at night. Inexpensive.*

South of Market   **S. Asimakopoulos Cafe.** Terrific Greek food at reasonable prices keeps the crowds waiting for seats at the counter or at bare-topped tables in this storefront café. The menu is large and varied, but lamb dishes are the stars. Convenient to Showplace Square. *288 Connecticut, Potrero Hill, tel. 415/552–8789. No reservations. Dress: informal. AE, MC, V. No lunch weekends. Closed major holidays. Inexpensive.*

Indian

The following restaurants serve the cuisine of northern India, which is more subtly seasoned and not as hot as its southern counterparts. They also specialize in succulent meats and crispy breads from the clay-lined tandoori oven.

Northern Waterfront and Embarcadero   **Gaylord's.** A vast selection of mildly spiced northern Indian food is offered here, along with meats and breads from the tandoori ovens and a wide range of vegetarian dishes. The dining rooms are elegantly appointed with Indian paintings and gleaming silver service. The Ghirardelli Square location offers bay views. *Ghirardelli Sq., tel. 415/771–8822. Embarcadero One, tel. 415/397–7775. Reservations advised. Dress: informal. AE, DC, MC, V. No lunch Sun. at Embarcadero. Ghirardelli closed Thanksgiving, Christmas; Embarcadero closed Labor Day, Christmas, New Year's Day. Validated parking at Ghirardelli Sq. garage and Embarcadero Center garage. Moderate.*

Pacific Heights   **North India.** Small and cozy, this restaurant has a more limited menu and hotter seasoning than Gaylord. Both tandoori dishes and curries are served, plus a range of breads and appetizers. Everything is cooked to order. *3131 Webster St., tel. 415/931–1556. Reservations advised. Dress: informal. AE, DC, MC, V. No lunch weekends. Parking behind restaurant. Moderate.*

International

The following restaurants are truly international in that they draw their inspiration from both Eastern and Western cuisines.

Embarcadero **Square One.** Chef Joyce Goldstein introduces an ambitious new
★ menu daily, with dishes based on the classic cooking of the
Mediterranean countries as well as that of Asia and Latin
America. The dining room, with its views of the open kitchen
and the Golden Gateway commons, is an understated setting
for some of the finest food in town. Bar menu. *190 Pacific Ave.,
tel. 415/788–1110. Reservations advised. Dress: informal. AE,
DC, MC, V. No lunch weekends. Closed major holidays. Valet
parking in evenings. Expensive.*

Union Square **Trader Vic's.** This is the headquarters of Vic's empire. You'll
find the usual tikis, the vast array of Cantonese and Polynesian
dishes, and the exotic drinks. Concentrate instead on simpler
fare, such as fresh seafood and Indonesian rack of lamb. The
Captain's Cabin is where the local celebs hang out, but you're
not likely to get a seat there unless you're known. *20 Cosmo
Pl., tel. 415/776–2232. Reservations advised. Jacket and tie required. AE, DC, MC, V. No lunch. Closed Thanksgiving,
Christmas. Valet parking. Moderate–Expensive.*

Italian

Italian food in San Francisco spans the "boot" from the mild
cooking of northern Italy to the spicy cuisine of the south. Then
there is the style indigenous to San Francisco, known as North
Beach Italian—such dishes as *cioppino* (a fisherman's stew)
and Joe's special (a mélange of eggs, spinach, and ground beef).

Embarcadero **Ciao.** Light, contemporary Italian food is the mainstay here:
graceful appetizers, a large selection of freshly made pastas,
grilled meats, and sausages. The high-tech decor of this popular trattoria is as modern as the food: all white splashed with
brass and chrome. *230 Jackson St., tel. 415/982–9500. Reservations advised. Dress: informal. AE, DC, MC, V. No lunch
Sun. Closed Thanksgiving, Christmas, New Year's Day. Valet
parking in the evening. Moderate.*

Il Fornaio. An offshoot of the Il Fornaio bakeries, this handsome tile-floored, wood-paneled complex combines a café, bakery, and upscale trattoria with outdoor seating. The cooking is
Tuscan, featuring pizzas from a wood-burning oven, superb
house-made pastas and gnocchi, and grilled poultry and seafood. Anticipate a wait for a table, but once seated, you won't
be disappointed—only surprised by the moderate prices.
*Levi's Plaza, 1265 Battery, tel. 415/986–0100. Reservations
advised. Dress: informal. MC, V. Closed Thanksgiving,
Christmas. Valet parking. Moderate.*

Financial District **Blue Fox.** This landmark restaurant was revitalized in 1988 by
John Fassio, son of a former owner, who redecorated the place
in a low-key, formal style. The classic cooking is from the Piedmont region of northern Italy, with a seasonally changing
menu. Pasta and gnocchi are made on the premises, as are the
luscious desserts. *659 Merchant St., tel. 415/981–1177. Reservations required. Jacket and tie required. AE, DC, MC, V.
Dinner only. Closed Sun. and major holidays. Valet parking.
Expensive–Very Expensive.*

Palio d'Asti. This moderately priced venture of Blue Fox owner
Gianni Fassio draws a lively Financial District lunch crowd.
Some specialties are Piedmontese, and a good show is provided
by the open kitchen and pizza oven, as well as the rolling carts

of antipasti. *640 Sacramento St., tel. 415/395–9800. Reservations advised. Dress: informal. MC, V. Moderate.*

Marina **Ristorante Parma.** This is a warm, wonderfully honest trattoria with excellent food at modest prices. The antipasti tray, with a dozen unusual items, is one of the best in town, and the pastas and veal are exceptional. Don't miss the spinach gnocchi, served only on weekends. *3314 Steiner St., tel. 415/567–0500. Reservations advised. Dress: informal. AE, MC, V. No lunch. Closed Sun. and some major holidays. Moderate.*

Midtown **Acquarello.** This exquisite restaurant is a new venture of the former chef and former maître 'd at Donatello. The service and food are exemplary, and the menu covers the full range of Italian cuisine, from northern Italy to the tip of the boot. Desserts are exceptional. *1722 Sacramento St., tel. 415/567–5432. Reservations advised. Dress: informal. DC, MC, V. No lunch. Closed Sun.–Mon. Validated parking across the street. Expensive.*

North Beach **Buca Giovanni.** Giovanni Leoni showcases the dishes of his
★ birthplace: the Serchio Valley in Tuscany. Pastas made on the premises are a specialty, and the calamari salad is one of the best around. The subterranean dining room is cozy and romantic. *800 Greenwich St., tel. 415/776–7766. Reservations advised. Dress: informal. AE, MC, V. No lunch. Closed Sun. and most major holidays. Moderate.*

Capp's Corner. One of the last of the family-style trattorias, diners sit elbow to elbow at long Formica tables to feast on bountiful six-course dinners. For the budget-minded or calorie-counters, a shorter dinner includes a tureen of soup, salad, and pasta. *1600 Powell St., North Beach, tel. 415/989–2589. Reservations advised. Dress: informal. DC, MC, V. No lunch weekends. Closed Thanksgiving, Christmas. Credit off meal check for parking in garage across the street. Moderate.*

Little City Antipasti Bar. This was the first place in San Francisco to introduce tapas-style dining, though the selection of appetizers spans many ethnic cuisines. The menu now also offers regular lunches and dinners featuring pastas and grilled dishes. Many fans still come, however, to make a meal of the appetizers—and many come just to drink at the big, crowded bar. *673 Union St., tel. 415/434–2900. Reservations accepted only for parties of 6 or more. Dress: informal. Open late. AE, MC, V. Closed major holidays. Moderate.*

South of Market **Etrusca.** The ancient Etruscan civilization inspired this popular new showplace in Rincon Center. Onyx chandeliers cast a warm glow on Siena gold walls, terrazzo floors and ceiling frescoes. The dishes from the giant wood-fired oven that dominates the open kitchen, however, recall modern Tuscany more than ancient Etruria. Bar menu. *Rincon Center, 101 Spear St., tel. 415/777–0330. Reservations advised. Dress: informal. MC, V. No lunch weekends. Validated parking in Rincon Center garage. Moderate.*

Undici. The robust flavors of Sicily and Sardinia dominate the menu of this new SoMa hot spot. Along with pastas and pizzas, look for earthy soups and stews. *374 11th St., tel. 415/431–3337. Reservations advised. Dress: informal. MC, V. No lunch Sat. Closed Sun. Moderate.*

Union Square **Donatello.** Much of the menu in this elegant restaurant in the Donatello Hotel is drawn from the Emilia-Romagna region of

Italy, which is famous for its food, especially the Bolognese pastas. The intimate dining rooms are exquisitely appointed with silk-paneled walls, paintings, and tapestries. Service is superb and low-keyed. Donatello also serves breakfasts that combine typical American fare with Italian-accented dishes. *Post and Mason Sts., tel. 415/441-7182. Reservations advised. Jacket and tie required. AE, DC, MC, V. No lunch. Validated parking in hotel garage. Expensive–Very Expensive.*

Kuleto's. The contemporary cooking of northern Italy, the atmosphere of old San Francisco, and an antipasti bar have made this spot off Union Square a hit since it opened during the 1980s. Grilled seafood dishes are among the specialties. Breakfast is served, too. Publike booths and a long open kitchen fill one side of the restaurant; a gardenlike setting with light splashed from skylights lies beyond. *221 Powell St., tel. 415/ 397-7720. Dress: informal. Reservations advised. AE, DC, MC, V. Closed Thanksgiving, Christmas. Moderate.*

Lascaux. Despite its Gallic name (after the primitive caves in France), the cuisine at this smart new restaurant is primarily Mediterranean, with a contemporary Italian accent. Changing menus offer fluffy polenta topped with steamed mussels, a torta of sun-dried tomatoes and mascarpone, and grilled seafood with imaginative sauces. Desserts are fabulous. A huge fireplace cheers the romantically lit subterranean dining room. *248 Sutter St., tel. 415/391-1555. Reservations advised. Dress: informal. AE, DC, MC, V. No lunch Sat. Closed Sun., Thanksgiving, Christmas. Moderate.*

Japanese

To understand a Japanese menu, you should be familiar with the basic types of cooking: *yaki*, marinated and grilled foods; *tempura*, fish and vegetables deep-fried in a light batter; *udon* and *soba*, noodle dishes; *domburi*, meats and vegetables served over rice; *ramen*, noodles served in broth; and *nabemono*, meals cooked in one pot, often at the table. Of course sushi bars are extremely popular in San Francisco; most offer a selection of *sushi*, vinegared rice with fish or vegetables, and *sashimi*, raw fish. Western seating refers to conventional tables and chairs; *tatami* seating is on mats at low tables.

Chinatown **Yamato.** The city's oldest Japanese restaurant is by far its most beautiful, with inlaid wood, painted panels, a meditation garden, and a pool. Both Western and tatami seating, in private shoji-screened rooms, are offered, along with a fine sushi bar. Come primarily for the atmosphere; the menu is somewhat limited, and more adventurous dining can be found elsewhere. *717 California St., tel. 415/397-3456. Reservations advised. AE, DC, MC, V. No lunch weekends. Closed Mon., Thanksgiving, Christmas, New Year's Day. Moderate.*

Japantown **Sanppo.** This small place has an enormous selection of almost every type of Japanese food: yakis, nabemono dishes, domburi, udon, and soba, not to mention feather-light tempura and interesting side dishes. Western seating only. *1702 Post St., tel. 415/346-3486. No reservations. Dress: informal. No credit cards. Closed Mon. and major holidays. Validated parking in Japan Center garage. Inexpensive.*

Mexican

In spite of San Francisco's Mexican heritage, until recently most south-of-the-border eateries were locked into the Cal-Mex taco-enchillada-mashed-beans syndrome. But now some newer places offer a broader spectrum of Mexican cooking.

Richmond District **Alejandro's.** Peruvian-Spanish dishes, especially seafood stews, are among the specialties here, although traditional Mexican combination plates are served as well. And there's an extensive tapas menu, too. The dining room is attractive—whitewashed walls and Peruvian artifacts—but noisy. *1840 Clement St., tel. 415/668–1184. Reservations advised. Dress: informal. AE, DC, MC, V. No lunch. Closed Thanksgiving, Christmas Eve, Christmas Day, New Year's Eve, New Year's Day. Moderate.*

South of Market **Chevys.** This first San Francisco branch of a popular Mexican minichain is decked out with funky neon signs and "El Machino" turning out flour tortillas. "Stop gringo food" is the motto here, and the emphasis is on the freshest ingredients and sauces. Of note are the fabulous fajitas and the grilled quail and seafood. *4th and Howard Sts., tel. 415/543–8060. Reservations accepted only for parties of 8 or more. Dress: informal. MC, V. Closed Thanksgiving, Christmas. Validated parking evenings after 5 PM and weekends at garage under bldg. (enter from Minna St.). Inexpensive.*

Union Square **Corona Bar & Grill.** The ever-changing menu offers light versions of regional Mexican dishes. Corona's paella, laden with shellfish and calamari, is sensational, as is the chocolate-coated flan. The atmosphere is a mix of old San Francisco (pressed tin ceilings and an antique bar) and old Mexico (hand-painted masks and Aztec motifs). *88 Cyril Magnin St., tel. 415/392–5500. Reservations advised. Dress: informal. AE, DC, MC, V. Closed Thanksgiving, Christmas. Moderate.*

Moroccan

San Francisco's Moroccan restaurants share a similarity of decor, menu, and ritual. Diners are seated on pillows or hassocks at low round tables for a sumptuous multicourse feast: spicy lentil-based soup, platters of vegetables scooped up with Arabic bread, *bastilla* (slivers of chicken, hard-cooked eggs, and almonds layered with honey and cinnamon in paper-thin pastry), and a choice of over a dozen entrees. Most of the main dishes are chicken or lamb stewed with various combinations of fruits and vegetables. The finale is sweet Moroccan pastries washed down with mint tea. The following restaurants, both in the Richmond District, offer these banquets at quite moderate prices, considering the abundance of food.

Richmond District **El Mansour.** *3123 Clement St., tel. 415/751–2312. Reservations advised. Dress: informal. AE, DC, MC, V. No lunch. Moderate.*
Mamounia. *4411 Balboa, tel. 415/752–6566. Reservations advised. Dress: informal. AE, MC, V. No lunch. Closed Mon. Moderate.*

Seafood

Like all port cities, San Francisco takes pride in its seafood, even though less than half the fish served here is from local waters. In winter and spring look for the fresh Dungeness crab, best served cracked with mayonnaise. In summer, feast upon Pacific salmon, even though imported varieties are available year-round. A recent development is the abundance of unusual oysters from West Coast beds and an outburst of oyster bars.

Civic Center **Hayes Street Grill.** Eight to 15 different kinds of seafood are
★ chalked on the blackboard each night at this extremely popular restaurant. The fish is served simply grilled, with a choice of sauces ranging from tartar to a spicy Szechuan peanut concoction. Appetizers are unusual, and desserts are lavish. *320 Hayes St., tel. 415/863–5545. Reservations should be made precisely 1 week in advance. Dress: informal. MC, V. No lunch Sat. Closed Sun. and major holidays. Moderate.*

Embarcadero **The Waterfront.** The dramatic, multilevel glass-walled dining room guarantees a bay view from every table. The food doesn't always match the fabulous view, but the fresh fish and pasta are usually above average. Very popular for weekend brunch. *Pier 7, Embarcadero, tel. 415/391–2696. Reservations required. Dress: informal. AE, DC, MC, V. Closed Christmas. Valet parking. Moderate.*

Financial District **Sam's Grill.** Sam's and Tadich (below) are two of the city's oldest restaurants and so popular for lunch that you must arrive before 11:30 to get a table. No frills here. The aura is starkly old-fashioned; some booths are enclosed and curtained. Although the menu is extensive and varied, those in the know stick with the fresh local seafood and East Coast shellfish. *374 Bush St., tel. 415/421–0594. Reservations not accepted. Dress: informal. DC, MC, V. Closed weekends and holidays. Moderate.*

Tadich Grill. Owners and locations have changed many times since this old-timer opened during the Gold Rush era, but the 19th-century atmosphere remains, as does the kitchen's special way with seafood. Seating at the counter or in private booths; long lines for a table at lunchtime. *240 California St., tel. 415/391–2373. No reservations. Dress: informal. MC, V. Closed Sun. and holidays. Moderate.*

Marina **Scott's Seafood Grill and Bar.** During peak dinner hours, you'll wait an hour for a table, but many fish lovers gladly do so for the grilled or sautéed catches of the day—usually about a dozen choices. Cioppino is another winner here. The atmosphere is pleasant, too, though sometimes a bit frantic. *2400 Lombard St., tel. 415/563–8988. No reservations after 6:30 PM. Dress: informal. AE, MC, V. Closed Thanksgiving, Christmas. Moderate.*

Pacific Heights **Pacific Heights Bar & Grill.** This is unquestionably the best oyster bar in town, with at least a dozen varieties available each day and knowledgeable shuckers to explain the mollusks' origins. In the small dining rooms, grilled seafood and shellfish stews head the bill of fare. Paella is a house specialty. *2001 Fillmore St., tel. 415/567–3337. Reservations advised. Dress: informal. AE, MC, V. No lunch Sat. Closed Thanksgiving, Christmas. Valet parking in the evening. Moderate.*

Union Square **Bentley's Oyster Bar & Restaurant.** The bustling bar downstairs dispenses at least 10 different types of oysters. An upstairs dining room offers the eclectic seafood concoctions of chef Amey Shaw, who mixes and matches the hot-and-spicy flavors of Southeast Asia, the American Southwest, and the Mediterranean. *185 Sutter St., tel. 415/989–6895. Reservations advised. Dress: informal. AE, DC, MC, V. Closed major holidays. Validated parking at downstairs garage in the evening. Moderate.*

Southeast Asian

In recent years San Franciscans have seen tremendous growth in the numbers of restaurants specializing in the foods of Thailand, Vietnam, and, most recently, Cambodia. The cuisines of these countries share many features, and one characteristic in particular: The cooking is always spicy and often very hot.

Marina **Angkor Palace.** This is one of the loveliest Cambodian restaurants in town and also the most conveniently located for visitors. The extensive family-style menu offers such exotic fare as fish-and-coconut mousse baked in banana leaves. You'll have questions, of course, but you'll find the staff eager to explain the contents of the menu. *1769 Lombard St., tel. 415/931–2830. Reservations advised. Dress: informal. AE, MC, V. No lunch. Inexpensive.*

Midtown **Golden Turtle.** This popular Vietnamese café is more accessible than the original restaurant on 5th Avenue. The menu is also more extensive, with some 50 items, and the decor is more elaborate. There's even a carp pond. *2211 Van Ness Ave., tel. 415/441–4419. Reservations accepted only for parties of 3 or more. Dress: informal. AE, MC, V. Closed Mon. and last week in Dec. Inexpensive.*

Richmond District **Khan Toke Thai House.** The city's first Thai restaurant has a ★ lovely dining room, furnished with low tables and cushions, and a garden view. The six-course dinners, with two entrees from an extensive choice, provide a delicious introduction to Thai cooking. (The seasoning will be mild, unless you request it hot.) Classical Thai dancing on Sunday. *5937 Geary Blvd., tel. 415/668–6654. Reservations advised. Dress: informal. AE, MC, V. No lunch. Closed Thanksgiving, Christmas, Labor Day. Inexpensive–Moderate.*

South of Market **Manora.** When Passarin Prassl opened this homey Thai café way out on Mission Street, she named it after her daughter, Manora. Soon crowds from all over town were lined up for a table to try the extensive selection of carefully prepared dishes. Now Manora has her own spot on Folsom Street, not far from the Performing Arts Center, with the same great food. *3226 Mission St., tel. 415/550–0856. 1600 Folsom St., tel. 415/861–6224. Dress: informal. MC, V. No lunch weekends. Closed Labor Day, Thanksgiving. Inexpensive.*

Steak Houses

Although San Francisco traditionally has not been a meat-and-potatoes town, the popularity of steak is on the rise. Following are some of the best steak houses, but you can also get a good piece of beef at some of the better French, Italian, and American restaurants.

Marina **Izzy's Steak & Chop House.** Izzy Gomez was a legendary San Francisco saloonkeeper, and his namesake eatery carries on the tradition with terrific steaks, chops, and seafood, plus all the trimmings—such as cheesy scalloped potatoes and creamed spinach. A collection of Izzy memorabilia and antique advertising art covers almost every inch of wall space. *3345 Steiner St., tel. 415/563–0487. Reservations accepted. Dress: informal. AE, DC, MC, V. No lunch. Closed Thanksgiving, Christmas. Validated parking at Lombard Garage. Moderate.*

Midtown **Harris'.** Ann Harris knows her beef. She grew up on a Texas
★ cattle ranch and was married to the late Jack Harris of Harris Ranch fame. In her own elegant restaurant she serves some of the best dry-aged steaks in town, but don't overlook the grilled seafood or poultry. Extensive bar menu. *2100 Van Ness Ave., tel. 415/673–1888. Reservations recommended. Dress: informal. AE, DC, MC, V. Lunch on Wed. only. Closed Christmas, New Year's Day. Valet parking. Expensive.*

Vegetarian

Marina **Greens at Fort Mason.** This beautiful restaurant with its bay
★ views is a favorite with carnivores as well as vegetarians. Owned and operated by the Tassajara Zen Center of Carmel Valley, the restaurant offers a wide, eclectic, and creative spectrum of meatless cooking, and the bread promises nirvana. Dinners are à la carte on weeknights, but only a five-course prix-fixe dinner is served on Friday and Saturday. *Bldg. A, Fort Mason, tel. 415/771–6222. Dress: informal. Reservations advised. MC, V. No dinner Sun. Closed Mon., Thanksgiving, Christmas, New Year's Day. Public parking at Fort Mason Center. Moderate.*

Vegetarians should also consider Gaylord's (*see* Indian restaurants, above), which offers a wide variety of meatless dishes from the Hindu cuisine.

7 Lodging

by Laura Del Rosso

Laura Del Rosso is San Francisco bureau chief for Travel Weekly, *a news magazine for the travel industry, and often writes about San Francisco for other publications.*

Few cities in the United States can rival San Francisco's variety in lodging. There are plush hotels ranked among the finest in the world, renovated older buildings that have the charm of Europe, bed-and-breakfast inns in the city's Victorian "Painted Ladies," and the popular chain hotels and low-rise motels that are found in most cities in the United States.

One of the brightest spots in the lodging picture is the transformation of handsome early 20th-century downtown high rises into small, distinctive hotels that offer personal service and European-style ambience. Another is the recent addition of ultradeluxe modern hotels such as the Nikko, Portman, and Mandarin Oriental, which promote their attentive Asian-style hospitality. On top of those offerings are the dozens of popular chain hotels, such as Holiday Inn, Sheraton, Hyatt, and Hilton, that continually undergo face-lifts and additions to keep up with the competition.

Because San Francisco is one of the top destinations in the United States for tourists as well as business travelers and convention goers, reservations are always advised, especially during the May–September peak season.

San Francisco's geography makes it conveniently compact. No matter their location, the hotels listed below are on or close to public transportation lines. Some properties on Lombard Street and in the Civic Center area have free parking, but a car is more a hindrance than an asset in San Francisco.

Although not as high as New York, San Francisco hotel prices may come as a surprise to travelers from less urban areas. Average rates for double rooms downtown and at the wharf are in the $110 range. Motel and hotel rooms can be found for less throughout the city, especially in the Civic Center and Lombard areas. Adding to the expense is the city's 11% transient occupancy tax, which can significantly boost the cost of a lengthy stay.

An alternative to hotels, inns, and motels is staying in private homes and apartments, available through two companies: **American Family Inn/Bed & Breakfast San Francisco** (Box 349, San Francisco, CA 94101, tel. 415/931–3083) and **Bed & Breakfast International–San Francisco** (1181–B Solano Ave., Albany, CA 94706, tel. 415/525–4569 or 800/872–4500).

The **San Francisco Convention and Visitors Bureau** each year publishes a free lodging guide with a map and listing of all hotels. Send $1 for postage and handling to the SFCVB, Box 6977, San Francisco, CA 94101-6977.

If you are looking for truly budget accommodations (under $50), consider the Adelaide Inn (*see* Union Square/Downtown, below) and the **YMCA Central Branch.** *220 Golden Gate Ave. 94102, tel. 415/885-0460. 102 rooms, 3 with bath. Facilities: health club, pool, sauna. MC, V.*

The most highly recommended hotels are indicated by a star ★.

Lodgings are listed by geographical area and price range.

Downtown San Francisco Lodging

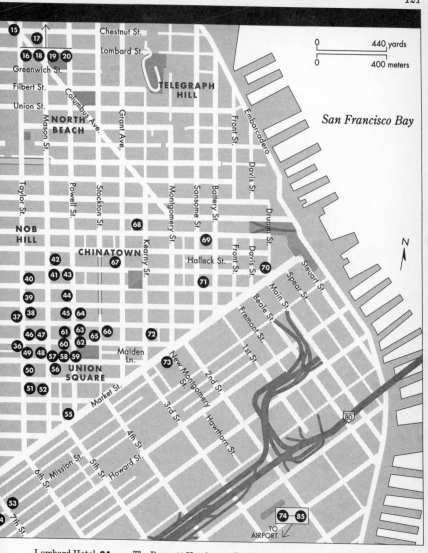

Lombard Hotel, **24**

Majestic Hotel, **22**

Mandarin Oriental, **71**

The Mansion, **11**

Marina Inn, **7**

Marina Motel, **1**

Mark Hopkins Inter-Continental, **41**

Miyako, **21**

Monticello Inn, **55**

New Richelieu Hotel, **25**

Pan-Pacific, **47**

Park Hyatt, **69**

Petite Auberge, **38**

The Phoenix Inn, **27**

The Prescott Hotel, **46**

Radisson Inn, **82**

Ramada Hotel-Fisherman's Wharf, **14**

Rancho Lombard Motel, **12**

The Raphael, **57**

San Francisco Airport Hilton, **76**

San Francisco Airport Marriott, **77**

San Francisco Hilton on Hilton Square, **51**

San Francisco Marriott-Fisherman's Wharf, **6**

San Remo Hotel, **18**

Sheraton Palace, **73**

Sheraton at Fisherman's Wharf, **19**

The Sherman House, **6**

Sir Francis Drake, **63**

Stouffer Stanford Court, **43**

Star Motel, **9**

Town House Motel, **8**

TraveLodge at the Wharf, **20**

Union Street Inn, **5**

U.N. Plaza Hotel, **35**

Vagabond Inn, **15**

Vagabond Inn (airport), **83**

Vintage Court, **44**

Westin Hotel, **78**

Westin St. Francis, **59**

White Swan, **39**

York Hotel, **31**

Category	Cost*
Very Expensive	over $175
Expensive	$100–$175
Moderate	$65–$100
Inexpensive	under $65

*All prices are for a standard double room, excluding 11% tax.

The following credit card abbreviations are used: AE, American Express; DC, Diners Club; MC, MasterCard; V, Visa.

Union Square/Downtown

The largest variety and greatest concentration of hotels are centered on the city's lovely downtown hub, Union Square, where hotel guests find the best shopping, the theater district, and transportation to every spot in San Francisco.

Very Expensive
★ **Campton Place.** Steps away from Union Square is one of the most highly rated and elegant hotels in San Francisco. Attentive, personal service takes off from the moment uniformed doormen greet guests outside the marble-floor lobby. *340 Stockton St., 94108, tel. 415/781–5555, 800/235–4300 in CA, or 800/647–4007 nationwide. 126 rooms. Facilities: restaurant, bar. AE, DC, MC, V.*

★ **Four Seasons Clift.** Probably San Francisco's most acclaimed hotel, this stately landmark is the first choice of many celebrities and discriminating travelers for its attentive personal service. Special attention is given to children, with fresh cookies and milk provided at bedtime. All rooms have been recently redecorated—the suites in elegant black and gray, others in bright beige and pink—in a somewhat updated contemporary style. *495 Geary St., 94102, tel. 415/775–4700 or 800/332–3442. 329 rooms. Facilities: restaurant, Redwood Room lounge. AE, DC, MC, V.*

Grand Hyatt. This hotel overlooks Union Square and Ruth Asawa's fantasy fountain in the garden (*see* Tour 1: Union Square in Chapter 3). The hotel, formerly the Hyatt on Union Square, recently underwent a $20 million renovation. *345 Stockton St., 94108, tel. 415/398–1234 or 800/233–1234. 693 rooms. Facilities: 2 restaurants, 2 lounges, shopping arcade. AE, DC, MC, V.*

Hotel Nikko–San Francisco. Trickling waterfalls and walls of white marble set a quiet, subtle mood at this fine Japanese Airlines–owned hotel. The rooms are pink and gray contemporary with an Oriental touch. *222 Mason St., 94102, tel. 415/394–1111 or 800/NIKKO–US. 525 rooms. Facilities: indoor pool, health club and spa, 2 restaurants, lounge. AE, DC, MC, V.*

San Francisco Hilton on Hilton Square. A huge expansion and renovation in 1988 made this by far the largest hotel in San Francisco. Popular with convention and tour groups. Free parking. *1 Hilton Sq. (O'Farrell and Mason Sts.), tel. 415/771–1400 or 800/445–8667. 1,907 rooms. Facilities: 5 restaurants, 2 lounges, pool, shopping arcade. AE, DC, MC, V.*

Westin St. Francis. This is one of the grand hotels of San Francisco and a Union Square landmark. Rooms in the original building have been redecorated but still retain some of the 1904 moldings and bathroom tiles. Rooms in the modern tower have brighter, lacquered furniture. *335 Powell St., 94102, tel. 415/*

397–7000 or 800/228–3000. 1,200 rooms. Facilities: 5 restaurants, 5 lounges, shopping arcade. AE, DC, MC, V.

Expensive   **Aston Regis Hotel.** This is one of the finest examples of the new generation of small, renovated hotels. Rooms are large and elegant, decorated in Louis XVI–style with French and Oriental antiques and canopy beds. *490 Geary St., 94102, tel. 415/928–7900 or 800/82–REGIS. 86 rooms. Facilities: restaurant, lounge. AE, DC, MC, V.*

Holiday Inn–Union Square. This hotel enjoys a good location on the cable car line only a block from Union Square. The decor of the Sherlock Holmes Lounge is 221-B Baker Street all the way. *480 Sutter St., 94108, tel. 415/398–8900 or 800/HOLIDAY. 400 rooms. Facilities: restaurant, lounge. AE, DC, MC, V.*

Hotel Diva. This hotel attracts the avant garde set with a high-tech look that sets it apart from any other hotel in San Francisco. *440 Geary St., 94102, tel. 415/885–0200 or 800/553–1900. 125 rooms. Facilities: restaurant, lounge. AE, DC, MC, V.*

Inn at Union Square. The individually decorated rooms with goosedown pillows and four-poster beds here are sumptuous. Continental breakfast and afternoon tea are served before a fireplace in the cozy sitting areas on each floor. *440 Post St., 04102, tel. 415/397–3510 or 800/288–4346. 30 rooms. AE, DC, MC, V.*

Kensington Park. A handsome, high-ceilinged lobby sets the mood of this fine hotel, where afternoon tea and sherry are served. The rooms are decorated with English Queen Anne–style furniture. *450 Post St., 94102, tel. 415/788–6400 or 800/553–1900. 90 rooms. AE, DC, MC, V.*

★ **Petite Auberge.** The French countryside was imported to downtown San Francisco to create this charming bed-and-breakfast inn. Calico-printed wallpaper, fluffy down comforters, and French reproduction antiques decorate each room. Most have wood-burning fireplaces. Next door is the sister hotel, the 27-room **White Swan**, similar in style but with an English country flavor. *845 Bush St., 94108, tel. 415/928–6000. 26 rooms. Facilities: breakfast rooms, parlors. AE, MC, V.*

The Prescott Hotel. The newest and plushest of the city's renovated old hotels, the Prescott may be most famous as home of Wolfgang Puck's Postrio restaurant. The hotel's emphasis is on personalized service, such as complimentary limousine service to the Financial District. *545 Post St., tel. 415/563–0303 or 800/283–7322. 167 rooms. Facilities: restaurant, lounge. AE, DC, MC, V.*

Sir Francis Drake. The rooms in this popular San Francisco hotel, famous for its Beefeater-costumed doormen, got a face-lift in 1986 during a multimillion-dollar renovation. They are decorated in an old English style, with mahogany furniture. The Starlight Roof is a lovely place for a drink. *450 Powell St., 94102, tel. 415/392–7755, 800/652–1668 in CA, or 800/227–5480 nationwide. 415 rooms. Facilities: restaurant, lounge, exercise room. AE, DC, MC, V.*

Moderate   **The Cartwright.** This is a family-owned hotel with a friendly,
★   personal touch in an ideal location. Renovated in 1986 after a five-year program to instill elegance and charm into the surroundings, this hotel offers rooms with brass or wood-carved beds, small refrigerators, and newly tiled bathrooms. *524 Sutter St., 94102, tel. 415/421–2865 or 800/227–3844. 114 rooms. Facilities: coffee shop. AE, DC, MC, V.*

★ **Chancellor Hotel.** This venerable hotel has been attracting a loyal clientele since it opened in 1924. Renovated in 1986, rooms have a new, elegant appearance with polished cherry-wood furniture. One of the best buys on Union Square. *433 Powell St., 94102, tel. 415/362–2004 or 800/428–4748. 140 rooms. Facilities: restaurant, lounge. AE, DC, MC, V.*

Handlery Union Square Hotel. The former Handlery Motor Inn and Stewart Hotel were combined and refurbished at a cost of $5 million in early 1988. The suitelike Handlery Club rooms are larger and more expensive. *351 Geary St., 94102, tel. 415/781–7800 or 800/223–0888. 378 rooms. Facilities: restaurant, outdoor heated pool, nonsmoking rooms. AE, DC, MC, V.*

Hotel Bedford. Big, cheery floral prints dominate the recently renovated guest rooms in this hotel, four blocks from Union Square. *761 Post St., 94109, tel. 415/673–6040, 800/652–1889 in CA, or 800/227–5642 nationwide. 144 rooms. Facilities: restaurant, English-style pub, in-room movie rentals. AE, DC, MC, V.*

★ **King George.** This charming midsize hotel was renovated in 1988 and 1989 to give it a more elegant, sophisticated look. The hotel's quaint Bread and Honey Tearoom serves traditional afternoon high tea. *334 Mason St., 94102, tel. 415/781–5050 or 800/288–6005. 144 rooms. Facilities: tearoom, lounge. AE, DC, MC, V.*

Monticello Inn. This hotel could boast "George Washington slept here" and most people would believe it. A little bit of the American Colonial period in the middle of downtown. Opened in 1987 after a complete renovation. The popular Corona Bar and Grill is off the lobby. *80 Cyril Magnin St., 94102, tel. 415/392–8800 or 800/669–7777. 91 rooms. Facilities: restaurant. AE, DC, MC, V.*

The Raphael. A favorite among repeat visitors to San Francisco, the Raphael was one of the first moderately priced European-style hotels in the city. Rooms were redecorated in 1988. The location is excellent. *386 Geary St., 94102, tel. 415/986–2000 or 800/821–5343. 151 rooms. Facilities: restaurant, lounge, in-room HBO. AE, DC, MC, V.*

Vintage Court. Beautifully furnished, elegant rooms, which were redecorated in 1989 in a Wine Country theme, are featured. Complimentary wine is served before crackling fire in the lobby in afternoons. *650 Bush St., 94108, tel. 415/392–4666, 800/654–7266 in CA, or 800/654–1100 nationwide. 106 rooms. Facilities: Masa's restaurant, lounge. AE, DC, MC, V.*

York Hotel. This very attractive, renovated old hotel is known for its Plush Room cabaret and as the site of a scene in Alfred Hitchcock's *Vertigo. 940 Sutter St., 94109, tel. 415/885–6800 or 800/227–3608. 96 rooms. Facilities: nightclub, fitness center, complimentary chauffeured limousine. AE, DC, MC, V.*

Inexpensive **Adelaide Inn.** The bedspreads may not match the drapes or carpets and the floors may creak, but the rooms are clean and cheap (under $50 for a double room) at this friendly small hotel that is popular with Europeans. Continental breakfast is complimentary. *5 Isadora Duncan Ct. (off Taylor between Geary and Post), 94102, tel. 415/441–2474. 16 rooms, all share bath. Facilities: sitting room, refrigerator for guest use. MC, V.*

Amsterdam. This European-style pension is in a Victorian building two blocks from Nob Hill. Rooms were renovated in 1988. *749 Taylor St., 94108, tel. 415/673–3277 or 800/637–3444.*

30 rooms, 8 with shared bath. Facilities: cable TV in rooms, reading room, breakfast room for complimentary breakfast. AE, MC, V.

Beresford Arms. Complimentary pastries and coffee are served in the hotel's grand old lobby. The suites with full kitchens are a good bargain for families. Standard rooms contain queen-size beds and small refrigerators. *701 Post St., 94109, tel. 415/673–2600 or 800/533–6533. 90 rooms. Facilities: some rooms have whirlpool baths. AE, DC, MC, V.*

Galleria Park. This very attractive hotel is convenient to the Union Square shopping district. The guest rooms were all redecorated in late 1988 in a simplified French country style. *191 Sutter St., 94104, tel. 415/781–3060, 800/792–9855 in CA, or 800/792–9636 nationwide. 177 rooms. Facilities: rooftop park and jogging track, 2 restaurants, lounge. AE, DC, MC, V.*

Holiday Inn–Financial District. This hotel boasts excellent location in Chinatown and is five minutes from Union Square and North Beach. Rooms on 12th floor and above have city and bay views. *750 Kearny St., 94108, tel. 415/433–6600 or 800/HOLI-DAY. 556 rooms. Facilities: pool, restaurant, lounge, free parking. AE, DC, MC, V.*

★ **Grant Plaza.** This bargain-priced hotel at the entrance of Chinatown has small but clean and attractively furnished rooms. No restaurant, but plenty of dining nearby. *465 Grant Ave., 94103, tel. 415/434–3883, 800/472–6805 in CA, or 800/472–6899 nationwide. 72 rooms. AE, MC, V.*

U.N. Plaza Hotel. This is a well-kept hotel for budget-conscious travelers who don't mind a less-than-desirable location. The large corner suites are ideal for families. Color TVs have in-room movies. *1112 Market St., 94102, tel. 415/626–5200 or 800/553–1900. 136 rooms. Facilities: tour desk in lobby. AE, DC, MC, V.*

Financial District

High-rise growth in San Francisco's Financial District has turned it into mini-Manhattan, a spectacular sight by night.

Very Expensive   **Hyatt Regency.** The stunning atrium-lobby architecture is the highlight here. Major renovations took place in late 1989 to upgrade the rooms and the lobby. *5 Embarcadero Center, 94111, tel. 415/788–1234 or 800/233–1234. 803 rooms. Facilities: 2 restaurants, coffee shop, lounge, 24-hour room service, shopping arcade. AE, DC, MC, V.*

Mandarin Oriental. The third-highest building in San Francisco's skyline is topped by a luxurious 11-story hotel on its 38th–48th floors. It's the best for spectacular views, especially from the bathrooms in the Mandarin rooms with their floor-to-ceiling windows flanking the tubs. *222 Sansome St., 94104, tel. 415/885–0999 or 800/622–0404. 160 rooms. Facilities: gourmet restaurant, lounge. AE, DC, MC, V.*

Park Hyatt. This is the Hyatt chain's candidate for competing with the ultraluxury of some of the city's best hotels. Service is highly personal and attentive and rooms are plush, with such goodies as gourmet chocolates and imported soaps. Many rooms have balconies and bay views. The hotel caters to corporate executives and the like. *333 Battery St., tel. 415/392–1234 or 800/228–9000. 360 rooms. Facilities: restaurant, lounge, library room. AE, DC, MC, V.*

Expensive   **Sheraton Palace.** One of the city's grand old hotels, the Sheraton reopened in 1991 after a $150 million reconstruction. New: air-conditioning, business center, health club, pool. Restored: the Garden Court restaurant with its leaded-glass ceiling, the Pied Piper lounge featuring Maxfield Parrish's painting of that name. *2 New Montgomery St., 94105, tel. 415/543–0671 or 800/325–3535. 550 rooms. Facilities: 24-hour room service, 2 restaurants, 2 lounges, fitness center. AE, DC, MC, V.*

Nob Hill

Synonymous with San Francisco's high society, Nob Hill contains some of the city's best-known luxury hotels. All offer spectacular city and bay views and noted gourmet restaurants. Cable car lines that cross Nob Hill make transportation a cinch.

Very Expensive   **Fairmont Hotel and Tower.** The regal "grande dame" of Nob Hill, the Fairmont has one of the most spectacular lobbies and public rooms in the city. All guest rooms are spacious and finely decorated. Those in the modern tower have the best views, while those in the old building have the stately ambience of another era. *950 Mason St., 94108, tel. 415/772–5000 or 800/527–4727. 596 rooms. Facilities: health club and spa, gift shops, 6 restaurants, 6 lounges, 24-hour room service. AE, DC, MC, V.*

★   **Huntington Hotel.** Understated class is found in this little jewel atop Nob Hill. Sumptuous rooms and suites are individually decorated. The only elevator operators in the city push buttons for guests 24 hours a day. *1075 California St., 94108, tel. 415/474–5400, 800/652–1539 in CA, or 800/227–4683 worldwide. 143 rooms. Facilities: restaurant, lounge with entertainment. AE, DC, MC, V.*

Mark Hopkins Inter-Continental. Another Nob Hill landmark, "The Mark" is lovingly maintained. Rooms were redone in late 1987 in dramatic neoclassical furnishings of gray, silver, and khaki and with bold leaf-print bedspreads. Bathrooms are lined with Italian marble. Even-numbered rooms have views of the Golden Gate Bridge. *999 California St., 94108, tel. 415/392–3434 or 800/327–0200. 392 rooms. Facilities: gift shops, restaurant, lobby lounge, Top of the Mark cocktail lounge with panoramic views. AE, DC, MC, V.*

★   **Stouffer Stanford Court Hotel.** This is one of the most highly acclaimed hotels in the United States. The service is so thoughtful that the general manager recently put dictionaries in each room for guests' convenience. One of the city's finest restaurants, Fournou's Ovens, is located here. *905 California St., 94108, tel. 415/989–3500 or 800/227–4726. 402 rooms. Facilities: gift shops, 2 restaurants, 2 lounges. AE, DC, MC, V.*

Fisherman's Wharf/North Beach

Fisherman's Wharf, San Francisco's top tourist attraction, is also the most popular area for accommodations. All are within a couple of blocks of restaurants, shops, and cable car lines. Because of city ordinances, none of the hotels exceed four stories; thus, this is not the area for fantastic views of the city or bay. Reservations are always necessary, sometimes weeks in advance during the peak summer months. Some streetside rooms can be noisy.

Very Expensive   **San Francisco Marriott–Fisherman's Wharf.** Elegant lobby and guest rooms set the mood in one of the wharf's newest and finest hotels. *1250 Columbus Ave., 94133, tel. 415/775–7555 or 800/228–9290. 256 rooms. Facilities: restaurant, lounge, gift shop. AE, DC, MC, V.*

Expensive **Holiday Inn–Fisherman's Wharf.** This large brick-faced hotel covers nearly two square blocks, including the 1984 addition, which has its own lobby and restaurant. Ongoing renovations keep rooms throughout the hotel upgraded. Charley's restaurant in the main building serves three excellent buffets; lunch brims with fresh seafood. *1300 Columbus Ave., 94133, tel. 415/ 771–9000 or 800/HOLIDAY. 580 rooms. Facilities: outdoor pool, laundry rooms, free parking. AE, DC, MC, V.*

Ramada Hotel–Fisherman's Wharf. The well-appointed public areas and guest rooms have all been renovated within the past few years. *590 Bay St., 94133, tel. 415/885–4700 or 800/228– 2828. 231 rooms. Facilities: parking, running track, Parcourse. AE, DC, MC, V.*

Sheraton at Fisherman's Wharf. Rooms and corridors were handsomely refurnished in 1987 at this sprawling full-service hotel. Streetside rooms can be noisy; interior courtyard rooms are the quietest. *2500 Mason St., 94133, tel. 415/362–5500 or 800/325–3535. 525 rooms. Facilities: outdoor pool, restaurant, cocktail lounge. AE, DC, MC, V.*

TraveLodge at the Wharf. This is an attractive hotel whose rooms were tastefully redecorated during the past few years. Higher priced interior rooms (third and fourth floors) have balconies overlooking the landscaped deck and swimming pool, as well as unobstructed views of Alcatraz. *250 Beach St., 94133, tel. 415/392–6700 or 800/255–3050. 250 rooms. Facilities: outdoor pool, restaurant, lounge, free parking. AE, DC, MC, V.*

Moderate **Columbus Motor Inn.** This is an attractive motel between the wharf and North Beach with suites that are ideal for families. *1075 Columbus Ave., 94133, tel. 415/885–1492. 45 rooms. Facilities: free parking. AE, DC, MC, V.*

Inexpensive **San Remo Hotel.** This cozy hotel is reminiscent of a European-
★ style pension. Renovated during recent years, its smallish rooms and narrow corridors are freshly painted and decorated with plants and antiques. It offers a good location on the border of Fisherman's Wharf and North Beach. *2237 Mason St., 94133, tel. 415/776–8688. 62 rooms, all with shared baths. Daily and weekly rates. Facilities: popular Italian restaurant. MC, V.*

Lombard Street/Cow Hollow

Lombard Street, a major traffic corridor leading to the Golden Gate Bridge, is sandwiched between two of San Francisco's poshest neighborhoods, Cow Hollow and the Marina District.

Very Expensive **The Sherman House.** In the middle of an elegant residential dis-
★ trict is this magnificent landmark mansion, the most luxurious small hotel in San Francisco. Each room is individually decorated with Biedermeier, English Jacobean, or French Second-Empire antiques, with tapestrylike canopies covering four-poster beds. Marble-top, wood-burning fireplaces and black granite bathrooms with whirlpool baths complete the picture. There is an in-house restaurant for guests only. *2160 Green St., 94123, tel. 415/563–3600. 15 rooms. Facilities: dining room, sitting rooms. AE, DC, MC, V.*

Moderate   **The Bed and Breakfast Inn.** The first of San Francisco's B&Bs, this is an ivy-covered renovated Victorian located in an alleyway off Union Street. Romantic, cheery rooms with flowery wallpaper include "The Mayfair," a flat with a spiral staircase leading to a sleeping loft. Some rooms are more modest and share baths. *4 Charlton Ct., 94123, tel. 415/921–9784. 10 rooms with baths. Facilities: breakfast room. No credit cards.*

Bel Aire TraveLodge. This attractive, well-kept motel is in a quiet location half a block from Lombard Street. *3201 Steiner St., 94123, tel. 415/921–5162 or 800/255–3050. 32 rooms. Facilities: free parking. AE, DC, MC, V.*

Cow Hollow Motor Inn. This is a large, modern motel with lovely rooms that were all renovated in 1988 with thick, new burgundy carpeting and rose-colored bedspreads. *2190 Lombard St., 94123, tel. 415/921–5800. 129 rooms. Facilities: restaurant, free parking. AE, DC, MC, V.*

★   **Marina Inn.** Here cute B&B-style accommodations are offered at motel prices. Dainty-flowered wallpaper, poster beds, country pine furniture, and fresh flowers give the rooms an English country air. Continental breakfast is served in the cozy central sitting room. Turned-down beds and chocolates greet guests at the end of the day. No parking. *3110 Octavia St. at Lombard St., 94123, tel. 415/928–1000. 40 rooms. Facilities: lounge. AE, MC, V.*

Rancho Lombard Motel. This motel has handsome, newly renovated rooms with Colonial-style furniture. Some rooms have kitchens and/or bay views. *1501 Lombard St., 94123, tel. 415/474–3030. 37 rooms. Facilities: free parking. AE, DC, MC, V.*

Union Street Inn. A retired schoolteacher has transformed this 1902 Edwardian home into a cozy inn. Antiques and fresh flowers are found throughout. *2229 Union St., 94123, tel. 415/346–0424. 6 rooms with private bath. Facilities: English garden, breakfast room, free parking. AE, MC, V.*

Vagabond Inn. This is a beautifully maintained motor inn that overlooks a central courtyard swimming pool. Some fourth- and fifth-floor rooms have views of the Golden Gate Bridge. *2550 Van Ness Ave. near Lombard St., 94109, tel. 415/776–7500 or 800/522–1555 in CA. 132 rooms. Facilities: outdoor pool, 24-hour restaurant, lounge. AE, DC, MC, V.*

Inexpensive   **Edward II Inn.** Standard rooms are smallish and parking is not available, but reasonable prices and a quaint pension atmosphere offset these drawbacks. *3155 Scott St. at Lombard St., 94123, tel. 415/922–3000. 29 rooms, 19 with bath. Facilities: restaurant, Italian bakery off the lobby. AE, MC, V.*

Marina Motel. This quaint Spanish-style stucco complex is one of the oldest motels on Lombard Street, but it is well kept. Each room has its own garage. *2576 Lombard St., 94123, tel. 415/921–9406. 45 rooms, some with kitchen. Facilities: free parking. AE, MC, V.*

Star Motel. This is a well-maintained motel with basic rooms. Free HBO. *1727 Lombard St., 94123, tel. 415/346–8250 or 800/835–8143. 52 rooms. Facilities: free parking. AE, MC, V.*

★   **Town House Motel.** A very attractive motel with recently redecorated rooms, this is one of the best values on Lombard Street. *1650 Lombard St., 94123, tel. 415/885–5163 or 800/255–1516. 24 rooms. Facilities: free parking. AE, DC, MC, V.*

Civic Center/Van Ness

The governmental heart of San Francisco has been undergoing a renaissance that has made it come alive with fine restaurants, trendy night spots, and renovated small hotels.

Expensive **Cathedral Hill Hotel.** Guest rooms were renovated in 1988 at this popular convention hotel. *1101 Van Ness Ave., 94109, tel. 415/776–8200, 800/622–0855 in CA, 800/227–4730 nationwide. 400 rooms. Facilities: free parking, pool, 2 restaurants, lounge. AE, DC, MC, V.*

★ **Inn at the Opera.** A music or ballet lover's heart may quiver at the sight of this lovely small hotel, where musicians and singers stay when they appear at San Francisco's performing arts centers a block away. There are billowing pillows, terry-cloth robes, microwave ovens, and servibars in each room. *333 Fulton St., 94102, tel. 415/863–8400, 800/423–9610 in CA, or 800/325–2708 nationwide. 48 rooms. Facilities: classy restaurant, lounge. AE, DC, MC, V.*

Miyako. In the heart of Japantown is this elegant, recently renovated hotel. The Japanese ambience is established by a greeting from a kimono-clad hostess. Traditional Japanese rooms with tatami mats are available. *1625 Post St. at Laguna St., 94115, tel. 415/922–3200 or 800/533–4567. 208 rooms. Facilities: Japanese baths, saunas, restaurant, 2 lounges. AE, DC, MC, V.*

Moderate **Abigail Hotel.** A former B&B inn, this hotel retains its homey
★ atmosphere with an eclectic mix of English antiques and mounted hunting trophies in the lobby. Hissing steam radiators and sleigh beds set the mood in the antiques-filled rooms. Room 211—the hotel's only suite—is the most elegant and spacious. *246 McAllister St., 94102, tel. 415/861–9728, 800/553–5575 in CA, or 800/243–6510 nationwide. 62 rooms. AE, DC, MC, V.*

Best Western Americania. This hotel is distinguished by its pink-and-turquoise Moorish facade. Rooms overlook inner courtyards with fountain or swimming pool. *121 7th St., 94103, tel. 415/626–0200 or 800/444–5816. 142 rooms. Facilities: outdoor pool, sauna, coffee shop, free parking, nonsmoking rooms available, evening shuttle to Union Square. AE, DC, MC, V.*

Holiday Inn–Civic Center. A 1989 renovation of the exterior, all rooms, lobby, and the restaurant has added a touch of elegance. The location is good—three blocks from the Civic Center and two blocks from Brooks Hall/Civic Auditorium. *50 8th St., 94103, tel. 415/626–6103 or 800/HOLIDAY. 390 rooms. Facilities: restaurant, lounge, outdoor pool. AE, DC, MC, V.*

★ **Lombard Hotel.** This is a European-style hotel with a handsome marble-floor lobby flanked on one side by the Gray Derby restaurant. Many of the rooms were refurbished in 1989 with blondwood furniture and new servibars. Quiet rooms are in the back. Complimentary evening cocktails and chauffeured limousine downtown are offered. *1015 Geary St., 94109, tel. 415/673–5232 or 800/227–3608. 100 rooms. Facilities: restaurant. AE, DC, MC, V.*

Majestic Hotel. One of San Francisco's original grand hotels, the Majestic was meticulously restored and reopened in 1985 with even more stately elegance. Romantic rooms have French and English antiques and four-poster canopy beds. Many have fireplaces and original claw-foot bathtubs. *1500 Sutter St.,*

94109, tel. 415/441–1100 or 800/869–8966. 60 rooms. Facilities: gourmet restaurant, lounge. AE, MC, V.

The Mansion. This twin-turreted Queen Anne Victorian was built in 1887 and today houses one of the most unusual hotels in the city. Rooms contain an oddball collection of furnishings and vary from the tiny "Tom Thumb" room to the opulent "Josephine" suite, the favorite of such celebrities as Barbra Streisand. Owner Bob Pritikin's pig paintings and other "porkabilia" are everywhere. *2220 Sacramento St., 94115, tel. 415/ 929–9444. 28 rooms. Facilities: dining room, weekend concerts, Bufano sculpture, and flower garden. AE, DC, MC, V.*

New Richelieu Hotel. The Richelieu's rooms acquired new beds, furniture, and carpeting in an extensive 1988 renovation. Rooms in the back building are larger and have new bathrooms. The lobby has been spruced up with an elegant gray-and-blue color scheme. *1050 Van Ness Ave., 94109, tel. 415/673–4711 or 800/227–3608. 150 rooms. Facilities: nonsmoking rooms available, gift shop and tour desk in lobby, 24-hour restaurant adjacent. AE, DC, MC, V.*

The Phoenix Inn. Resembling more of a '50s-style beachside resort than a hotel in San Francisco's government center, the Phoenix bills itself aptly as an "urban retreat." Bungalow-style rooms, decorated with casual Filipino bamboo and original art by San Francisco artists, all face a pool courtyard and sculpture garden. *601 Eddy St., 94109, tel. 415/776–1380. 44 rooms. Facilities: free parking, lounge, heated pool; restaurant offers room service. AE, DC, MC, V.*

Inexpensive **The Atherton Hotel.** A clean, low-price hotel with bilevel Mediterranean-style lobby. *685 Ellis St., 94109, tel. 415/474–5720 or 800/227–3608. 75 rooms. Facilities: restaurant, bar. AE, DC, MC, V.*

The Essex Hotel. New Italian marble floors in the lobby give this otherwise simple tourist hotel a touch of class. The friendliness of the Australian couple who own it is also a big plus. Popular with German and English tourists. *684 Ellis St., 94109, tel. 415/474–4664, 800/44–ESSEX in CA, or 800/45–ESSEX nationwide. 100 rooms, 52 with bath. AE, MC, V.*

★ **Hotel Britton.** This hotel is clean and comfortable, with good rates, and is close to the Civic Center. Rooms are attractively furnished, and color TVs offer in-room movies. *112 7th St. at Mission St., 94103, tel. 415/621–7001 or 800/444–5819. 80 rooms. Facilities: coffee shop. AE, DC, MC, V.*

The Airport

A construction boom near San Francisco International Airport during the mid-'80s added several luxury-class hotels. Rates are about 20% less than at San Francisco counterparts. Airport shuttle buses are provided by all of the following hotels. Because they cater primarily to midweek business travelers, the airport hotels often cut weekend prices drastically. Be sure to inquire.

Expensive ★ **Embassy Suites–Burlingame.** Slow-turning fans and jungle landscaping provide the ambience of a pink-and-turquoise "Paradise Island" resort. Bayside rooms have views of the airport and distant San Francisco. *150 Anza Blvd., Burlingame 94010, tel. 415/342–4600 or 800/EMBASSY. 344 2-room suites. Facilities: popular restaurant and lounge with live enter-*

tainment, jogging path, indoor pool, health club, in-room movies, gift shop. AE, DC, MC, V.

Hyatt Regency–Burlingame. A 10-story open-air atrium lobby is the centerpiece of this convention-oriented hotel, which opened in July 1988. *1333 Old Bayshore Hwy., Burlingame 94010, tel. 415/347–1234 or 800/233–1234. 791 rooms. Facilities: pool, health club, concierge floor, 3 restaurants, 2 lounges. AE, DC, MC, V.*

San Francisco Airport Hilton. This newly renovated hotel is the only one at the airport's doorstep. *San Francisco International Airport, Box 8355, 94128, tel. 415/589–0770 or 800/445–8667. 529 rooms. Facilities: 2 restaurants, lounge, fitness center, landscaped grounds, pool. AE, DC, MC, V.*

San Francisco Airport Marriott. This hotel's elegant lobby has picture windows that overlook the bay and airport runways; half of the rooms have the same view. *1800 Old Bayshore Hwy., Burlingame 94010, tel. 415/692–9100 or 800/228–9290. 684 rooms. Facilities: indoor pool, health club, jogging path, 2 restaurants, 2 lounges, 24-hour room service, in-room movies, concierge floor. AE, DC, MC, V.*

Hotel Sofitel–San Francisco Bay. A 15-minute drive south of the airport congestion, this hotel carries out a French theme in its courtyard, lobby, and restaurants. It faces a bayside lagoon, where there are jogging trails and nearby tennis courts. *223 Twin Dolphin Dr., Redwood City, 94065, tel. 415/598–9000, 800/221–4542, fax 415/598–0459. 324 rooms, 42 suites. Facilities: 2 restaurants, lounge, concierge, valet/laundry service, pool, health club, spa. AE, DC, MC, V.*

Westin Hotel. Built in 1987, this deluxe, service-oriented hotel has a palm-tree-lined entrance and Japanese-inspired interior decor. Theme restaurants include a '50s-style diner and a plush steak house. *1 Bayshore Blvd., Millbrae 94030, tel. 415/692–3500 or 800/228–3000. 388 rooms. Facilities: concierge floor, 2 restaurants, 2 lounges, health club, pool. AE, DC, MC, V.*

Moderate **Clarion Hotel.** This hotel in a garden setting five minutes south of the airport has been upgraded in recent years. *401 E. Millbrae Ave., Millbrae 94030, tel. 415/692–6363 or 800/CLARION. 435 rooms. Facilities: in-room movies, lounge, 2 restaurants, health club, heated pool, spa. AE, DC, MC, V.*

Comfort Suites. This is an attractive low-rise hotel whose rooms are divided into sitting areas and bedrooms. Complimentary Continental breakfast is served in a Mexican-style lobby with tile floors and an adobe fireplace. *121 E. Grand Ave., South San Francisco 94080, tel. 415/589–7766 or 800/228–5150. 164 rooms. Facilities: health club/spa, in-room movies. AE, DC, MC, V.*

Holiday Inn Crowne Plaza. Built in 1984, this bayside hotel fulfills the chain's desire to offer more sophisticated accommodations. *600 Airport Blvd., Burlingame 94010, tel. 415/340–8500 or 800/HOLIDAY. 407 rooms. Facilities: restaurant, lounge, concierge floor, in-room movies, pool, health spa with weight room, business center. AE, DC, MC, V.*

Radisson Inn. Formerly the Airport Executive Inn, this hotel was thoroughly refurbished under Radisson management. A breakfast buffet is included in the rates. *275 S. Airport Blvd., South San Francisco 94080, tel. 415/873–3550 or 800/333–3333. 221 rooms. Facilities: 2 restaurants, fitness center, concierge floor, car-rental office/pick-up/drop-off station. AE, DC, MC, V.*

Vagabond Inn. This well-maintained motel offers bayfront rooms with terraces (they are $10 more but worth it). *1640 Bayshore Blvd., Burlingame 94010, tel. 415/692–4040 or 800/522–1555. 91 rooms. Facilities: in-room movies, sauna, restaurants adjacent. AE, DC, MC, V.*

Inexpensive **Days Inn.** This is a three-story, redbrick hotel with an attractive pool area. *777 Airport Blvd., Burlingame 94010, tel. 415/342–7772 or 800/325–2525. 200 rooms. Facilities: nonsmoking rooms, in-room movies, pool, 24-hour restaurant. AE, DC, MC, V.*

La Quinta Motor Inn. Opened in late 1987, this economy lodge offers attractively furnished rooms. *20 Airport Blvd., South San Francisco 94080, tel. 415/583–2223 or 800/531–5900. 174 rooms. Facilities: 24-hour restaurant adjacent, pool. AE, DC, MC, V.*

8 The Arts and Nightlife

The Arts

by Robert Taylor

Longtime San Franciscan Robert Taylor writes about the arts for the Oakland Tribune.

The best guide to arts and entertainment events in San Francisco is the "Datebook" section, printed on pink paper, in the Sunday *Examiner and Chronicle*. The *Bay Guardian*, a free weekly newspaper available in racks around the city, lists more neighborhood, avant-garde, and budget-priced events. For up-to-date information about cultural and musical events, call the Convention and Visitors Bureau Cultural Events Calendar (tel. 415/391–2001).

Half-price tickets to many local and touring stage shows go on sale at noon Tuesday–Saturday at the **STBS** booth on the Stockton Street side of Union Square, between Geary and Post streets. STBS is also a full-service ticket agency for theater and music events around the Bay Area (open until 7:30 PM). While the city's major commercial theaters are concentrated downtown, the opera, symphony, and ballet perform at the Civic Center. For recorded information about STBS tickets, call 415/433–7827.

The city's two charge-by-phone ticket services are **BASS** (tel. 415/762–2277), with one of its centers in the STBS booth, and **Ticketron** (tel. 415/392–7469), with a center in the Emporium store, 835 Market Street. Other agencies downtown are the **City Box Office**, 141 Kearny Street in the Sherman-Clay store (tel. 415/392–4400) and **Downtown Center Box Office** in the parking garage at 320 Mason Street (tel. 415/775–2021). The opera, symphony, the ballet's *Nutcracker*, and touring hit musicals are often sold out in advance; tickets are usually available within a day of performance for other shows.

Theater

San Francisco's "theater row" is a single block of Geary Street west of Union Square, but a number of commercial theaters are located within walking distance, along with resident companies that enrich the city's theatrical scene. The three major commercial theaters are operated by the Shorenstein-Nederlander organization, which books touring plays and musicals, some of them before they open on Broadway. The most venerable is the **Curran** (445 Geary St., tel. 415/673–4400), which is used for plays and smaller musicals. The **Golden Gate** is a stylishly refurbished movie theater (Golden Gate Ave. at Taylor St., tel. 415/474–3800), primarily a musical house. The 2,500-seat **Orpheum** (1192 Market St. near the Civic Center, tel. 415/474–3800) is used for the biggest touring shows.

The smaller commercial theaters, offering touring shows and a few that are locally produced, are the **Marines Memorial Theatre** (Sutter and Mason Sts., tel. 415/441–7444) and **Theatre on the Square** (450 Post St., tel. 415/433–9500). For commercial and popular success, nothing beats *Beach Blanket Babylon*, the zany revue that has been running for years at **Club Fugazi** (678 Green St. in North Beach, tel. 415/421–4222). Conceived by imaginative San Francisco director Steve Silver, it is a lively, colorful musical mix of cabaret, show-biz parodies, and tributes to local landmarks. (*See* Cabarets in Nightlife, below.)

The city's major theater company is the **American Conservatory Theatre (ACT)**, which quickly became one of the nation's leading regional theaters when it was founded during the mid-1960s. It presents a season of approximately eight plays in rotating repertory from October through late spring. The ACT's ticket office is at the **Geary Theatre** (415 Geary St., tel. 415/749–2228), though the theater itself was closed following the 1989 earthquake. The rebuilt Geary is expected to reopen in 1993, and in the meantime, the ACT is performing at the nearby **Stage Door Theater** (420 Mason St.) and other theaters around the city.

At the next level are several established theaters in smaller houses and with lower ticket prices that specialize in contemporary plays. The most reliable are the **Eureka Theatre** (2730 16th St. in the Mission District, tel. 415/558–9898) and the **Magic Theatre** (Bldg. D, Fort Mason Center, Laguna St. at Marina Blvd., tel. 415/441–8822).

The city boasts a wide variety of specialized and ethnic theaters that work with dedicated local actors and some professionals. Among the most interesting are **The Lamplighters**, the delightful Gilbert and Sullivan troupe that often gets better reviews than touring productions of musicals, performing at Presentation Theater (2350 Turk St., tel. 415/752–7755); the **Lorraine Hansberry Theatre**, which specializes in plays by African-American writers (620 Sutter St., tel. 415/474–8800); the **Asian American Theatre** (405 Arguello Blvd., tel. 415/346–8922); and the gay and lesbian **Theatre Rhinoceros** (2926 16th St., tel. 415/861–5079). The **San Francisco Shakespeare Festival** offers free performances on summer weekends in Golden Gate Park (tel. 415/221–0642).

Avant-garde theater, dance, opera, and "performance art" turn up in a variety of locations, not all of them theaters. The major presenting organizations are **Life on the Water** (Bldg. B, Fort Mason Center, Laguna St. at Marina Blvd., tel. 415/776–8999) and **Theater Artaud** (499 Alabama St. in the Mission District, tel. 415/621–7797) in a huge, converted machine shop. One more trendy performance center is the **Climate** theater (252 9th St., tel. 415/626–9196), in the neighborhood of the newest cafés, clubs, and galleries.

Berkeley Repertory Theatre across the bay is the American Conservatory Theatre's major rival for leadership among the region's resident professional companies. It performs a more adventurous mix of classics and new plays in a more modern, intimate theater at 2025 Addison Street near BART's downtown Berkeley station (tel. 415/845–4700). It's a fully professional theater, with a fall–spring season and special events during the summer. Tickets are available at the STBS booth in San Francisco's Union Square. The Bay Area's most professional outdoor summer theater is **California Shakespeare Festival**, formerly based in Berkeley, which in 1991 moved to a new amphitheater east of Oakland, on Gateway Boulevard just off state Highway 24 (tel. 510/548–3422).

Music

The completion of Davies Symphony Hall at Van Ness Avenue and Grove Street finally gave the San Francisco Symphony a home of its own. It solidified the base of the city's three major performing arts organizations—symphony, opera, and ballet—in the Civic Center. The symphony and other musical groups also perform in the smaller, 928-seat Herbst Theatre in the Opera's "twin" at Van Ness Avenue and McAllister Street, the War Memorial Building. Otherwise the city's musical ensembles can be found all over the map: in churches and museums, in restaurants and outdoors in parks, and in outreach series in Berkeley and on the peninsula.

San Francisco Symphony (Davies Symphony Hall, Van Ness Ave. at Grove St., tel. 415/431-5400. Tickets at the box office or through BASS, tel. 415/762-2277). The city's most stable performing arts organization plays from September to May, with music director Herbert Blomstedt conducting for about two-thirds of the season. Guest conductors often include Michael Tilson Thomas, Edo de Waart, and Riccardo Mutti. Guest soloists include artists of the caliber of Andre Watts, Leontyne Price, and Jean-Pierre Rampal. The symphony has stayed with the standard repertoire in recent years as Blomstedt concentrates on the ensemble's stability and focus. Special events include a Mostly Mozart festival during the spring, a Beethoven festival during the summer, a New and Unusual Music series during the spring in the more intimate Herbst Theatre, and summer Pops Concerts in the nearby Civic Auditorium. Throughout the season, the symphony presents a Great Performers Series of guest soloists and orchestras.

Philharmonia Baroque (Herbst Theatre, Van Ness Ave. at McAllister St., tel. 415/552-3656. Tickets also at STBS booth in Union Square). This stylish ensemble has been called the local baroque orchestra with the national reputation. Its season of concerts, fall–spring, celebrates composers of the 17th and 18th centuries, including Handel, Vivaldi, and Mozart.

Chamber Symphony of San Francisco (various locations, tel. 415/441-4636). Under musical director Jean-Louis Le Roux, this group has become known for the variety of its programming, which can include composers from Handel to Villa-Lobos.

Kronos Quartet (Herbst Theatre and other locations, tel. 415/731-3533). Twentieth-century works and a number of premieres make up the programs for this group that goes as far as possible to prove that string quartets are not stodgy.

Midsummer Mozart (Herbst Theatre and occasionally at Davies Symphony Hall, tel. 415/781-5931). This is one of the few Mozart festivals that haven't filled programs with works by other composers. It performs in July and August under George Cleve, conductor of the San Jose Symphony.

Old First Concerts (Old First Church, Van Ness Ave. at Sacramento St., tel. 415/474-1608. Tickets also at STBS booth, Union Square). This is a well-respected Friday evening and Sunday afternoon series of chamber music, vocal soloists, new music, and jazz.

Pops Concerts (Polk and Grove Sts., tel. 415/431-5400). Many members of the symphony perform in the July pops series in the 7,000-seat Civic Auditorium. The schedule includes light classics, Broadway, country, and movie music. Tickets cost as little as a few dollars.

Stern Grove (Sloat Blvd. at 19th Ave., tel. 415/398-6551). This is the nation's oldest continual free summer music festival, offering 10 Sunday afternoons of symphony, opera, jazz, pop music, and dance. The amphitheater is in a eucalyptus grove below street level; remember that summer in this area near the ocean can be cool.

There are also free organ concerts on Saturday and Sunday at 4 PM in the **Palace of the Legion of Honor** (34th Ave. at Clement St. in Lincoln Park, tel. 415/750–3600) and free band concerts on Sunday and holiday afternoons in the **Golden Gate Park bandshell** (tel. 415/558–3706) opposite the de Young Museum.

Opera

San Francisco Opera (Van Ness Ave. at Grove St., tel. 415/864–3330). Founded in 1923, and the resident company at the War Memorial Opera House in the Civic Center since it was built in 1932, the Opera has expanded to a fall season of 13 weeks. Approximately 70 performances of 10 operas are given, beginning on the first Friday after Labor Day. For many years the Opera was considered a major international company and the most artistically successful operatic organization in the United States. International competition and management changes have made recent seasons uneven; the company has revitalized under general director Lofti Mansouri, formerly head of Toronto's Canadian Opera Company. International opera stars frequently sing major roles here, but the Opera is also well known for presenting the American debuts of singers who have made their name in Europe. In the same way, the company's standard repertoire is interspersed with revivals of rarely heard works.

The Opera was one of the first to present "supertitles," projecting English translations above the stage during performances. The system is used for almost all operas not sung in English. In addition to the fall season, the Opera performs Wagner's *Ring* cycle every five summers—next in 1995. Ticket prices range from about $28 to a high of about $90, and many performances are sold out far in advance. Standing-room tickets are always sold, however, and patrons often sell extra tickets on the Opera House steps just before curtain time.

Pocket Opera (tel. 415/346–2780). This lively, modestly priced alternative to "grand" opera gives concert performances, mostly in English, of rarely heard works. Offenbach's operettas are frequently on the bill during the winter-spring season. Concerts are held at various locations.

Another operatic alternative is the **Lamplighters** (*see* Theater, above), which specializes in Gilbert and Sullivan but presents other light operas as well.

Dance

San Francisco Ballet (War Memorial Opera House, Van Ness Ave. at Grove St., tel. 415/621–3838). The ballet has regained much of its luster under artistic director Helgi Tomasson, and both classical and contemporary works have won admiring reviews. The company's primary season runs February–May; its repertoire includes such full-length ballets as *Swan Lake* and a new production of *Sleeping Beauty*. The company is also intent on reaching new audiences with bold new dances, what it likes to call "cutting-edge works that will make you take a second look." Like many dance companies in the nation, the ballet presents *The Nutcracker* in December, and its recent production is one of the most spectacular.

Oakland Ballet (Paramount Theatre, 2025 Broadway, Oakland, near BART's 19th St. station, tel. 510/452–9288). Founded in 1965, this company is not simply an imitation of the larger San

Francisco Ballet across the bay. It has earned an outstanding reputation for reviving and preserving ballet masterworks from the early 20th century and presenting innovative contemporary choreography. It has recreated historic dances by such choreographers as Diaghilev, Bronislava Nininska, and Mikhail Fokine. The company also presents its own *Nutcracker* in December; its season begins in September.

Margaret Jenkins Dance Company (Theater Artaud, 450 Florida St., tel. 415/863–1173). This is one of the most reliable of the city's modern experimental dance troupes, in which the dancers themselves help shape the choreography.

Ethnic Dance Festival (Palace of Fine Arts Theatre, Bay and Lyon Sts., tel. 415/474–3914). Approximately 30 of the Bay Area's estimated 200 ethnic dance companies and soloists perform on several programs in June. Prices are modest for the city-sponsored event.

San Francisco and the Bay Area support innumerable experimental and ethnic dance groups. Among them are **ODC/San Francisco** (tel. 415/863–6606), performing at Herbst Theatre (Van Ness Ave.); the **Joe Goode Performance Group** (tel. 415/648–4848); **Kulintang Arts,** (tel. 415/553–8824), a Philippine troupe; and **Rosa Montoya Bailes Flamenco** (tel. 415/931–7374), which often performs at Herbst Theatre.

Film

The San Francisco Bay Area, including Berkeley and San Jose, is considered to be one of the nation's most important movie markets. If there is a film floating around the country or around the world in search of an audience, it is likely that it will eventually turn up on a screen in San Francisco. The Bay Area is also a filmmaking center: Documentaries and experimental works are being produced on modest budgets, feature films and television programs are shot on location, and some of Hollywood's biggest directors prefer to live here, particularly in Marin County. In San Francisco, about a third of the theaters regularly show foreign and independent films. The city is also one of the last strongholds of "repertory cinema," showing older American and foreign films on bills that change daily.

San Francisco's traditional movie theater center, downtown on Market Street, is pretty much given over to sex and action movies nowadays. First-run commercial movie theaters are now scattered throughout the city, although they are concentrated along Van Ness Avenue, near Japantown, and in the Marina District. All are accessible on major Muni bus routes, as are the art-revival houses. Several of the most respected and popular independent theaters have been taken over by chains recently, and their policy could change. The San Francisco International Film Festival (tel. 415/931–3456), the oldest in the country, continues to provide an extensive selection of foreign films each spring. The Pacific Film Archive in Berkeley is an incomparable source for rare American and foreign films.

Foreign and Independent Films The most reliable theaters for foreign and independent films are **Opera Plaza Cinemas** (Van Ness Ave. at Golden Gate Ave., tel. 415/771–0102); **Lumiere** (California St. near Polk St., tel. 415/885–3200); **Clay** (Fillmore and Clay Sts., tel. 415/346–1123); **Gateway** (215 Jackson St. at Battery St., tel. 415/421–3353); **Castro** (Castro St. near Market St., tel. 415/621–6120), the last remaining movie palace from the 1920s that is still showing movies, with an extensive schedule of revivals; and **Bridge** (3013 Geary Blvd. near Masonic Ave., tel. 415/751–3212).

Festival **The San Francisco International Film Festival** (tel. 415/931–3456) takes over several theaters for two weeks in late March at the AMC Kabuki complex at Post and Fillmore streets. The festival schedules about 75 films from abroad, many of them American premieres, along with a variety of independent American documentaries. During recent years there has been an emphasis on films from the Soviet Union and Asia.

Other showcases for films out of the commercial mainstream include **The Roxie** (3116 16th St., tel. 415/863–1087), which specializes in social and political documentaries; the **Cinematheque** at the San Francisco Art Institute (800 Chestnut St., tel. 415/558–8129), which often features films by avant-garde artists; and **New Langton Arts** (1246 Folsom St., tel. 415/626–5416), which offers experimental videos.

The most extensive screening schedule for both American and foreign, old and new films is the **Pacific Film Archive** (2625 Durant Ave., Berkeley, tel. 510/642–1124). It often shows films from New York's Museum of Modern Art collection.

Nightlife

by Dan Spitzer

A Bay Area resident, Dan Spitzer has written travel books about South America and the Far East.

San Francisco provides a tremendous potpourri of evening entertainment ranging from ultrasophisticated cabarets to bawdy bistros that reflect the city's gold rush past. With the exception of the hotel lounges and discos noted below, the accent is on casual dress—call ahead if you are uncertain.

For information on who is performing where, check the following sources: The Sunday San Francisco *Examiner and Chronicle*'s pink "Datebook" insert lists major events and cultural happenings. The free alternative weekly, the *Bay Guardian*, is a terrific source for current music clubs and comedy. Another handy reference for San Francisco nightlife is *Key* magazine, offered free in most major hotel lobbies. For a phone update on sports and musical events, call the Convention and Visitor Bureau's *Cultural Events Calendar* (tel. 415/391–2001). Those seeking weekly jazz headliners should dial the *KJAZ Jazz Line* (tel. 415/769–4818).

Although San Francisco is a compact city with the prevailing influences of some neighborhoods spilling into others, the following generalizations should help you find the kind of entertainment you're looking for. **Nob Hill** is noted for its plush piano bars and panoramic skyline lounges. **North Beach,** infamous for its topless and bottomless bistros, also maintains a sense of its beatnik past and this legacy lives on in atmospheric bars and coffeehouses. **Fisherman's Wharf,** while touristy, is great for people-watching and provides plenty of impromptu entertainment from street performers. **Union Street** is home away from home for singles in search of company. **South of Market** (SoMa, for short) has become a hub of nightlife, with a bevy of highly popular nightclubs, bars, and lounges in renovated warehouses and auto shops. Gay men will find the **Castro** and **Polk Street** scenes of infinite variety, while lesbian bars abound on and around **Valencia Street.**

Rock, Pop, Folk, and Blues

DNA Lounge. Mainly rock is featured, but country and jazz groups occasionally play here, too. Representative of DNA's bands are Beatnik Beach and the Sea Hags. *375 11th St. near Harrison St., tel. 415/626–1409. Live bands most nights at 10 PM. Other nights the club is open for dancing to recorded music. Cover: weeknights $3, Fri.–Sat. $7. No credit cards.*

Fillmore Auditorium. Bastion of the great bands of the '60s, the Fillmore is being refurbished and will feature some of the hottest names on the contemporary rock scene as well as survivors of an earlier era. Headliners include Little Feat and Jimmy Cliff. *1805 Geary St., tel. 415/922–FILL. Call for show times and prices. No credit cards.*

Freight and Salvage Coffee House. This is one of the finest folk houses in the country; it's worth a trip across the bay. Some of the most talented practitioners of folk, blues, Cajun, and bluegrass perform at the Freight, among them U. Utah Phillips and Rosalie Sorrels. *1111 Addison St., Berkeley, tel. 415/548–1761. Shows: weeknights 8 PM, Fri. and Sat. 8:30. Cover: $1 Tues. for open mike, $6–$10 other nights. No credit cards.*

Great American Music Hall. This is one of the great eclectic nightclubs, not only in San Francisco but in the entire country. Here you will find truly top-drawer entertainment, running the gamut from the best in blues, folk, and jazz to rock with a sprinkling of outstanding comedians. This colorful marble-pillared emporium will also accommodate dancing to popular bands. Past headliners here include Carmen McCrae, B.B. King, Tom Paxton, and Doc Watson. *859 O'Farrell St. between Polk and Larkin Sts., tel. 415/885–0750. Shows usually at 8 PM, but this may vary, so call. Cover: $10–$20. No credit cards.*

I-Beam. One of the most popular of San Francisco's rock dance clubs, the I-Beam features new-wave bands and high-energy rock 'n' roll in a spacious setting. Spectacular lights and lasers enhance your dancing pleasure here. *1748 Haight St., tel. 415/668–6006. Open nightly 9 PM. Cover: $5–$10; occasionally free. No credit cards.*

Last Day Saloon. In an attractive setting of wooden tables and potted plants, this club offers some major entertainers and a varied schedule of blues, Cajun, rock, and jazz. Some of the illustrious performers who have appeared here are Taj Mahal, the Zazu Pitts Memorial Orchestra, Maria Muldaur, and Pride and Joy. *406 Clement St. between 5th and 6th Aves. in the Richmond District, tel. 415/387–6343. Shows 9 PM nightly. Cover: $4–$6; some weeknights free. No credit cards.*

Lou's Pier 47. This Wharf restaurant features cool music and hot food on the waterfront. *300 Jefferson St., Fisherman's Wharf, tel. 414/771–0377. Afternoon and evening shows, usually 4 PM and 9 PM. Cover: $6 in evening. AE, MC, V.*

Paradise Lounge. This quirky lounge has three stages for eclectic live music and dancing, plus an upstairs cabaret featuring offbeat performers. *1501 Folsom St. tel. 415/861–6906. Live music 10 PM nightly. Cover: $3 Thurs. and Fri., $5 Sat. and Sun. No credit cards.*

Paul's Saloon. At Paul's, bluegrass is the specialty of the house. *3251 Scott St. in the Marina, tel. 415/922–2456. Shows 8 PM Sun.–Thurs. and 9 PM Fri.–Sat. No cover. No credit cards.*

Plush Room. This cabaret club affords elegant environs for patrons. Such big-name entertainers as Billie Barnes and Jim Bailey play here. *In the Hotel York, 940 Sutter St., tel. 415/885–*

6800. Shows Fri.–Sat. 8:30 and 10:30 PM. Cover: $15–$20, 2-drink minimum. AE, MC, V.

Slim's. One of the most popular newcomers to the SoMa scene, Slim's specializes in what it labels "American roots music"— blues, jazz, classic rock, and the like. Co-owner Boz Scaggs helps bring in the crowds. *333 11th St., tel. 415/621–3330. Shows nightly 9 PM. Cover $10–$15. AE, MC, V.*

The Saloon. Some locals consider the historic Saloon the best spot in San Francisco for the blues. Headliners here include Roy Rogers. *1232 Grant St. near Columbus Ave. in North Beach, tel. 415/989–7666. Shows 9:30 PM nightly. Cover: $5–$8. No credit cards.*

The Stone. This club features primarily rock groups, with occasional jazz and blues performers. *412 Broadway in North Beach, tel. 415/547–1954. Shows Wed.–Sun., 8 PM. Cover: $6–$10, 2-drink minimum. No credit cards.*

The Warfield. This old Art Deco theater was completely renovated in 1988 to become a showcase for mainstream rock and roll. There are tables and chairs downstairs, and theater seating upstairs. Such contemporary acts as Robert Palmer, Simply Red, and K.D. Lang have played here recently. *982 Market St. tel. 415/775–7722. Shows most nights at 8 PM. Tickets $15–$20. V.*

Jazz

Kimball's. Such jazz greats as Freddie Hubbard play at this club, which is also a restaurant. *300 Grove St. at Franklin St. in the Civic Center, tel. 415/861–5555. Shows 9 PM and 11 PM Wed.–Sat. Cover: $12–$15. The additional $5 minimum for food and drink is generally not enforced. AE, MC, V.*

Pasand Lounge. Features jazz and rhythm and blues. *1875 Union St., Pacific Heights, tel. 415/922–4498. Shows nightly, 7 PM–1 AM. No cover. 2-drink minimum. AE, MC, V.*

Pier 23. Pier 23 offers the best in bebop, ranging from the Brian Melvin Trio to Kitty Margolis. *At Embarcadero and Pier 23, across from the Fog City Diner, tel. 415/362–5125. Shows Tues.–Sat. 10 PM, Sun. 4–8 PM. No cover. 2-drink minimum. MC, V.*

Yoshi's. Although located in Oakland, Yoshi's is well worth the trip over to the East Bay because it features some of the biggest names in jazz. The likes of Carmen McCrae, Dizzy Gillespie, and Cecil Taylor have played in this pleasant club with excellent acoustics. There is a Japanese restaurant adjacent. *6030 Claremont St. in north Oakland, just over the Berkeley line, tel. 415/652–9200. Shows Tues.–Thurs. and Sun. 8 PM, Fri.–Sat. 9 and 11 PM. Cover: $5–$18. AE, MC, V.*

Cabarets

Club Fugazi. *Beach Blanket Babylon Goes around the World* is a wacky musical revue that has become the longest running show of its genre in the history of the theater. It has run now for well over a decade, outstripping the Ziegfeld Follies by years. While the choreography is colorful and the songs witty, the real stars of the show are the exotic costumes—worth the price of admission in themselves. Order tickets as far in advance as possible; the revue has been sold out up to a month in advance. *678 Green St., 94133, tel. 415/421–4222. Shows 8 PM Wed.–Thurs., 8 and 10:30 PM Fri.–Sat., 3 and 7:30 PM Sun. Cover: $15–$30,* *depending upon date and seating location. Note: those under 21 are admitted only to the Sun. matinee performance. MC, V.*

Finocchio's. Are you ready for the truly outrageous? You will redefine "queen" once you see Finocchio's female impersonators—among the finest on the planet. Finocchio's has been generating general confusion for 50 years. *506 Broadway, North Beach, tel. 415/982–9388. Note: those under 21 not admitted. Shows nightly at 8:30, 10, and 11:30, closed Mon. and Wed. Cover: $15. MC, V.*

Josie's Cabaret and Juice Joint. This small stylish café and cabaret in the predominantly gay Castro District books performers who reflect the countercultural feel of the neighborhood. *3583 16th St., at Market St., tel. 415/861–7933. Shows nightly, times vary. Cover: $6–$10. No credit cards.*

Comedy Clubs

Cobb's Comedy Club. Bobby Slayton, Paula Poundstone, and Dr. Gonzo are among the super stand-up comics who perform here. *In the Cannery, 2801 Leavenworth St. at the corner of Beach St., tel. 415/928–4320. Shows Mon. 8 PM, Tues.–Thurs. 9 PM, Fri.–Sat. 9 and 11 PM. Cover: $7 weeknights, $9 Fri. and Sat. 2-drink minimum Fri. and Sat. MC, V.*

Holy City Zoo. Robin Williams ascended like a meteor from an improv group that gained fame here, and terrific stand-up comics, such as local favorite Michael Prichard, headline now. The "Zoo" features comedy nightly, with an open mike for pros and would-be comedians every Tuesday. *408 Clement St. in the Richmond District, tel. 415/386–4242. Shows Sun.–Thurs. 9 PM, Fri.–Sat. 9 and 11 PM. Cover: $3 Sun.–Thurs., $8 Fri. and Sat., 2-drink minimum. MC, V.*

The Punch Line. A launching pad for the likes of Jay Leno and Whoopie Goldberg, the Punch Line features some of the top talents around—several of whom are certain to make a national impact. Note that weekend shows often sell out, and it is best to buy tickets in advance at BASS outlets (tel. 415/762–BASS). *444-A Battery St. between Clay and Washington Sts., tel. 415/ 397–PLSF. Shows Sun.–Thurs. 9 PM, Fri. 9 and 11 PM, Sat. 7, 9, and 11 PM. Cover: $7 Tues.–Thurs.; $10 Fri. and Sat.; special $5 showcases Mon. and Sun. 2-drink minimum. MC, V.*

Dancing Emporiums

Cesar's Palace. Salsa-style Latin music attracts all kinds of dancers to this popular club in the city's Hispanic Mission District. *3140 Mission St., tel. 415/648–6611. Open Thurs. 8 PM–2 AM; Fri.–Sun. 9 PM–5 AM. Cover: $7.*

Club DV8. One of the largest of the trendy SoMa clubs, DV8 attracts scores of stylish young people to its 25,000 square feet (two levels) of dance floors. *540 Howard St., tel. 415/957–1730. Open Wed.–Sat. 9 PM–3 AM. Cover: $5–$10.*

Club O. This dance spot gets its name from the swimming pool adjacent. It was the original SoMa crossover bar. The cover charge varies. Note: You must be 21 to enter. *278 11th St., South of Market, tel. 415/621–8119. Opens 9:30 PM.*

Firehouse 7. This popular Mission District club plays reggae, rock and roll, modern dance music, house music, and soul. Live music and open mike on Sundays. *3160 16th St., tel. 415/621– 1617. Opens at 9. Cover: $3 Mon.–Thurs.; $5 Fri. and Sat.; $1 Sun.*

Oz. The most popular upscale disco in San Francisco, the land of Oz is reached via a glass elevator. Then, surrounded by a splendid panorama of the city, you dance on marble floors and recharge on cushy sofas and bamboo chairs. The fine sound system belts out oldies, disco, Motown, and new wave. *335 Powell St. between Geary and Post Sts. on the top floor of the Westin St. Francis Hotel, tel. 415/397–7000. Open nightly 9 PM–2 AM. Cover: $8 Sun.–Thurs.; $15 Fri.–Sat.*

The Kennel Club. Alternative rock and funk rule in this small, steamy room: Everyone's dancing! On Thursdays and Saturdays this space is known as The Box, and a very gay mixed-gender, mixed-race crowd takes over. *628 Divisadero, tel. 415/931–1914. Open nightly 9 PM–2 AM. Cover: $2–$10.*

Townsend. This big industrial space has an edgy but fashionable feel, complemented by a house mix of rock and modern dance music. *177 Townsend, near the train depot, tel. 415/974–6020. Open Thurs. 10 PM–3 AM, Fri.–Sat. 10 PM–4AM. Cover: around $10.*

Piano Bars

Act IV Lounge. A popular spot for a romantic rendezvous, the focal point of this elegant lounge is a crackling fireplace. *At the Inn of the Opera, 333 Fulton St. near Franklin St., tel. 415/863–8400. Pianist nightly 6–9. No cover.*

Club 36. Relax to piano music or jazz combos while enjoying the view from the top floor of the newly renovated Grand Hyatt at Union Square. *345 Stockton St., tel. 415/398–1234. Piano or jazz nightly 9 PM–1 AM. No cover.*

Redwood Room. You will find an easy-listening atmosphere here in this sumptuous Art Deco setting. *In the Clift Hotel, Taylor and Geary Sts., tel. 415/775–4700. No cover. Dress: formal.*

Skyline Bars

Carnelian Room. At 781 feet above the ground, enjoy dinner or cocktails here on the 52nd floor, where you may drink from the loftiest view of San Francisco's magnificent skyline. Reservations are a must for dinner here. *Top of the Bank of America Building, 555 California St., tel. 415/433–7500. Open Mon.–Fri. 3–11:30 PM; Sat. 4–11:30 PM; Sun. 10 AM–10:30 PM.*

Cityscape. At the top of the Hilton's tower, a live band plays rock, pop, and jazz for dancing beneath the stars. *In the Hilton Hotel, Mason and O'Farrell Sts., tel. 415/771–1400. Open nightly 5 PM–1 AM. No cover.*

Crown Room. Just ascending to the well-named Crown Room is a drama in itself as you take the Fairmont's glass-enclosed Skylift elevator to the top. Some San Franciscans maintain that this lounge is the most luxurious of the city's skyline bars. Lunches, dinners, and Sunday brunches are served as well as drinks. *29th floor of the Fairmont Hotel, California and Mason Sts., tel. 415/772–5131. Open daily 11 AM–1 AM.*

Equinox. What's distinctive about the Hyatt's skyline-view bar is its capacity to revolve. The Hyatt is also home to the **Other Phineas T. Barnacle.** This bar offers a unique panorama with views not of rooftops but of seal rocks and the horizon of the great Pacific Ocean. *In the Cliff House, 1090 Point Lobos Ave., tel. 415/386–7630. Open Mon.–Sat. 11 AM–2 AM, Sun. 10AM–2 AM.*

Starlite Roof. In this 21st-story glassed-in lounge, you may dance to a band playing primarily '50s and '60s hits. *In the Sir Francis Drake Hotel, Powell and Sutter Sts., tel. 415/392-7755. Open daily 4:30 PM–1:30 AM. No cover.*

Top of the Mark. This fabled landmark affords fabulous views in an elegant 19th-floor setting. *In the Mark Hopkins Hotel, California and Mason Sts., tel. 415/392-3434. Open nightly 4 PM–1:30 AM. Dress: formal.*

Trellis Lounge. There is no cover charge here for music ranging from classical to jazz. *Both are open 11 AM–1:30 AM; both are in the Hyatt Regency, Embarcadero Center No. 5, tel. 415/788-1234.*

Singles Bars

Balboa Cafe. A jam-packed hang-out for the young, upwardly mobile crowd, this bar/restaurant is famous for its burgers and single clientele. *2199 Fillmore St., tel. 415/921-3944. Open nightly until 2 AM.*

Blue Light Cafe. Pop star Boz Skagg's establishment, this super-trendy bar has savory appetizers and delicious daiquiris. The Blue Light is a celebrity hangout where many of the famous come to unwind. *1979 Union St., tel. 415/922-5510. Open weekdays 4 PM–midnight, weekends 4 PM–2 AM.*

Hard Rock Cafe. Part of the famous chain of youth-oriented bars, this crowded saloon is filled with a collection of rock 'n' roll memorabilia that won't disappoint Hard Rock fans. *1699 Van Ness Ave., tel. 415/885-1699. Open Sun.–Thurs. until 12:30 AM, Fri.–Sat. until 1 AM.*

Harrington's. This Irish drinking saloon is *the* place to be on St. Patrick's Day. *245 Front St., tel. 415/392-7595. Open Mon. and Tues. 9 AM–10 PM; Wed. and Thurs. 9 AM–11 PM; Fri. 9 AM–midnight; Sat. 11 AM–7 PM. Closed Sun.*

The Holding Company. This is one of the most popular weeknight Financial District watering holes, where scores of office workers enjoy friendly libations. *In 2 Embarcadero Center, tel. 415/986-0797. Open Mon.–Tues. until midnight, Wed.–Fri. until 2 AM. Closed Sat.–Sun.*

Perry's. Usually jam-packed, Perry's is the most famous of San Francisco's singles bars. You can dine here on great hamburgers as well as more substantial fare. *1944 Union St. at Buchanan St., tel. 415/922-9022. Open daily 9 AM–2 AM.*

San Francisco's Favorite Bars

Buena Vista. Even though the Buena Vista's claim of having introduced Irish Coffee to the New World may be dubious, this is the Wharf area's most popular bar. Usually packed with tourists, it has a fine view of the waterfront. *2765 Hyde St. near Fisherman's Wharf, tel. 415/474-5044.*

Edinburgh Castle. This is a delightful Scottish drinking emporium, with a jukebox that breathes Scottish airs and live bagpipes on weekends. The decor is Scottish, the bartender is Scottish, and there are plenty of Scottish brews from which to choose. The fare is of the fish-and-chips variety, which you can work off at the dart board. *950 Geary St. near Polk St., tel. 415/885-4074.*

House of Shields. For a taste of an authentic old-time San Francisco saloon, try this SoMa bar. *39 New Montgomery St., tel. 415/392-7732.*

John's Grill. Located on the fringe of the Tenderloin, this bar was featured in *The Maltese Falcon* and mystery fans will revel in its Hammett memorabilia. *63 Ellis St., tel. 415/986–0069.*

Peer Inn. If you want to get away from the tourist scene while at the waterfront, this is a good place in which to imbibe. Peer Inn has an adjacent restaurant. *Pier 33 at the Embarcadero at the end of Bay St., tel. 415/788–1411.*

Spec's. It's worth looking for this somewhat hard-to-find hangout for artists, poets, and seamen. Spec's is a wonderful watering hole hideaway, reflecting a sense of the North Beach of days gone by. *12 Adler Place near the intersection of Broadway and Columbus Ave., tel. 415/421–4112.*

Vesuvio Cafe. Near the legendary City Lights Bookstore, this quintessentially North Beach bar is little altered from its heyday as a haven for the Beat poets. *255 Columbus Ave. between Broadway and Pacific Ave., tel. 415/362–3370.*

Gay Bars

Amelia's. One of San Francisco's busiest lesbian bars, dancing and a show are offered here. *647 Valencia St., tel. 415/552–7788.*

Kimo's. This relaxed establishment affords an elegant ambience. *1351 Polk St., tel. 415/885–4535.*

The Midnight Sun. This is one of the Castro's longest-standing and most popular bars, with giant video screens riotously programmed. *4067 18th St., tel. 415/861–4186.*

The Stud. This is a popular, jam-packed SoMa bar. *399 9th St., tel. 415/863–6623.*

Twin Peaks. A pleasant mirrored fern bar, Twin Peaks is a tranquil place in which to drink and converse. *401 Castro St., tel. 415/864–9470.*

9 Excursions from San Francisco

Sausalito

by Robert Taylor

The San Francisco Convention and Visitors Bureau describes Sausalito's location as "the Mediterranean side of the Golden Gate." With its relatively sheltered site on the bay in Marin County, just 8 miles from San Francisco, it appeals to Bay Area residents and visitors for the same reason: It is so near and yet so far. As a hillside town with superb views, an expansive yacht harbor, the aura of an artist's colony, and ferry service, Sausalito might be a resort within commuting distance of the city. It is certainly the primary excursion for visitors to San Francisco, especially those with limited time to explore the Bay Area. Mild weather encourages strolling and outdoor dining, although afternoon winds and fog can roll over the hills from the ocean, funneling through the central part of town once known as Hurricane Gulch.

There are substantial homes, including Victorian mansions, in Sausalito's heights, but the town has long had a more colorful and raffish reputation. Discovered in 1775 by Spanish explorers and named Saucelito (Little Willow) for the trees growing around its springs, Sausalito was a port for whaling ships during the 19th century. In 1875, the railroad from the north connected with ferryboats to San Francisco and the town became an attraction for the fun-loving. Even the chamber of commerce recalls the time when Sausalito sported 25 saloons, gambling dens, and bordellos. Bootleggers flourished during Prohibition in the 1920s, and shipyard workers swelled the town's population during the 1940s, when tour guides divided the residents into "wharf rats" and "hill snobs." Ensuing decades brought a bohemian element with the development of an artists' colony and a houseboat community. Sausalito has also become a major yachting center, and restaurants attract visitors for the fresh seafood as well as the spectacular views. Sausalito remains a friendly and casual small town, although summer traffic jams can fray nerves. If possible, visit Sausalito on a weekday—and take the ferry.

Arriving and Departing

By Car Cross the Golden Gate Bridge and go north on Highway 101 to the Sausalito exit, then go south on Bridgeway to municipal parking near the center of town. The trip takes ½ hour to 45 minutes one-way. (You will need change for the parking lots' meters.)

By Bus **Golden Gate Transit** (tel. 415/332–6600) travels to Sausalito from 1st and Mission streets and other points in the city.

By Ferry **Golden Gate Ferry** (tel. 415/332–6600) crosses the bay from the Ferry Building at Market Street and the Embarcadero; **Red and White Fleet** (tel. 415/546–2896) leaves from Pier 41 at Fisherman's Wharf. The trip takes 15–30 minutes.

Guided Tours

Most tour companies include Sausalito on excursions north to Muir Woods and the Napa Valley Wine Country. Among them are **Gray Line** (tel. 415/558–9400) and **Great Pacific Tour Co.** (tel. 415/626–4499).

The Bay Area

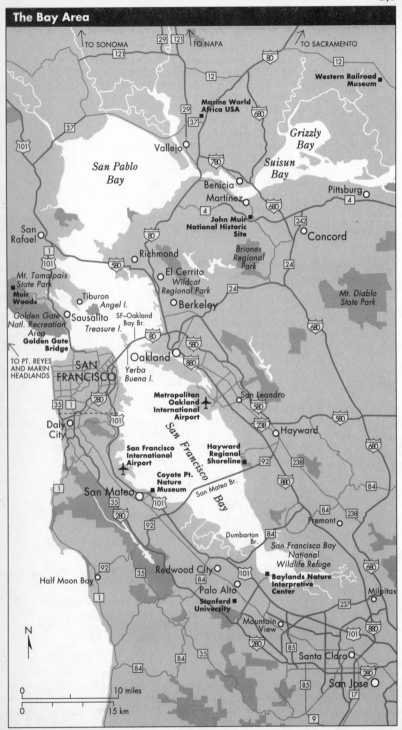

TO SONOMA

29 121 TO NAPA

TO SACRAMENTO

121

80

12

12

Western Railroad Museum

29

Marine World Africa USA

680

37

Grizzly Bay

101

Vallejo

780

Suisun Bay

San Pablo Bay

Benicia

Pittsburg

Martinez

680

4

San Rafael

4

John Muir National Historic Site

242

Concord

101

Richmond

80

Briones Regional Park

Mt. Tamalpais State Park

El Cerrito

24

Muir Woods

Tiburon

Angel I.

Wildcat Regional Park

Mt. Diablo State Park

Golden Gate Natl. Recreation Area

Sausalito

Berkeley

24

680

Treasure I.

SF-Oakland Bay Br.

Golden Gate Bridge

80

580

TO PT. REYES AND MARIN HEADLANDS

Oakland

880

SAN FRANCISCO

Yerba Buena I.

Metropolitan Oakland International Airport

San Leandro

580

35 1

280

Daly City

101

238

Hayward

580

San Francisco International Airport

Hayward Regional Shoreline

92

238

680

880

Coyote Pt. Nature Museum

San Mateo Br.

San Francisco Bay

84

1

San Mateo

35

280

92

101

Dumbarton Br.

84

Fremont

238

San Francisco Bay National Wildlife Refuge

680

Half Moon Bay

92

35

Redwood City

101

Milpitas

1

84

Baylands Nature Interpretive Center

237

Palo Alto

Stanford University

Mountain View

880

N

35

85

280

101

84

84

35

Santa Clara

280

10 miles

85

17

0

15 km

San Jose

9

Exploring

Numbers in the margin correspond with points of interest on the Sausalito map.

Bridgeway is Sausalito's main thoroughfare and prime destination, with the bay, yacht harbor, and waterfront restaurants on one side, and more restaurants, shops, hillside homes, and hotels on the other. It is only a few steps from the ferry terminal to the tiny landmark park in the center of town: the **Plaza Vina del Mar,** named for Sausalito's sister city in Chile. The park features a fountain and two 14-foot-tall statues of elephants created for the 1915 Panama-Pacific International Exposition in San Francisco.

Across the street to the south is the Spanish-style **Sausalito Hotel,** which has been refurbished and filled with Victorian antiques. Between the hotel and the **Sausalito Yacht Club** is another unusual historic landmark, a drinking fountain with the invitation Have a Drink on Sally. It's in remembrance of Sally Stanford, the former San Francisco madam who later ran Sausalito's Valhalla restaurant and became the town's mayor. Actually, the monument is also in remembrance of her dog. There is a sidewalk-level bowl that suggests Have a Drink on Leland.

South on Bridgeway, toward San Francisco, there is an esplanade along the water with picture-perfect views. Farther south are a number of restaurants on piers, including—near the end of Bridgeway at Richardson Street—what was the **Valhalla** and is the oldest restaurant in Sausalito. Built in 1893 as "Walhalla," it was one of the settings for the film *The Lady from Shanghai* in the 1940s, Sally Stanford's place in the 1950s, and most recently a Chart House restaurant.

North on Bridgeway from the ferry terminal are yacht harbors and, parallel to Bridgeway a block to the west, the quieter Caledonia Street, with its own share of cafés and shops. There is a pleasant, grassy park with a children's playground at Caledonia and Litho streets, with a food shop nearby for picnic provisions.

Here and there along the west side of Bridgeway are flights of steps that climb the hill to Sausalito's wooded, sometimes rustic and sometimes lavish residential neighborhoods. The stairway just across the street from Vina del Mar Park is named Excelsior, and it leads to the **Alta Mira,** a popular Spanish-style hotel and restaurant with a spectacular view. However, there are vistas of the bay from all these streets.

Where there isn't a hillside house or a restaurant or a yacht in Sausalito, there is a shop. Most are along Bridgeway and Princess Street, and they offer a wide assortment of casual and sophisticated clothing, posters and paintings, imported and handcrafted gifts, and the expected variety of T-shirts, ice cream, cookies, and pastries. The **Village Fair** (777 Bridgeway) is a four-story former warehouse that has been converted into a warren of clothing, craft, and gift boutiques. Crafts workers often demonstrate their talents in the shops, and a winding brick path—Little Lombard Street—connects various levels. The shopping complex is a haven during wet weather.

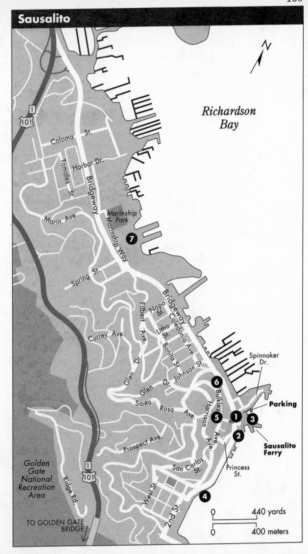

Sausalito's reputation as an art colony is enhanced by the **Art Festival** held during the three-day Labor Day weekend in September. It attracts more than 35,000 visitors to the waterfront area, and there are plans to expand the site and offer direct ferry service from San Francisco. Details are available from the Sausalito Chamber of Commerce (333 Caledonia St., 94965, tel. 415/332–0505).

7 North on Bridgeway, within a few minutes' drive, is the **Bay Model**, a re-creation in miniature of the entire San Francisco Bay and the San Joaquin–Sacramento River delta. It is actually nearly 400 feet square and is used by the U.S. Army Corps of Engineers to reproduce the rise and fall of tides, the flow of currents, and the other physical forces at work on the bay. It is housed in a former World War II shipyard building, and there is a display of shipbuilding history. At the same site is the Wapama, a World War I–era steam freighter being restored by volunteers. *2100 Bridgeway, tel. 415/332–3871. Open Tues.– Fri. 9–4, weekends 10–6. Closed Sun. in winter.*

Along the shore of Richardson Bay, between the Bay Model and U.S. 101, are some of the 400 houseboats that make up Sausalito's "floating homes community." In the shallow tidelands, most of them float only about half the time, but they are always a fanciful collection of the rustic, the eccentric, the flamboyant, and the elegant.

Dining

Restaurants and cafés line Bridgeway, Sausalito's main street, and specialize in seafood. A variety of sandwiches, salads, and snack foods are also available. The favored restaurants are directly on the bay or on Sausalito's hillside.

Restaurants are listed according to price category.

Category	Cost*
Very Expensive	$30 and up
Expensive	$20–$30
Moderate	$10–$20
Inexpensive	under $10

*per person, excluding drinks, service, and 6.5% sales tax

The following credit card abbreviations are used: AE, American Express; DC, Diners Club; MC, MasterCard; V, Visa.

Moderate– Expensive
Alta Mira. This is a smart restaurant, with a more formal atmosphere than the downtown cafés, in a Spanish-style hotel a block above Bridgeway. The Alta Mira serves three meals a day, and the specialties are fresh scallops and Pacific salmon, grilled meats, and large crab and shrimp salads. The terrace offers one of Sausalito's best views and is popular for lunch and Sunday brunch. *125 Bulkley Ave., tel. 415/332–1350. Reservations advised. AE, DC, MC, V.*

Casa Madrona. Another restaurant in a charming hotel, this is a Victorian surrounded by a landscaped walk and newer rooms stepping down the hill to Bridgeway. Casa Madrona serves American cuisine, with an appealing selection of breakfast and brunch dishes. *801 Bridgeway, tel. 415/331–5888. MC, V. No lunch Sat.*

Moderate
The Spinnaker. Seafood specialties and homemade pastas are offered in a quietly contemporary building in a spectacular setting on a point beyond the harbor, near the yacht club. You may see a pelican perched on one of the pilings just outside. *100 Spinnaker Dr., tel. 415/332–1500. AE, MC, V.*

Inexpensive– Moderate
Winship Restaurant. Here seafood, pasta, steaks, burgers, and salads are served in a casual nautical setting directly on the Bridgeway shopping strip. *670 Bridgeway, tel. 415/332–1454. AE, DC, MC, V. No dinner Mon., Tues.*

Tiburon

Located on a peninsula called Punta de Tiburon (Shark Point) by the Spanish explorers, this Marin County community has maintained its village atmosphere. The harbor faces Angel Island across Raccoon Strait, and San Francisco is directly south, 6 miles across the bay. The view from the decks of restaurants on the harbor may be the town's major attraction to visitors. No matter how crowded it gets on weekends, Tiburon remains more low-key than Sausalito. Tiburon has always been a waterfront settlement, beginning in 1884 when ferryboats from San Francisco connected here with a railroad to San Rafael. Especially during the summer and on weekends during pleasant weather year-round, the ferry is the most relaxing way to visit and avoid traffic and parking problems.

Arriving and Departing

By Car Take U.S. 101 north to the Tiburon Boulevard exit. The trip takes about 45 minutes to one hour one-way.

By Ferry **Red and White Fleet** (tel. 415/546–2896) ferries depart weekdays early mornings, late afternoon, and evenings from the Ferry Building. Ferries also depart Monday–Friday midday and Saturday and Sunday all day from Pier 41. The trip takes ½ hour.

Ferry service is available across the strait from Tiburon to Angel Island (tel. 415/435–2131).

By Bus **Golden Gate Transit** (tel. 415/332–6600) sends buses to Tiburon from First and Mission streets and other points in San Francisco and also from Sausalito.

Exploring

Tiburon's main street is indeed called **Main Street.** It's lined on the bay side with restaurants that overlook the harbor and offer views of San Francisco from outdoor decks. Sunday brunch is especially popular. On the other side of the narrow street are shops and galleries that sell casual clothing, gifts, jewelry, posters, and paintings. One gallery is devoted to a visual celebration of food. West along Main Street is **Ark Row.** During the 19th century these buildings were houseboats on the bay. Later they were beached and transformed into shops; now they are antiques and specialty stores along a tree-lined walk.

On a hill above town is **Old St. Hilary's Historic Preserve,** a Victorian-era church operated by the Landmarks Society as a historical and botanical museum. The surrounding area is a wildflower preserve. *Esperanza and Alemany Sts., tel. 415/435–1853. Open Wed., Sun. 1–4.*

Between Tiburon Boulevard and Richardson Bay, in a wildlife sanctuary on the route into town, is the 1876 **Lyman House** (tel. 415/388–2524), a Victorian fantasy that is now the western headquarters for the National Audubon Society. House tours are conducted.

Dining

Tiburon's restaurants offer seafood prepared simply or with Mexican, Italian, or Chinese touches. The informal dining and drinking cafés along Main Street also serve a wide variety of lunch and brunch fare.

The Red and White Fleet (tel. 415/546–2803) offers a weeknight dinner package that includes round-trip ferry rides from San Francisco and a meal at a selection of Tiburon restaurants.

Restaurants are listed according to price category.

Category	Cost*
Very Expensive	$30 and up
Expensive	$20–$30
Moderate	$10–$20
Inexpensive	under $10

*per person, excluding drinks, service, and 6.5% sales tax

The following credit card abbreviations have been used: AE, American Express; DC, Diners Club; MC, MasterCard; V, Visa.

Moderate– Expensive **Guaymas.** Mexican-style seafood is the specialty of this stylish restaurant. The adobe walls are whitewashed and decorated with colorful Mexican toys; there is a bay view and a terrace bar. Familiar Mexican dishes prepared with a contemporary eye for visual presentation and grilled California specialties are on the menu. *5 Main St., at the ferry terminal, tel. 415/435–6300. AE, DC, MC, V.*

Moderate **Mr. Q's.** Located on an upper level over the harbor, this casual and crowded restaurant is best known for the view from a deck that extends farther onto the bay than do its competitors. Jazz and rock groups play on weekends. Seafood, pasta, sandwiches, salads, and a variety of drinks are offered for lunch and dinner. Brunch is served on Sunday. *25 Main St., tel. 415/435–5088. AE, DC, MC, V.*

Inexpensive– Moderate **Sam's Anchor Cafe.** This longtime favorite remains the most amiable and informal of Tiburon's waterfront dining and drinking spots. Seafood, sandwiches, soups, salads, and a variety of brunch dishes are served. Brunch is served on Sunday. *27 Main St., tel. 415/435–4527. AE, MC, V.*

Inexpensive **Sweden House.** Pastries, breakfast specialties, and sandwiches, along with espresso and cappuccino, are served here. There is a take-out bakery and a full-service café with seating inside or on a secluded deck where a sign warns Please Watch Your Food or the Birds Will Eat It. *35 Main St., tel. 415/435–9767. No credit cards.*

The Marin Headlands

"The Golden Gate" originally referred not to a bridge painted "international orange" but to the grassy and poppy-strewn hills flanking the passageway into San Francisco Bay. This is the one break in the Coast Range Mountains that allows the rivers of California's 400-mile-long Central Valley to reach the ocean. The most dramatic scenery is on the north side of the gate—the Marin Headlands. Once the site of military installations, they are now open to the public as part of the Golden Gate National Recreation Area. The most spectacular photographs of San Francisco are taken from the headlands, with the Golden Gate Bridge in the foreground and the city skyline on the horizon. There are remarkable views east across the bay, north along the coast, and out to sea, with the Farralon Islands visible on a clear day.

Arriving and Departing

By Car The headlands are a logical side trip on the way to Sausalito, but reaching them can be tricky. Take U.S. 101 across the Golden Gate Bridge to the first exit, Alexander Avenue, just past Vista Point. Then take the first left turn through a tunnel under the highway and look for signs to Fort Barry and Fort Cronkhite. Conzelman Road follows the cliffs that face the gate; Bunker Road is a less spectacular route through Rodeo to the headlands headquarters at Fort Cronkhite.

By Bus **San Francisco Muni** (tel. 415/673–6864) No. 76 runs hourly from Fourth and Townsend streets on Sundays and holidays only. The trip takes 45 minutes one-way.

Exploring

Although they are only a short distance from San Francisco, the headlands are a world apart—a vast expanse of wild and open terrain. There are windswept ridges, stretches of shrubs and wildflowers, protected valleys, and obscure beaches. The views can be breathtaking, even when fog is rushing over the hills into the bay. The weather can change dramatically within a few hours, however. Dress warmly and wear appropriate shoes for walking. Stay on marked paths and park in designated areas.

Conzelman Road offers the most spectacular views of the gate, and craggy **Hawk Hill** is the best place on the West Coast from which to watch the migration of eagles, hawks, and falcons as they fly south for the winter from mid-August to mid-December. As many as 1,000 have been sighted in a single day. The viewing area is about 2 miles up Conzelman Road; look for a sign denoting former military Battery 129.

The **Marin Headlands Visitors Center** at Fort Cronkhite (tel. 415/331–1540; open daily, 9:30–4:30) is the center for exploring the region, which includes Rodeo Beach, Rodeo Lagoon, and the Point Bonita lighthouse. Also at Fort Cronkhite is the **California Marine Mammal Center,** which rescues and rehabilitates sick and injured seals and dolphins. Campsites are available, and at nearby Fort Barry there is the Golden Gate Hostel (415/331–2777). For advance planning, detailed maps are available at the Golden Gate National Recreation Area headquarters in

Fort Mason, Bay and Franklin streets, in San Francisco (tel. 415/556–0560).

Muir Woods

One hundred and fifty million years ago, ancestors of redwood and sequoia trees grew throughout the United States. Today the *Sequoia sempervirens* can be found only in a narrow, cool coastal belt from Monterey to Oregon. (*Sequoiadendron gigantea* grows in the Sierra Nevada.) **Muir Woods National Monument,** 17 miles northwest of San Francisco, is a 550-acre park that contains one of the most majestic redwood groves in the world. Some redwoods in the park are nearly 250 feet tall and 1,000 years old. This grove was saved from destruction in 1908 and named for naturalist John Muir, whose campaigns helped to establish the National Park system. His response: "This is the best tree-lover's monument that could be found in all of the forests of the world. Saving these woods from the axe and saw is in many ways the most notable service to God and man I have heard of since my forest wandering began."

Arriving and Departing

By Car Take U.S. 101 north to the Mill Valley–Muir Woods exit. The trip takes 45 minutes one-way when the roads are open, but traffic can be heavy on summer weekends so allow more time.

By Bus **Golden Gate Transit** (tel. 415/332–6600) sends buses from 1st and Mission streets and other points in San Francisco to Muir Woods.

Guided Tours

Most tour companies include Muir Woods on excursions to the Wine Country, among them **Gray Line** (tel. 415/558–9400) and **Great Pacific** (tel. 415/626–4499).

Exploring

Muir Woods is a park for walking; no cars are allowed in the redwood grove itself. There are 6 miles of easy trails from the park headquarters. The paths cross streams and pass through ferns and azaleas as well as magnificent stands of redwoods such as Bohemian Grove and the circular formation called Cathedral Grove. No picnicking or camping is allowed, but snacks are available at the visitor center. The weather is usually cool and often wet, so dress warmly and wear shoes appropriate for damp trails. *Tel. 415/388–2595. Open daily 8 AM–sunset.*

Mt. Tamalpais State Park

Although the summit of Mt. Tamalpais is less than ½-mile high, the mountain rises practically from sea level and dominates the topography of Marin County. Located about 18 miles northwest of San Francisco, adjacent to Muir Woods National Monument, Mt. Tamalpais offers views of the entire Bay Area and west to the Pacific Ocean from its summit. On foggy days lower elevations are sometimes blanketed by the fog, with other peaks just visible above. For years this 6,400-acre park has been a favorite destination for hikers. There are 50 miles of trails, some rugged but many developed for easy walking through meadows, grasslands, and forests, and along creeks.

Arriving and Departing

By Car   Take U.S. 101 north over the Golden Gate Bridge to the Mill Valley–Muir Woods exit. From this road (Shoreline Hwy.), take Panoramic Highway into the park. The trip takes one hour one-way.

By Bus   **Golden Gate Transit** (tel. 415/332–6600) from 1st and Mission streets and other points in the city.

Exploring

Panoramic Highway—the winding "Pan Toll Road" was once a toll road—and Ridgecrest Boulevard eventually lead to the three peaks and the 2,571-foot summit of Mt. Tamalpais. Along the route are numerous parking areas, picnic spots, scenic overlooks and trailheads. **The Mountain Theater** is a natural amphitheater with terraced stone seats that is used for plays and musicals in May and June. The relatively gentle **West Point Trail** begins here. A map of hiking trails is available from the ranger station, about 4 miles from the intersection of Panoramic Highway and the road down the hill to Muir Woods. *Tel. 415/ 388–2070. Open daily 7 AM–sunset.*

Point Reyes

by Dan Spitzer

Point Reyes frames the northern end of Drake's Bay. When Sir Francis sailed down the California coast in 1579 he missed the Golden Gate and San Francisco Bay, but he did land at what he described as a convenient harbor. It may have been Drake's Bay, Bolinas Bay, Bodega Bay, or somewhere else along Point Reyes. With its high rolling grassland above spectacular cliffs, Point Reyes probably reminded him of Scotland. Today Point Reyes National Seashore is a spectacularly beautiful park and one of the favorite spots for whale-watching.

Arriving and Departing

Take U.S. 101 north over the Golden Gate Bridge to the Mill Valley–Muir Woods exit and take Highway 1 north. You'll pass the turnoffs for Muir Woods and Mt. Tamalpais. If you have the energy for a long day of exploring, you can combine a trip to Point Reyes with a trip to Muir Woods or Mt. Tamalpais, but you'll need well over an hour to get to the visitor center and two hours to get all the way from San Francisco to the end of the point.

Exploring

Past the turnoff for Muir Woods, Highway 1 takes you past the town of **Stinson Beach,** which takes its name from one of the longest (4,500 feet) and most popular stretches of sand in Marin County. Along Bolinas Lagoon, just north of Stinson Beach, you'll find the **Audubon Canyon Ranch,** a 1,000-acre bird sanctuary. During the spring the public is invited to view great blue heron and great egret tree nests. There is also a small museum with displays on the geology and natural history of the region as well as a picnic area. *Tel. 415/383-1644. Admission free. Open weekends and holidays Mar. 1–July 4.*

At the northern edge of Bolinas Lagoon, a couple of miles beyond the Audubon Canyon Ranch, follow the unmarked road running west from Highway 1. This leads to the sleepy town of **Bolinas.** Some residents are so wary of tourism that whenever the state tries to post signs, they tear them down. Birders should take Mesa Road until they reach the **Point Reyes Bird Observatory,** a sanctuary that harbors nearly 350 species. *Tel. 415/868-1221. Admission free. Open daily Apr. 1–Sept. 1; Wed., weekends Sept. 2–Mar. 31.*

As you drive back to Bolinas, go right on Overlook Drive and right again on Elm Avenue until you come to **Duxberry Reef,** known for its fine tide pools.

Returning to Highway 1, you will pass a number of horse farms. About a third of a mile past Olema, look for a sign marking the turnoff for **Point Reyes National Seashore's Bear Valley Visitors Center.** The center has some fine exhibits of park wildlife, and helpful rangers can advise you on beaches, visits to the lighthouse for whale-watching (the season for grey-whale migration is mid-Dec.–Mar.), as well as on hiking trails and camping. (Camping is free, but reservations should be made through the visitor center.) A brilliantly reconstructed **Miwok Indian Village** is situated a short walk from the center. It provides insight into the daily lives of the first inhabitants of this region. The lighthouse is a very pretty, 30–40-minute drive from the visitor center, across rolling hills that resemble Scottish heaths. On busy weekends, parking at the lighthouse may be difficult. If you don't care to walk down—and back up—hundreds of steps, you may want to skip the descent to the lighthouse itself. You *can* see whales from the cliffs above the lighthouse, but it's worth the effort to get the lighthouse view. *Tel. 415/663-1092. Admission free. Open daily 9–5.*

Dining

Fresh seafood and local produce are best bets on a trip up to Point Reyes, and most of the following restaurants make good use of these ingredients in their meals. This area is also perfect for picnicking. So if you prefer the great outdoors, consider packing a lunch to take along on your wanderings.

Restaurants are listed according to price category.

Category	Cost*
Expensive	$15–$20
Moderate	$10–$15
Inexpensive	under $10

per person, excluding drinks, service and 6.5% sales tax

The following credit card abbreviations are used: AE, American Express; DC, Diners Club; MC, MasterCard; V, Visa.

Moderate–Expensive **Chez Madeline.** This restaurant features fine French cuisine and excellent seafood, and (as an added treat) its proprietor sometimes entertains by playing classical flute. *Hwy. 1, Point Reyes Station, tel. 415/663–9177. No lunch. Closed Mon. MC, V.*

Manka's. Excellent Czech cuisine is served in wood-paneled dining rooms warmed by a sizable fireplace. This is the best of Inverness's Eastern European restaurants. *30 Calendar Way, Inverness, tel. 415/669–1034. Dinner Thurs.–Mon. Brunch Sun. Reservations advised in summer. MC, V.*

Pelican Inn. Delicious basic English fare—from fish and chips to prime rib and Yorkshire pudding—is served with a fine selection of imported beers and ales. The ambience is wonderful: the wood-paneled dining room warmed by a great stone fireplace; a glass-enclosed solarium ideal for sunny lunches. *Hwy. 1, Muir Beach, tel. 415/383–6000. Reservations advised for 6 or more. MC, V.*

Station House Cafe. This favorite local hangout serves breakfast, lunch, and dinner. Fresh fish and expertly grilled meats highlight the dinner menu. *Hwy. 1, Point Reyes Station, tel. 415/663–1515. MC, V.*

Stinson Beach Grill. This grill serves excellent nouvelle cuisine. *Hwy. 1, Stinson Beach, tel. 415/868–2002. MC, V.*

Moderate   **Sand Dollar.** This pleasant pub serves great hamburgers and other sandwiches for lunch and decent seafood for dinner. An added attraction is an outdoor dining deck. *Hwy. 1, Stinson Beach, tel. 415/868–0434. No credit cards.*

Inexpensive   **Grey Whale.** This is a good place for pizza, salad, pastries, and coffee, at lunch or dinner. *On Sir Francis Drake Blvd. in the center of Inverness, tel. 415/669–1244. No credit cards.*

Berkeley

by Robert Taylor   Berkeley and the University of California are not synonymous, although the founding campus of the state university system dominates the city's heritage and contemporary life. The city of 100,000 facing San Francisco across the bay has other interesting features for visitors. Berkeley is culturally diverse and politically adventurous, a breeding ground for social trends, a continuing bastion of the counterculture, and an important center for Bay Area writers, artists, and musicians. The city's liberal reputation and determined spirit has led detractors to describe it in recent years as the People's Republic of Berkeley. Wooded groves on the university campus, neighborhoods of shingled bungalows, and landscaped hillside homes temper the environment.

The city was named for George Berkeley, the Irish philosopher and clergyman who crossed the Atlantic to convert the Indians and wrote "Westward, the course of empire takes its way." The city grew with the university, which was created by the state legislature in 1868 and established five years later on a rising plain of oak trees split by Strawberry Canyon. The central campus occupies 178 acres of the scenic 1,282-acre property, with most buildings located from Bancroft Way north to Hearst Street and from Oxford Street east into the Berkeley Hills. The university has more than 30,000 students and a full-time faculty of 1,600. It is considered one of the nation's leading intellectual centers and a major site for scientific research.

Note that the telephone area code for Berkeley, Oakland, and other cities on the east side of San Francisco Bay changed from 415 to 510 in 1991.

Arriving and Departing

By Car Take I–80 east across the Bay Bridge, then the University Avenue exit through downtown Berkeley to the campus, or take the Ashby Avenue exit and turn left on Telegraph Avenue to the traditional campus entrance; there is a parking garage on Channing Way. The trip takes ½ hour one-way (except in rush hour).

By Public Transportation **BART** (tel. 415/788–2278) trains run under the bay to the downtown Berkeley exit; transfer to the Humphrey GoBart shuttle bus to campus. The trip takes from 45 minutes to one hour one-way.

Exploring

Numbers in the margin correspond with points of interest on the Berkeley map.

❶ The Visitors Center (tel. 510/642–5215) in **University Hall** at University Avenue and Oxford Street, is open weekdays 8–5. There are maps and brochures for self-guided walks; student-guided tours leave weekdays at 1 PM.

❷ The throbbing heart of the University of California is **Sproul Plaza,** just inside the campus at Telegraph Avenue and Bancroft Way. It's a lively panorama of political and social activists, musicians, food vendors along Bancroft Way, children, dogs, and students on their way to and from classes at this "university within a park."

The university's suggested tour circles the upper portion of the central campus, past buildings that were sited to take advantage of vistas to the Golden Gate across the bay. The first campus plan was proposed by Frederick Law Olmsted, who designed New York's Central Park, and over the years the university's architects have included Bernard Maybeck and Julia Morgan (who designed Hearst Castle at San Simeon). Be-
❸ yond Sproul Plaza is the bronze **Sather Gate,** built in 1909 and the south entrance to the campus until expansion during the
❹ 1960s. Up a walkway to the right is vine-covered **South Hall,** one of two remaining buildings that greeted the first students in 1873.

❺ Just ahead is **Sather Tower,** popularly known as the Campanile, the campus landmark that can be seen for miles. The 307-foot tower was modeled on St. Mark's tower in Venice and was completed in 1914. The carillon, which was cast in England, is played three times a day. In the lobby of the tower is a photographic display of campus history. An elevator takes visitors 175 feet up to the observation deck. *Open daily except university holidays 10–4:30. Admission: 50¢.*

❻ Opposite the Campanile is **Bancroft Library,** with a rare-book collection and a changing series of exhibits that may include a Shakespeare first folio or a Gold Rush diary. On permanent display is a gold nugget purported to be the one that started the rush to California when it was discovered on January 24, 1848.

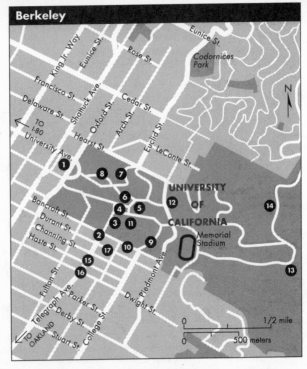

Berkeley

7 Across University Drive to the north is the **Earth Sciences Building,** with a seismograph for measuring earthquakes. The **8** building also contains the **Paleontology Museum,** which has displays of dinosaur bones and the huge skeleton of a plesiosaur. *Open when the university is in session, weekdays 8–5, weekends 1–5.*

9 The university's two major museums are on the south side of campus near Bancroft Way. **The Lowie Museum of Anthropology,** in Kroeber Hall, has a collection of more than 4,000 artifacts. Items on display may cover the archaeology of ancient America or the crafts of Pacific Islanders. The museum also houses the collection of artifacts made by Ishi, the lone survivor of a California Indian tribe who was brought to the Bay Area in 1911. *Tel. 510/642–3681. Open Tues.–Fri. 10–4:30, weekends noon–4:30.*

10 **The University Art Museum** is a fan-shaped building with a spiral of ramps and balcony galleries. It houses a collection of Asian and Western art, including a major group of Hans Hofmann's abstract paintings, and also displays touring exhibits. On the ground floor is the Pacific Film Archive, which offers daily programs of historic and contemporary films. *2626 Bancroft Way, tel. 510/642–0808. Museum open Wed.–Sun. 11–5. Free museum admission. Film-program information, tel. 415/642–1124.*

11 Many of the university's notable attractions are outdoors. Just south of the Campanile near the rustic Faculty Club is **Faculty Glade** on the south fork of Strawberry Creek, one of the best examples of the university's attempt to preserve a parklike atmosphere. East of the central campus, across Gayley Road, is (12) the **Hearst Greek Theatre,** built in 1903 and seating 7,000. Sarah Bernhardt once performed here; now it is used for major musical events.

Above the Greek Theatre in Strawberry Canyon is the 30-acre (13) **Botanical Garden,** with a collection of some 25,000 species. It's a relaxing gathering spot with benches and picnic tables. *Open daily 9–5, except Christmas.*

Perched on a hill above the campus on Centennial Drive is the (14) fortresslike **Lawrence Hall of Science,** which is a laboratory, a science education center, and—most important to visitors—a dazzling display of scientific knowledge and experiments. Displays are updated regularly. On weekends there are additional films, lectures, and demonstrations, especially for children. *Tel. 510/642–5132. Nominal admission charge. Open Mon.– Sat. 10–4:30, Sun. noon–5.*

Berkeley is a rewarding city to explore beyond the university. Just south of the campus on **Telegraph Avenue** is the busy, student-oriented district, full of cafés, bookstores, poster shops, and street vendors with traditional and trendy crafts items. Shops come and go with the times, but among the neighbor- (15) hood landmarks are **Cody's Books** (2454 Telegraph Ave.), with (16) its adjacent café; **Moe's** (2476 Telegraph Ave.), with a huge se- (17) lection of used books; and **Leopold Records** (2518 Durant Ave.). This district was the center of student protests during the 1960s, and on the street it sometimes looks as if that era still lives. People's Park, one of the centers of protest, is just east of Telegraph between Haste Street and Dwight Way.

Downtown Berkeley around University and Shattuck avenues is nondescript. However, there are shops for browsing along College Avenue near Ashby Avenue south of campus and in the Walnut Square development at Shattuck and Vine streets northwest of campus. Berkeley's shingled houses can be seen on tree-shaded streets near College and Ashby avenues. Hillside houses with spectacular views can be seen on the winding roads near the intersection of Ashby and Claremont avenues, around the Claremont Hotel (*see* Exploring in Oakland, below). At the opposite side of the city, there are views across the bay from the Berkeley Marina at the foot of University Avenue, west of I–80.

Dining

Berkeley's major restaurants, including those on Shattuck Avenue north of the university, are known for their innovative use of fresh local produce. There is an eclectic variety of low-cost international cafés and snack stands in the student area along Telegraph Avenue and more cafés downtown on Shattuck Avenue near the central Berkeley BART station.

Restaurants are listed according to price category.

Category	Cost*
Very Expensive	$30 and up
Expensive	$20–$30

| Moderate | $10–$20 |
| Inexpensive | under $10 |

per person, excluding drinks, service, and 6.5% sales tax

The following credit card abbreviations are used: AE, American Express; DC, Diners Club; MC, MasterCard; V, Visa.

Moderate–Expensive **Cafe at Chez Panisse.** Fresh and innovative light meals (lunch and dinner) are served, including pasta, pizza, salads, and light grilled dishes, upstairs from the mecca for California cuisine. *1517 Shattuck Ave., north of University Ave., tel. 510/548–5525. Same-day reservations accepted. Closed Sun. AE, DC, MC, V.*

Moderate **Spenger's Fish Grotto.** This is a rambling, boisterous seafood restaurant, with daily specials and hearty portions. *1919 Fourth St., near University Ave. and I–80, tel. 510/845–7771. Reservations for 5 or more. AE, DC, MC, V.*

Inexpensive **Kip's.** This is a student hangout but it is open to everyone, upstairs near Telegraph Avenue, with big wooden tables and burgers, pizza, and—of course—beer on tap. *2439 Durant Ave., tel. 510/848–4340. No reservations. No credit cards.*

New Delhi Junction. A popular Indian restaurant, New Delhi Junction offers Tandoori-roasted meats, curries, and regional specialties. *2556 University Ave., tel. 510/486–0477. Open daily. MC, V.*

Oakland

Originally the site of ranches, farms, a grove of redwood trees, and, of course, clusters of oaks, Oakland has long been a warmer and more spacious alternative to San Francisco. By the end of the 19th century, Mediterranean-style homes and gardens had been developed as summer estates. With swifter transportation, Oakland became a bedroom community for San Francisco; then it progressed to California's fastest-growing industrial city. In recent decades, Oakland has struggled to redefine its identity. However, the major attractions remain: the parks and civic buildings around Lake Merritt, which was created from a tidal basin in 1898; the port area, now named Jack London Square, where the author spent much of his time at the turn of the century; and the scenic roads and parks along the crest of the Oakland-Berkeley hills. Also in the hills is the castlelike Claremont Resort Hotel, a landmark since 1915, as well as more sprawling parks with lakes and miles of hiking trails.

Arriving and Departing

By Car Take I–80 across the Bay Bridge, then I–580 to the Grand Avenue exit for Lake Merritt. To reach downtown and the waterfront, take the I–980 exit from I–580. The trip takes 45 minutes.

By Public Transportation Take the BART to Oakland City Center station or to Lake Merritt station for the lake and Oakland Museum. The trip takes 45 minutes one-way.

Exploring

Numbers in the margin correspond with points of interest on the Oakland map.

❶ If there is one reason to visit Oakland, it is to explore the **Oakland Museum,** an inviting series of landscaped buildings that display the state's art, history, and natural science. It is the best possible introduction to a tour of California, and its dramatic and detailed exhibits can help fill the gaps on a brief visit. The natural science department displays a typical stretch of California from the Pacific Ocean to the Nevada border, including plants and wildlife. There is a breathtaking film, *Fast Flight,* that condenses the trip into five minutes. The museum's sprawling history section includes everything from Spanish-era artifacts and a gleaming fire engine that battled the flames in San Francisco in 1906 to 1960s souvenirs of the "summer of love." The California Dream exhibit recalls a century of inspirations. The museum's art department includes mystical landscapes painted by the state's pioneers, as well as contemporary visions. There is a pleasant museum café for lunch and outdoor areas for relaxing. *1000 Oak St. at 10th St., tel. 510/834–2413. Admission free. Open Wed.–Sat. 10–5, Sun. noon–7.*

❷ Near the museum, **Lake Merritt** is a 155-acre oasis surrounded by parks and paths, with several outdoor attractions on the **❸** north side. The **Natural Science Center and Waterfowl Refuge** attracts birds by the hundreds during winter months. *At the foot of Perkins St., tel. 510/273–3739. Ope Mon. noon–5, Tues.–Sun. 10–5.*

❹ **Children's Fairyland** is a low-key amusement park with a puppet theater, small merry-go-round, and settings based on nursery rhymes. *Grand Ave. at Park View Terr., tel. 510/832–3609. Open daily in summer, 10–4:30. Closed weekdays in winter.*
❺ The **Lakeside Park Garden Center** includes a Japanese garden and many native flowers and plants. *666 Bellevue Ave., tel. 510/273–3208. Open daily 10–3 or later in summer. Closed Thanksgiving, Christmas, New Year's Day.*

Jack London, although born in San Francisco, spent his early years in Oakland before shipping out for adventures that inspired *The Call of the Wild, The Sea Wolf, Martin Eden,* and *The Cruise of the Snark.* He is commemorated with a bronze **❻** bust in **Jack London Square** at the foot of Broadway. A livelier **❼** landmark is **Heinhold's First and Last Chance Saloon,** one of his hangouts. Next door is the reassembled Klondike cabin in which he spent a winter. The square is mainly for drinking and dining. Next door, Jack London Village has specialty shops and restaurants. The best local collection of the author's letters, manuscripts, and photographs is in the Jack London Room at the Oakland Main Library (125 14th St., tel. 510/273–3134).

Oakland's downtown has been undergoing redevelopment for many years. More stable and pleasant areas for shopping and browsing, with a selection of cafés, can be found on Lake Shore Avenue northeast of Lake Merritt, Piedmont Avenue near the Broadway exit from I–580, and College Avenue west of Broadway in North Oakland. College Avenue is lined with antiques stores, boutiques, and cafés. The neighborhood surrounds BART's Rockridge station. Transferring there to the local No.

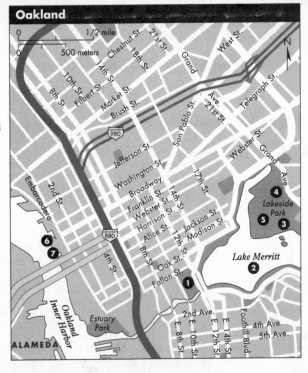

51 bus will take visitors to the University of California campus, about 1½ miles away in Berkeley.

Time Out   A drive through the Oakland Hills is spectacular, with open-space parks and bay views, and a stop on the way at the **Claremont Hotel** (Ashby and Domingo Aves., tel. 510/843–3000) offers fine views, a spot in which to relax, and good food. Drive north on Claremont Avenue to Ashby Avenue and on up the hill to the hotel. From a distance, this sprawling white building with towers and gables looks like a castle. Surrounded by 22 acres of lush grounds tucked into the south Berkeley hills, the Claremont is on the Oakland-Berkeley border, and for years both cities have claimed it. When a new entrance was built on a different side of the building, the address changed from Berkeley to Oakland. The 1915 hotel has been restored and refurbished and turned into a resort spa facility. The dining room is large and elegant, with pressed linen, large contemporary paintings, and views across the bay to San Francisco and the peninsula and north to Mt. Tamalpais. Meals, which fall into the Moderate–Expensive category, feature California cuisine, with seasonal fresh seafood for Sunday brunch and creative sandwiches for lunch.

The East Bay Regional Park District (tel. 510/531–9300) offers 46 parks in an area covering 60,000 acres to residents and visitors. In the Oakland hills is **Redwood Regional Park,** accessible from Joaquin Miller Road off Highway 13, to which Ashby Avenue will lead you. In the Berkeley hills is the 2,000-acre **Tilden Park,** which includes a lake and children's playground and is accessible from Grizzly Peak Boulevard off Claremont Avenue. There are scenic views of the Bay Area from roads that link the hilltop parks: Redwood Road, Skyline Boulevard, and Grizzly Peak Boulevard. Parks are open daily during daylight hours.

Dining

Oakland's ethnic diversity is reflected in its restaurants and cafés. There is a thriving Chinatown a few blocks northwest of the Oakland Museum, a number of seafood restaurants at Jack London Square, and a variety of international fare on Piedmont and College Avenues.

Restaurants are listed according to price category.

Category	Cost*
Very Expensive	over $30
Expensive	$20–$30
Moderate	$10–$20
Inexpensive	under $10

*per person, excluding drinks, service, and 6.5% sales tax

The following credit card abbreviations are used: AE, American Express; DC, Diners Club; MC, MasterCard; V, Visa.

Moderate– Expensive   **The Bay Wolf.** French inspiration and fresh, regional specialties mark one of the city's best restaurants, in a converted home. *3853 Piedmont Ave., tel. 510/655–6004. Reservations advised. No lunch weekends. MC, V.*

Moderate   **Pacific Coast Brewing Co.** This pub/restaurant/brewery serves a fine selection of sandwiches and salads. *906 Washington St., tel. 510/836–2739. MC, V.*

Inexpensive   **Ratto's.** Salads, sandwiches, soups, and pasta are served in a big, cheerful room adjacent to one of the Bay Area's best international grocery stores, in the Old Oakland Victorian Row restoration. *821 Washington St., tel. 510/832–6503. Lunch weekdays; take-out orders prepared in the deli, Mon.–Sat. No credit cards.*

The San Francisco Peninsula

During the morning and evening rush hours, the peninsula south of San Francisco resembles nothing so much as a vast commuter corridor. At other times and on the network of less-traveled roads, the area offers a remarkable variety of scenic attractions. Redwood forests remain, although they were heavily logged during the 19th century. In San Mateo and Half Moon Bay there are small adobe houses from California's Spanish and Mexican eras. The peninsula's most dramatic development came later with the grand country estates built by the "bonanza kings" who made their fortunes in mining and transportation. Many mansions survive: Ralston Hall, built by the owner of San Francisco's Palace Hotel, now the College of Notre Dame on Ralston Avenue in Belmont; La Dolphine on

Manor Drive in Burlingame, inspired by Le Petite Trianon at Versailles; and the Uplands, built by banker C. Templeton Crocker, now the Crystal Springs School for Girls on Uplands Drive in Burlingame. The only estate open to the general public is Filoli in Woodside, which has 16 acres of gardens. Another major attraction is Stanford University at Palo Alto, with a campus that stretches from the flatlands of the Santa Clara Valley into the Santa Cruz Mountains.

Arriving and Departing

By Car The most pleasant direct route down the peninsula is I–280, the Junipero Serra Freeway, which passes along Crystal Springs reservoir. Take the Edgewood Road exit for Filoli, and Alpine Road for Stanford. Highway 101 along the bay shore can be congested, but from there take Highway 93 west to Filoli and University Avenue or Embarcadero Road to Stanford. Skyline Boulevard (Hwy. 35), which begins near the San Francisco Zoo, is the most scenic route through the peninsula, following the crest of the Santa Cruz Mountains and offering views of both the bay and the Pacific Ocean. Highway 1 follows a relatively unknown section of the coast from San Francisco to Santa Cruz, a route including rugged cliffs, public beaches, communities such as Pescadero that began as fishing villages, and several 19th-century lighthouses.

By Public Transportation CalTrain (tel. 415/557–8661) from 4th and Townsend streets to Palo Alto, then shuttle bus to Stanford campus. Other attractions on the peninsula are difficult to reach except by car.

Exploring

One of the few great country houses in California that remains intact in its original setting is **Filoli** in Woodside. Built for wealthy San Franciscan William B. Bourn in 1916–1919, it was designed by Willis Polk in a Georgian style, with redbrick walls and a tile roof. The name is not Italian but Bourn's acronym for "fight, love, live." As interesting to visitors as the house (which you might remember from the television series "Dynasty") are the 16 acres of formal gardens. The gardens were planned and developed over a period of more than 50 years and preserved for the public when the last private owner, Mrs. William P. Roth, deeded Filoli to the National Trust for Historic Preservation.

The gardens rise south from the mansion to take advantage of the natural surroundings of the 700-acre estate and its vistas. Among the designs are a sunken garden, walled garden, woodland garden, yew alley, and a rose garden developed by Mrs. Roth with more than 50 shrubs of all types and colors. A focal point of the garden is a charming teahouse designed in the Italian Renaissance style. Spring is the most popular time to visit, but daffodils, narcissi, and rhododendrons are in bloom as early as February, and the gardens remain attractive in October and November. *Canada Rd., near Edgewood Rd., Woodside, tel. 415/364–2880. Admission: $8. Children under 12 not admitted. Open for tours mid-Feb.–mid-Nov., Mon.–Sat. Reservations necessary; spring tours may fill several weeks in advance. Call for openings. Filoli is often open for unguided visits and nature hikes on the estate, but call for information.*

Stanford University, 30 miles south of San Francisco, also has its roots among the peninsula's estates. Originally the property was former California governor Leland Stanford's farm for breeding horses. For all its stature as one of the nation's leading universities, Stanford is still known as "the farm." Founded and endowed by Leland and Jane Stanford in 1885 as a memorial to their son, Leland, Jr., who died of typhoid fever, the university was opened in 1891. Frederick Law Olmsted conceived the plan for the grounds and Romanesque sandstone buildings, joined by arcades and topped by red-tile roofs. Variations on this solid style persist in newer buildings, which, along with playing fields, now cover about 1,200 acres of the 8,200-acre campus. The center of the university is the inner quadrangle, a group of 12 original classroom buildings later joined by Memorial Church, with its facade and interior walls covered with mosaics of biblical scenes.

The university is organized into seven schools made up of 70 departments. In addition, there are several institutes on campus, including the Hoover Institution on War, Revolution, and Peace. Its 285-foot tower is a landmark; there is an elevator to an observation deck. Except for the central cluster of buildings, the campus is remarkably uncongested—enrollment is only about 15,000.

Free walking tours leave daily at 11 AM and 3:15 PM from the **Visitor Information Booth** (tel. 415/723–2560 or 723–2053) at the front of the quadrangle. The main campus entrance, Palm Drive, is an extension of University Avenue from Palo Alto.

The **Stanford Museum of Art,** on Lomita Drive, contains an outstanding collection of Egyptian and Oriental works along with the original golden spike that Leland Stanford drove in at Promontory Point, Utah, in 1869, uniting the Central Pacific and Union Pacific railroads to complete the transcontinental railroad. Adjacent to the museum is a gallery of student art and an outdoor garden of Rodin bronzes. *Tel. 415/723–4177. Open Tues.–Fri. 10–5, weekends 1–5. Closed Aug.*

Two miles west of the main campus, on Sand Hill Road, is the **Stanford Linear Accelerator** (tel. 415/926–3300, ext. 2204). There are tours of the 2-mile-long electron accelerator used for elementary-particle research.

Just north of the main campus, facing El Camino Real, is the **Stanford Shopping Center,** one of the Bay Area's first and still one of the most pleasant and inviting. The Nature Company has a fascinating collection of artifacts and gadgets reflecting an interest in the natural world, a large collection of natural-history books, and a good poster selection. The Palo Alto Roasting Company roasts a variety of coffees in three strengths. Crate and Barrel is a large kitchen and housewares store with a fine contemporary and moderately priced selection.

Dining

El Camino Real (Hwy. 82) is the peninsula's major commercial thoroughfare, with many cafés, restaurants, and fast-food franchises. There are several pleasant cafés, some with outdoor dining, in downtown Palo Alto along University Avenue and its cross streets, just east of El Camino Real. The Stanford Shopping Center has a variety of upscale cafés: Gaylord's serves moderately priced Indian food in a relaxed and elegant atmosphere, and the nearby Fresh Choice offers inexpensive gourmet salads and sandwiches.

Restaurants are listed according to price category.

Category	Cost*
Very Expensive	over $30
Expensive	$20–$30
Moderate	$10–$20
Inexpensive	under $10

per person, excluding drinks, service, and 6.5% sales tax

The following credit card abbreviations are used: AE, American Express; DC, Diners Club; MC, MasterCard; V, Visa.

Expensive **Flea Street Cafe.** The decor is a flowery mixture of Victorian and Art Deco styles, and the fare is imaginative, featuring fresh produce and freshly baked breads. Specialties sometimes include raspberry chicken sautéed in a port wine and raspberry vinegar sauce, vegetable frittata, and—for Sunday brunch—sweet-potato pancakes topped with pecans, yogurt, and syrup. *Alameda de las Pulgas, Menlo Park (take Sand Hill Rd. west from the Stanford shopping center or east from I–280, turn right on Alameda), tel. 415/854–1226. MC,V. No lunch Sat. Closed Mon.*

Inexpensive– **Village Pub.** This is a pleasant restaurant near Filoli that fea-
Moderate tures Continental cuisine, including a variety of seafood and luncheon salads. *2967 Woodside Rd., Woodside, tel. 415/851–1294. Reservations advised. AE, DC, MC, V. No lunch weekends.*

Inexpensive **Tressider Memorial Union.** Two cafés in Stanford's student union welcome visitors, and there is an adjacent shop for take-out snacks. The cafés serve breakfast, lunch, and dinner. *Santa Teresa St. at west side of central campus, tel. 415/723–4311. No credit cards.*

San Jose and Santa Clara

San Jose, founded in 1777, was California's first town apart from a Spanish mission or fortification. It was (briefly) the state's first capital during the American occupation, but until the middle of the 20th century it remained primarily an agricultural center. San Jose, 50 miles south of San Francisco, was touted as "the garden city in the valley of heart's delight" when the Santa Clara Valley was filled with orchards. Vineyards and wineries continue to flourish, but the area became "Silicon Valley" with the advent of high-tech industries based on the silicon chip. Santa Clara and nearby Sunnyvale are the high-tech centers, but sprawling San Jose has become the state's fourth-largest city. Many of the area's attractions are family-oriented and are widely separated in this "Los Angeles of the north," but San Jose has embarked on a massive building project to redefine the city center, the area around First and San Carlos streets. Already completed are the first link in a light-rail transportation system that reaches the Great America theme park to the north, the high-rise Fairmont Hotel, and a cultural center. Meanwhile, among the shopping centers and residential subdivisions, the valley's history endures at such sites as Mission Santa Clara on the tree-shaded campus of the University of Santa Clara.

Arriving and Departing

By Car Drive south on I–280 to downtown San Jose exits or south on Highway 101 to Great America, Santa Clara, and downtown San Jose. The trip takes one hour one-way; however, traffic south of Mountain View can be congested and slow during morning and evening rush hours.

By Public Transportation A car is almost a necessity, but **CalTrain** (tel. 415/557–8661) commuter service is available from 4th and Townsend streets to Santa Clara or San Jose. San Jose–based **Go Anywhere Tours** (tel. 408/241–8687) covers the valley and its historic wineries.

Exploring

The Technology Center of Silicon Valley offers high-tech information and hands-on lab exhibits to demystify microelectronics, biotechnology, robotics, and space exploration. *145 W. San Carlos at the convention center, San Jose, tel. 408/279–7150. Admission, $6 adults, $4 students and senior citizens. Open Tues.–Sun. 10–5.*

The Children's Discovery Museum encourages interaction with exhibits on space, technology, the humanities, and the arts. *180 Woz Way at Auzerais St., near the convention center, San Jose, tel. 408/298–5495. Admission, $6 adults, $3 children. Open Tues.–Sat. 10–5, Sun. noon–5.*

The Winchester Mystery House has long been a favorite family attraction, although it is not as mysterious as it was when the land around it was overgrown countryside. Now it's brightly painted, with well-tended gardens and a historical museum. The history remains: a bizarre, 160-room Victorian-era labyrinth built by firearms heiress Sarah Winchester, a widow who was convinced that spirits would harm her if construction ever stopped. Building began in 1884 and continued for 38 years, with hundreds of carpenters often working around the clock. *525 S. Winchester Blvd., near I–280, San Jose, tel. 408/247–2101. Admission: $10.95 adults, $8.95 senior citizens, $5.95 children 6–12. Open daily 9–4:30; extended summer hours. Closed Christmas.*

The Rosicrucian Egyptian Museum offers some mysteries of its own in the West Coast's largest collection of Egyptian antiquities, including mummies, shrunken heads, and a walk-in replica of a nobleman's tomb. Children find it fascinating. The museum's entrance is a reproduction of the avenue of ram sphinxes from the temple at Karnak in Egypt, and the complex is set in a garden filled with palms, papyrus, and other plants associated with ancient Egypt. *1600 Park Ave., San Jose, tel. 408/287–2807. Admission: $4 adults, $2 children. Open Tues.–Sun. 9–5.*

On the east side of San Jose, **Kelly Park** offers a variety of family attractions on 176 acres of rolling grasslands with tree-shaded picnic sites. **Happy Hollow Park and Zoo** is a creative park with theme rides, puppet shows, a riverboat replica, and events specially planned for children from 2 to 10 years old. *1300 Senter Rd., tel. 408/295–8383. Open Mon.–Sat. 10–5, Sun. 11–6. Closed Christmas.*

The **San Jose Historical Museum** is also an outdoor attraction, a collection of restored Victorian homes, San Jose businesses, and even a gas station from the 1920s. It's reminiscent of small-town America without the gloss of amusement-park reproductions. *635 Phelan Ave., tel. 408/287–2290. Open weekdays 10–4:30, weekends noon–4:30.*

Also in the park is the **Japanese Friendship Garden,** with fish ponds and a teahouse. *Open daily 10 AM–sunset.*

Another nearby outdoor attraction is **Hakone Gardens,** on a hillside in Saratoga about 10 miles west of San Jose. The picturesque gardens were designed in 1918 by a man who had been an imperial gardener in Japan. It has been carefully maintained and restored, and the site includes a traditional Japanese teahouse. The park is a quiet refuge from the busy valley below. *21000 Big Basin Way, Saratoga, tel. 408/867–3438, ext. 43. Nominal admission fee. Open weekdays 10–5, weekends 11–5. Tours available.*

Santa Clara offers two major attractions at opposite ends of the spectrum: the mission, founded in 1777, and Great America, Northern California's answer to Disneyland, which continues to add multimillion-dollar adventure rides.

The Mission Santa Clara de Assis was the eighth in the chain of 21 California missions founded under the direction of Father Junipero Serra, and it is located in one of the most pleasant settings, on the campus of Santa Clara University. The mission has a dramatic history. Several early settlements were flooded, the present site was the fifth chosen, and the permanent mission chapel was destroyed by fire in 1926. The current building is a replica of the original, with roof tiles salvaged from earlier buildings that dated from the 1790s and 1820s. There is also a wooden cross from 1777 and early adobe walls and gardens. The surrounding campus provides a pleasant excursion; it was California's first college, established in 1851 by the Jesuits. On campus is a notable northern California art museum, the de Saisset, with a permanent collection that includes California mission artifacts. *Campus: Franklin St. and the Alameda, Santa Clara, Mission, tel. 408/554–4023. Open daily 10–5. De Saisset Museum, tel. 408/554–4528. Admission free. Open Tues.–Sun. 11–4. Closed major holidays.*

Great America is a 100-acre theme park on the edge of San Francisco Bay with attractions designed to reflect regional North America: Hometown Square, Yukon Territory, Yankee Harbor, County Fair, and Orleans Place. A double-decked carousel, the Columbia, is located just inside the entrance, but other rides are more adventurous. There are five roller coasters, a triple-armed Ferris wheel, and several exciting rides that splash through water. The latest are the $4 million "Rip Roaring Rapids," which simulates a white-water journey in oversize inner tubes; and the "Vortex" stand-up roller coaster. For the less adventurous, there is the Skytower, an observation platform that rises 200 feet and gently revolves for a view of the valley on a clear day. *Entrance on Great America Pkwy., between Hwy. 101 and Hwy. 237, tel. 408/988–1776. Admis-*

sion: $20.95 adults, $13.95 senior citizens 55 and over, $10.95 children 3–6. Open Easter week and Memorial Day–Labor Day, daily 10–varying closing time; spring and fall, weekends. AE, MC, V. The park is served by Santa Clara County Transit (tel. 415/287–4210) from throughout the San Jose area and from the Fremont BART station.

Dining

San Jose may be the fast-food franchise capital of California, and its major streets are also scattered with Mexican, Asian, and Italian restaurants. There is also a variety of restaurants in the area's major shopping centers: The Pruneyard at South Bascom and Campbell avenues, Vallco Fashion Park on Wolfe Road near I–280, and Valley Fair on Stevens Creek Boulevard at I–880.

Restaurants are listed according to price category.

Category	Cost*
Very Expensive	$30 and up
Expensive	$20–$30
Moderate	$10–$20
Inexpensive	under $10

per person, excluding drinks, service, and 6.5% sales tax

The following credit card abbreviations are used: AE, American Express; DC, Diners Club; MC, MasterCard; V, Visa.

Moderate–Expensive **Sebastian's.** Classic as well as innovative French and Italian dishes are served in a restaurant on the 17th floor of an office building in the Pruneyard, one of the valley's charming shopping centers. *1901 S. Bascom Ave., Campbell, tel. 408/377–8600. No lunch Sat. AE, DC, MC, V.*

Moderate **Scott's Seafood Grill.** A good selection of reliably fresh seafood, with a number of daily specials, is available for lunch and dinner. *185 Park Ave., downtown San Jose, tel. 408/971–1700. No lunch weekends. AE, DC, MC, V.*

Inexpensive **Original Joe's.** Hearty Italian specialties, along with steaks, chops, and hamburgers, are served. Serves three meals a day. *301 S. 1st St., downtown San Jose, tel. 408/292–7030. No credit cards.*

On and Around the Bay

A ferry ride to Sausalito or Tiburon or a drive across the Golden Gate or Bay bridge only suggests the many opportunities to enjoy and explore San Francisco Bay and its nearby waterways. The bay, 60 miles long and between 3 and 13 miles wide, was the area's transportation hub before there were passable roads and rails. Richard Henry Dana described sailing and shipping during the 1830s in *Two Years Before the Mast*. The bay, the inland delta, and the Sacramento River were the gateway to the goldfields. Now they are an equally thriving area for weekend and vacation excursions. Around the bay are miles of shoreline parks and wildlife refuges, easily accessible but almost never seen by travelers on the busy Bayshore and East Shore freeways.

Yerba Island provides the center anchorage for the Bay Bridge and is connected by a causeway to man-made Treasure Island, with its military museum and relics of the island's 1939 World's Fair. There are excursions available to the Farallon Islands, which are rich with wildlife, 23 miles outside the Golden Gate. Other boating excursions explore the bay and the delta's maze of waterways as far as Stockton and Sacramento. Back on land is the town of Benicia, about an hour's drive northeast of San Francisco, where an early state capitol has been meticulously restored. Across Carquinez Strait is the former home of naturalist John Muir. Scenic river roads, particularly Highway 160, offer slower paced alternatives to freeway travel between the Bay Area and Sacramento.

Exploring

Every day 250,000 people pass through **Yerba Buena Island** on their way across the San Francisco–Oakland Bay Bridge, yet it remains a mystery to most of them. Yerba Buena and the adjacent Treasure Island are primarily military bases, but they are accessible to the public. **Treasure Island** provides a superb bay-level view of the San Francisco skyline. The **Navy-Marine Corps–Coast Guard Museum** focuses on the military role in the Pacific; it is housed in one of the remaining buildings from the 1939 Golden Gate International Exposition. *Bldg. 1, Treasure Island, tel. 415/395-5067. Admission free. Open daily 10-3:30.*

Recently developed wildlife refuges offer welcome access to the bay's shore, which can appear to be a congested commercial strip from surrounding freeways. Among the best of the free public parks are **Coyote Point Nature Museum** just off U.S. 101 south of San Francisco Airport (tel. 415/342-7755; open Wed.–Fri. 10-5, weekends 1-5); the **Baylands Nature Interpretive Center** (tel. 415/881-6751) in the marshes at the east end of Embarcadero Road in Palo Alto; the **San Francisco Bay National Wildlife Refuge** on Thornton Avenue in Fremont, at the east end of the Dumbarton Bridge/Highway 84 (tel. 510/792-0222; open daily 10-5); and the **Hayward Regional Shoreline,** the largest marsh restoration project on the West Coast, on West Winton Avenue at the east end of the San Mateo Bridge/Highway 92 (open daily 6 AM–sunset; for guided walks, call the Interpretive Center).

Another major wildlife center is outside the bay, the islands of the **Gulf of the Farallones National Maritime Sanctuary.** Rare nesting birds and passing seals and whales are visible from cruise boats, but the islands are off limits to visitors. Cruises are operated by Oceanic Society Expeditions (tel. 415/474-3385). Cost: $30–$50.

A cruise line offers riverboat excursions through San Francisco, San Pablo, and Suisun bays, and along the Sacramento–San Joaquin River Delta as far as Sacramento. **Delta Riverboats** uses Harbor Tours ferries for the daylong voyage, with sightseeing on land in Old Sacramento before returning to San Francisco by bus. Or passengers may stay overnight and return on the ferry. *1540 W. Capitol Ave., Box 813, West Sacramento 95691, tel. 916/372-3690. Cost: $50-$120. Tours on weekends May–Oct.*

Houseboats can be rented to explore the 1,000 miles of delta waterways. Prices are about $600–$2,000 a week. Boats accommodate up to 14 persons, and a "test drive" with an operator is included in the rental. A list of houseboat operators is available from the California Office of Tourism (801 K St., Suite 1600, Sacramento 95814, tel. 916/322–1396).

The historic port city of Benicia is worth a detour for travelers on I–80 between San Francisco and Sacramento. (Take the I–780 exit in Vallejo, then Benicia's East 2nd Street exit.) The old town center is on 1st Street, and at the foot of the street there is a fishing pier with a view through Carquinez Strait to San Pablo Bay. Benicia was named for the wife of General Mariano Vallejo, who owned the surrounding 99,000 acres. Benicia was the state capital in 1852 and 1853, and the handsome brick Greek Revival **capitol** has been splendidly restored. *1st and W. G Sts. Nominal admission fee. Open Mon.–Fri. 8:30–5, Sat–Sun. 11–3.*

There is a pleasant garden and Federal-style home next door to the capitol that is open to the public. Nearby are scattered historic buildings, art galleries, crafts workshops, and antiques stores. The **Chamber of Commerce** (831 1st St.) distributes a helpful map and guide to the old waterfront district. It may be one of the few city guides that list former brothels. The restored **Union Hotel** (401 1st St., tel. 707/746–0100) is a prime example of restoration, and its restaurant is the area's finest.

Just across Carquinez Strait from Benicia is Martinez, another historic port city (now increasingly industrial) with at least one inviting landmark: **John Muir National Historic Site,** the Victorian-era residence of conservationist John Muir. Carefully restored and maintained, it sits atop a hill and is still surrounded by orchards and gardens. *Alhambra Valley Rd., near Hwy. 4, tel. 510/228–8860. Nominal admission fee. Open daily 10–4:30. Closed Thanksgiving, Christmas, New Year's Day.*

Another historic note: Martinez claims to be the birthplace of the martini, which according to legend was invented as the "Martinez cocktail" and was later slurred into its present designation.

North of the delta, about halfway between San Francisco and Sacramento, is the **Western Railroad Museum,** which has collected and restored more than 100 pieces of railway equipment, including steam engines, suburban railroad commuter cars, and a variety of streetcars that make excursions around the 25-acre site. *Hwy. 12 at Rio Vista Junction 10 mi east of Fairfield, tel. 415/346–2310 weekdays; 707/374–2978 weekends. Admission: $1–$3, plus excursion fares. Open 11–5 weekends and most holidays.*

Marine World Africa USA

This wildlife theme park is one of northern California's most popular attractions. It has been a phenomenal success since moving in 1986 from a crowded site south of San Francisco to Vallejo, about an hour's drive northeast. The 160-acre park features animals of the land, sea, and air performing in shows, roaming in natural habitats, and accompanying their trainers to stroll among park visitors. Among the "stars" are killer whales, dolphins, a dozen Bengal tigers, elephants, sea lions, chimpanzees, and a troupe of human water-skiers. There are cockatoos, macaws, flamingos, cranes, and ostriches. There is a whale and dolphin show, a sea lion show, a tiger and lion show, and an elephant and chimpanzee show.

The park is owned by the Marine World Foundation, a nonprofit organization devoted to educating the public about the world's wildlife. The shows and close-up looks at exotic animals serve that purpose without neglecting entertainment. The park is a family attraction, so it's not just for youngsters. For additional sightseeing, visitors can reach the park on a high-speed ferry from San Francisco, a trip that offers unusual vistas through San Francisco Bay and San Pablo Bay. *Marine World Pkwy., Vallejo, tel. 707/643–6722. Admission: $15–$20; tickets at Ticketron outlets. Open daily 9:30–5 or later in summer; Wed.–Sun. rest of year and some school holidays.*

Arriving and Departing

By Car Take I–80 east to Marine World Parkway in Vallejo. The trip takes one hour one-way.

By Bus **Greyhound Lines** (tel. 415/558–6789) from 1st and Mission streets, San Francisco, to Vallejo, or the **BART** train (415/781–BART) to El Cerrito Del Norte Station; transfer to **Vallejo Transit** line (tel. 707/643–7663) to the park.

By Ferry **Red and White Fleet's** (tel. 415/546–2896) high-speed ferry departs mornings each day that the park is open from Pier 41 at Fisherman's Wharf. It arrives in Vallejo an hour later. Round-trip service allows five hours to visit the park. Excursion tickets are $20–$38 and include park admission.

10 The Wine Country

In 1862, after an extensive tour of the wine-producing areas of Europe, Count Agoston Haraszthy de Mokcsa reported to his adopted California with a promising prognosis: "Of all the countries through which I passed," wrote the Father of California's viticulture, "not one possessed the same advantages that are to be found in California. . . . California can produce as noble and generous a wine as any in Europe; more in quantity to the acre, and without repeated failures through frosts, summer rains, hailstorms, or other causes."

The "dormant resources" that Haraszthy saw in the temperate valleys of Sonoma and Napa, with their balmy days and cool nights, are in full fruition today. While its wines are savored by connoisseurs throughout the world, the area is a fermenting vat of experimentation, a crucible for the latest techniques of grape-growing and wine-making.

In the Napa Valley, it seems that every available inch of soil is combed with neat rows of vines; would-be wine-makers with very little acreage can rent the cumbersome, costly machinery needed to stem and press the grapes. Many say making wine is one way to turn a large fortune into a small one, but that hasn't deterred the doctors, former college professors, publishing tycoons, and airline pilots who come to try their hand at the process.

Twenty years ago the Napa Valley had no more than 20 wineries; today there are almost 10 times that number. In Sonoma County, where the web of vineyards is looser, there are more than 100 wineries, and development is now claiming the cool Carneros region at the head of the San Francisco Bay, deemed ideal for growing the currently favored Chardonnay grape.

All this has meant some pretty stiff competition, and the wine makers are constantly honing their skills. They are aided by the scientific know-how of graduates of the nearby University of California at Davis, as well as by the practical knowledge of the grape-growers. They experiment with planting the vine stock closer together and with "canopy management" of the grape cluster, as well as with "cold" fermentation in stainless steel vats and new methods of fining, or filtering, the wine.

In the past the emphasis was on creating wines to be cellared, but today "drinkable" wines that can be enjoyed relatively rapidly are in demand. This has led to the celebration of dining as an art in the Wine Country. Many wineries boast first-class restaurants, which showcase excellent California cuisine and their own fine wines.

With the depredations of increased excise taxes and the health lobbyists, business has felt the pinch lately, but the stretch of highway from Napa to Calistoga rivals Disneyland as the biggest tourist draw in the state. Two-lane Highway 129 slows to a sluggish crawl on weekends throughout the year, and there are acres of vehicles parked at the picnic places, upscale gift shops, and restaurants in the area.

The pace in Sonoma County is less frenetic. While Napa is upscale and elegant, Sonoma is overalls-and-corduroy, with an air of rustic innocence. But the County's Alexander, Dry Creek, and Russian River valleys are no less productive of award-winning vintages. The Sonoma countryside also offers excellent opportunities for hiking, biking, camping, and fishing.

In addition to state-of-the-art viticulture, the Wine Country also provides a look at California's history. In the town of Sonoma, you'll find remnants of Mexican California and the solid, ivy-covered, brick wineries built by Haraszthy and his disciples. The original attraction here was the water, and the rush to the spas of Calistoga, promoted by the indefatigable Gold Rush entrepreneur Samuel Brannan in the late 19th century, left a legacy of fretwork, clapboard, and Gothic architecture. More recent architectural details can be found at the Art Nouveau mansion of the Beringer brothers in St. Helena and the latter-day neoclassical extravaganza of Clos Pegase in Calistoga.

The courting of the tourist trade has produced tensions, and some residents wonder whether projects like the *Wine Train*, finally running between Napa and St. Helena, brings the Disneyland atmosphere a little too close to home. These fears may or may not be realized, but the natural beauty of the landscape will always draw tourists. Whether in the spring, when the vineyards bloom yellow with mustard flowers, or in the fall, when fruit is ripening, this slice of California has a feel not unlike the hills of Tuscany or Provence. Haraszthy was right: This is a chosen place.

Getting Around

By Plane The San Francisco and Oakland airports are closest to the Wine Country. **Greyhound-Trailways** (tel. 415/558–6789) runs buses from the San Francisco Terminal at 7th and Mission streets to Napa (one each day), Sonoma (one each day), and Santa Rosa (three each day).

By Bus **Sonoma County Area Transit** (tel. 707/585–7516) and **The Vine** (tel. 707/255–7631), Napa's bus service, provide local transportation within towns in the Wine Country.

By Car Although traffic on the two-lane country roads can be heavy, the best way to get around the Wine Country is by private car. Rental cars are available at the airports and in San Francisco, Oakland, Santa Rosa, and Napa.

The Rider's Guide (484 Lake Park Ave., Box 255, Oakland 94610, tel. 415/653–2553) produces tapes about the history, landmarks, and wineries of the Sonoma and Napa valleys that you can play in your car. The tapes are available for $11.95, plus $2 postage at Waldenbooks, Brentanos, and Books Inc. in San Francisco, as well as at selected locations (wineries and hotels) in the Wine Country itself. Call to inquire about current availability.

Guided Tours

Full-day guided tours of the Wine Country usually include lunch and cost about $50. The guides, some of whom are winery owners themselves, know the area well and may show you some lesser-known cellars.

Gray Line Inc. (425 Mission St., San Francisco 94105, tel. 415/558–9400) has bright-red double-deckers that tour the Wine Country. Reservations are required.

Great Pacific Tour Co. (518 Octavia St., San Francisco 94102, tel. 415/626–4499) offers full-day tours, including a picnic lunch, to Napa and Sonoma, in passenger vans that seat 13.

Maxi Tours (545 Eddy St., Box 59046, San Francisco 94159, tel. 415/441–6294) provides air-conditioned van tours of the Wine Country.

Starlane Tours (416 Francisco St., San Francisco 94133, tel. 415/982–2223) provides full-day tours of Napa and Sonoma wineries; they offer group and senior-citizen rates.

Superior Sightseeing (642 Alvarado St., Suite 100, San Francisco 94114, tel. 415/550–1352) limits its full-day excursions to 20 passengers. The company offers personalized itineraries on request and provides free hotel pickup as well as group and senior-citizen rates. Reservations are required.

Wine Train (1275 McKinstry St., Napa 94559, tel. 707/253–2111, 800/427–4124 in CA, 800/522–4142 outside CA) allows you to enjoy lunch, dinner, or a weekend brunch on one of several restored 1915 Pullman railroad cars that now run between Napa and St. Helena on tracks that were formerly owned by the Southern Pacific Railroad. Round-trip fare is $29; a three-course brunch or luncheon costs $22, and a five-course dinner costs $45 (train fare is reduced to $14.50 for dinner parties of two or more). During the winter service is limited to Thursday through Sunday. There is a special car for families with children on the Saturday or Sunday brunch trip.

Horse-Drawn Vineyard Tours through the Alexander Valley are offered by Five Oaks Farm (15851 Chalk Hill Rd., Healdsburg 95448, tel. 707/433–2422). The tours run Thursday–Sunday from April through November, weather permitting, and include lunch or dinner.

Important Addresses and Numbers

Tourist Information

Redwood Empire Association (785 Market St., 15th floor, San Francisco 94103, tel. 415/543–8334). The *Redwood Empire Visitors' Guide* is available free at the office or for $2 by mail.

Napa Chamber of Commerce (1556 1st St., Napa 94559, tel. 707/226–7455).

Sonoma Valley Visitors Bureau (453 1st St. E, Sonoma 95476, tel. 707/996–1090).

Sonoma County Convention and Visitors Bureau (10 4th St., Suite 100, Santa Rosa 95401, tel. 707/575–1191 or 800/326–7666).

Calistoga Chamber of Commerce (1458 Lincoln Ave., Calistoga 94515, tel. 707/942–6333).

Healdsburg Chamber of Commerce (217 Healdsburg Ave., Healdsburg 95448, tel. 707/433–6935 or 800/648–9922 in CA).

St. Helena Chamber of Commerce (1080 Main St., Box 124, St. Helena 94574, tel. 707/963–4456 or 800/767–8528).

Emergencies

The emergency number for fire, police, ambulance, and paramedics is 911; or dial 0 for operator and ask to be connected with the appropriate agency.

Exploring

There are three major paths through the Wine Country: U.S. 101 north from Santa Rosa, Highways 12 and 121 through Sonoma County, and Highway 29 north from Napa.

From San Francisco, cross the Golden Gate Bridge and follow Highway 101 to Santa Rosa and points north. Or cross the Golden Gate, go north on Highway 101, east on Highway 37, and north on Highway 121 into Sonoma. Yet another route runs over the San Francisco Bay Bridge and along I–80 to Vallejo, where Highway 29 leads north to Napa.

If you approach the Wine Country from the east, you'll travel along I–80 and then turn northwest on Highway 12 for a 10-minute drive through a hilly pass to Highway 29. From the north, take Highway 101 south to Geyserville, turn southeast on Highway 128, and drive down into the Napa Valley.

Wineries

Choosing which of the 400 or so wineries to visit will be difficult, and the range of opportunities makes it tempting to make multiple stops. Being adventurous will pay off. The wineries along the more frequented arteries of the Napa Valley tend to charge nominal fees for tasting, but in Sonoma County, where there is less tourist traffic, fees are the exception rather than the rule. In Sonoma, you are more likely to run into a wine-grower who is willing to spend part of an afternoon in convivial conversation than you are along the main drag of Napa Valley, where the waiter serving yards of bar has time to do little more than keep track of the rows of glasses.

Unless otherwise noted, visits to the wineries listed are free.

Highway 29 The town of Napa is the gateway into the famous valley, with its unrivaled climate and neat rows of vineyards. The towns in the area are small, and their Victorian Gothic architecture adds to the self-contained and separate feeling that permeates the valley.

A few miles north of Napa is the small town of Yountville. Turn west off Highway 2 at the Veterans Home exit and then up California Drive to **Domaine Chandon,** owned by the French champagne producer Moet-Hennessy and Louis Vuitton. You can tour the sleek modern facilities of this beautifully maintained property and sample flutes of the *methode champenoise* sparkling wine. Champagne is $4 per glass, the hors d'oeuvres are complimentary, and there is an elegant restaurant. *California Dr., Yountville, tel. 707/944–2280. Restaurant closed Mon.– Tues. Nov.–Apr. No dinner Mon.–Tues. May–Oct. Tours daily 11–5 except Mon.–Tues., Nov.–Apr. Closed major holidays.*

Vintage 1870, a 22-acre complex of boutiques, restaurants, and gourmet stores is on the east side of Highway 29. The vine-covered brick buildings were built in 1870 and originally housed a winery, livery stable, and distillery.

The adjacent **Vintage Cafe** is housed in the depot Samuel Brannan built in 1868 for his privately owned Napa Valley Railroad; the remodeled railroad cars of the **Napa Valley Railway Inn** accommodate guests (*see* Lodging, below).

Washington Square, at the north end of Yountville, is a new complex of shops and restaurants; **Pioneer Cemetery,** where the town's founder George Yount is buried, is across the street.

Many premier wineries lie along the route from Yountville to St. Helena.

At **Robert Mondavi,** tasters are required to take the 40–60 minute tour before they imbibe. There are concerts on the grounds during the summer. *7801 St. Helena Hwy., Oakville, tel. 707/*

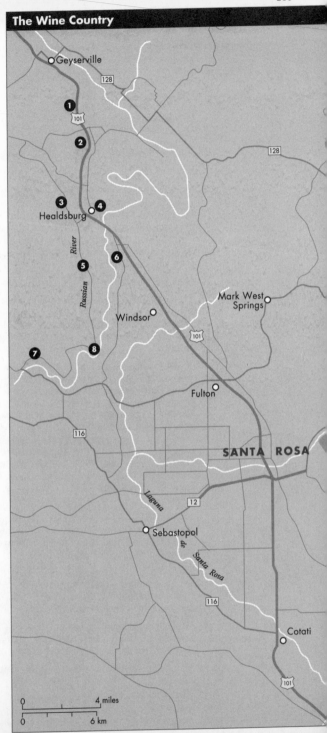

The Wine Country

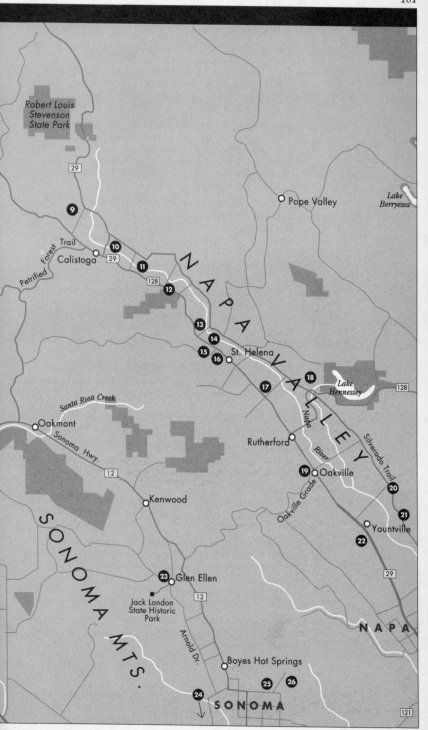

Robert Louis
Stevenson
State Park

29

Pope Valley

Lake
Berryessa

9

Petrified   Forest   Trail
Calistoga
29
10
11
128
12

N A P A

13
14
St. Helena
15
16

18
Lake
Hennessey
128

17

Napa

Santa Rosa Creek

Oakmont
Sonoma Hwy.

Rutherford

River

V A L L E Y

Silverado Trail

12

Kenwood

19 Oakville

Oakville Grade

20

21
Yountville
22

S O N O M A   M T S.

23 Glen Ellen

Jack London
State Historic
Park

12

Arnold Dr.

29

N A P A

Boyes Hot Springs

25   26

24

S O N O M A

121

963–9611. Open daily 10–4:30. Reservations advised in summer. Closed major holidays.

The **Charles Krug Winery** opened in 1861 when Count Haraszthy loaned Krug a small cider press. It is the oldest winery in the Napa Valley. Run by the Peter Mondavi family, it offers vineyard tours on Friday mornings and has a gift shop. *2800 N. Main St., St. Helena, tel. 707/963–5057. Open daily 10–5. Closed major holidays.*

The wine made at **V. Sattui** is sold only on the premises; the tactic draws crowds, as does the huge delicatessen with its exotic cheeses. Award-winning wines include Dry Johannisberg Rieslings, Zinfandels and Madeiras. *Main St. at White La., St. Helena, tel. 707/963–7774. Open daily 9–5. Tours by appointment. Closed Christmas.*

The town of St. Helena boasts many Victorian buildings; don't overlook the **Silverado Museum,** two blocks east from Main Street on Adams, with Robert Louis Stevenson memorabilia, including first editions, manuscripts, and photographs. *1490 Library La., tel. 707/963–3757. Admission free. Open Tues.–Sun. noon–4. Closed major holidays.*

Beringer Vineyards has been operating continually since 1876. Tastings are held in the Rhine House mansion, where hand-carved oak and walnut and stained glass show Belgian Art Nouveau at its most opulent. The Beringer brothers, Frederick and Joseph, built the mansion in 1883 for the princely sum of $30,000. Tours include a visit to the deep limestone tunnels in which the wines mature. *2000 Main St., St. Helena, tel. 707/963–4812. Open daily 9:30–5. Closed major holidays.*

Christian Brothers Greystone Cellars is housed in an imposing stone building, built in 1889 and recently renovated. There are tours every half hour, displays on wine-barrel making, and an unusual collection of corkscrews. *2555 Main St., St. Helena, tel. 707/967–3112. Open daily 10–5. Closed major holidays.*

Freemark Abbey Winery was founded in the 1880s by Josephine Tychson, the first woman to establish a winery in California. *3022 St. Helena Hwy. N, St. Helena, tel. 707/963–9694. Open daily 10–4:30. One tour daily at 2 PM.*

The **Hurd Beeswax Candle Factory** is next door, with two restaurants and a gift shop that specializes in handcrafted candles made on the premises.

The **Sterling Vineyards** lies on a hilltop to the east as you near Calistoga. The pristine white Mediterranean-style buildings are reached by an enclosed gondola from the valley floor; the view from the tasting room is superb. *1111 Dunaweal La., Calistoga, tel. 707/942–5151. Tram fee: $5 for adults, children under 16 free. Open daily 10:30–4:30. Closed major holidays.*

At **Clos Pegase,** neoclassicism sets the tone. The new winery, designed by architect Michael Graves, the exemplar of post-modernism, and commissioned by Jan Schrem, a publisher and art collector, pays homage to art, wine, and mythology. *1060 Dunaweal La., Calistoga, tel. 707/942–4981. Open 10:30–4:30. Closed major holidays.*

Calistoga, at the head of the Napa Valley, is noted for its mineral water, hot mineral springs, mud baths, steam baths, and massages. The Calistoga Hot Springs Resort was founded in

1859 by the maverick entrepreneur Sam Brannan, whose ambition was to found "the Saratoga of California." He tripped up over the name at a formal banquet, and it stuck. One of his cottages, preserved as the **Sharpsteen Museum,** has a magnificent diorama of the resort in its heyday. *1311 Washington St., tel. 707/942–5911. Donations accepted. Open May–Oct., daily 10–4; Nov.–Apr., daily noon–4.*

Chateau Montelena, a vine-covered building built in 1882, is set in Chinese-inspired gardens complete with a lake, red pavilions, and arched bridges. It's a romantic spot for a picnic if you reserve ahead. *1429 Tubbs La., Calistoga, tel. 707/942–5105. Open daily 10–4. Tours at 11 and 2 by appointment only.*

The **Silverado Trail,** which runs parallel to Highway 29, takes you away from the madding crowd to some distinguished wineries as you travel north from Napa:

Clos du Val. Bernard Portet, the French owner, produces a celebrated Cabernet Sauvignon. *5330 Silverado Trail, tel. 707/252–6711. Open daily 10–4:30.*

Stag's Leap Wine Cellars. The Cabernet Sauvignon was rated higher than many venerable Bordeaux wines at a blind tasting in Paris in 1976. *5766 Silverado Trail, tel. 707/944–2020. Open daily 10–4. Tours by appointment. Closed major holidays.*

Rutherford Hill Winery. The wine ages in French oak barrels stacked in more than 30,000 square feet of caves. You can tour the nation's largest such facility and picnic on the grounds. *200 Rutherford Hill Rd., Rutherford, tel. 707/963–7194. Open weekdays 10–4:30, weekends 10–5. Tours on the half hour 11:30–3:30. Cave tours at 11:30, 1, 2:30.*

Hanns Kornell Champagne Cellars. Kornell opened his winery in 1952; he still checks in on the operation run by his family. *1091 Larkmead Ln., just east of Hwy. 29, 4 mi north of St. Helena, tel. 707/963–1237. Open daily 10–4:30.*

The **Calistoga Soaring Center** will give you a bird's-eye view of the entire valley, offering rides in gliders and biplanes, as well as tandem skydiving. *1546 Lincoln Ave., tel. 707/942–5000. Fee: $70–$160. Open daily 9 AM–sunset, weather permitting.*

You don't have to be a guest at a spa to experience a mud bath. At **Dr. Wilkinson's Hot Springs** the $27 fee includes individual mineral-water showers and a mineral-water whirlpool, followed by time in the steam room and a blanket wrap. For $49, you also get a half-hour massage. Reservations are recommended. *1507 Lincoln Ave., Calistoga, tel. 707/942–4102. Open daily 8:30–3:30.*

Highway 12 Rustic Sonoma is anchored by its past. It is the site of the last and the northernmost of the 21 missions established by the Franciscan order of Fra Junipero Serra, and its central plaza includes the largest group of old adobes north of Monterey. The **Mission San Francisco Solano,** whose chapel and school labored to bring Christianity to the Indians, is now a museum that contains a collection of 19th-century watercolors. *114 Spain St. E, tel. 707/938–1519. Admission: $2 adults, $1 children 6–17; includes the Sonoma Barracks on the central plaza and General Vallejo's home, Lachryma Montis (see below). Open daily 10–5. Closed Thanksgiving, Christmas, New Year's Day.*

Time Out The four-block **Sonoma Plaza** is the largest of its kind in California. An inviting array of shops and food stores look out onto the shady park and attract gourmets from miles around. Many pick up the makings for a first-rate picnic. The **French Bakery** (466 1st St. E) is famous for its sourdough bread and cream puffs. The **Sonoma Sausage Co.** (453 1st St. W) produces a mind-boggling selection of bratwurst, bologna, boudin, bangers, and other Old World sausages. There are good cold cuts, too. The **Sonoma Cheese Factory** (2 Spain St.), run by the same family for four generations, makes Sonoma jack cheese and a tangy new creation, Sonoma Teleme. You can peer through the glass windows at the cheese-making process: great swirling baths of milk and curds and the wheels of cheese being pressed flat to dry.

A few blocks west (and quite a hike) is the tree-lined approach to **Lachryma Montis,** which General Mariano Vallejo, the last Mexican governor of California, built for his large family in 1851. The Victorian Gothic house is secluded in the midst of beautiful gardens; opulent Victorian furnishings, including a white marble fireplace in every room, are particularly noteworthy. The state purchased the home in 1933. *Spain St. W, tel. 707/938–1578. Admission: $2 adults, $1 children 6–17. Open daily 10–5. Closed Thanksgiving, Christmas, New Year's Day.*

The **Sebastiani Vineyards,** planted by Franciscans of the Sonoma Mission in 1825 and later owned by General Vallejo, were bought by Samuele Sebastiani in 1904. The Sebastianis recently helped popularize "blush" wines, and Sylvia Sebastiani has recorded her good Italian home cooking in a family recipe book, *Mangiamo.* Tours include an unusual collection of impressive carved oak casks. *389 4th St. E, tel. 707/938–5532. Open daily 10–5. Closed major holidays.*

The landmark **Buena Vista Winery** (follow signs from the Plaza), set among towering trees and fountains, is a must-see in Sonoma. This is where, in 1857, Count Agoston Haraszthy de Mokcsa laid the basis for modern California wine making, bucking the conventional wisdom that vines should be planted on well-watered ground by planting on well-drained hillsides. Chinese laborers dug the cool aging tunnels 100 feet into the hillside, and the limestone they extracted was used for the main house. Although the wines are produced elsewhere today, there are tours, a gourmet shop, art gallery, wine museum, and great picnic spots. *18000 Old Winery Rd., tel. 707/938–1266. Open daily 10–5.*

In the Carneros region of the Sonoma Valley, south of Sonoma, the wines at **Gloria Ferrer Champagne Caves** are aged in a "cava," or cellar, where several feet of earth maintain a constant temperature. *23555 Hwy. 121, tel. 707/996–7256. Tasting $3.50. Open daily 10:30–5:30.*

The well-known **Glen Ellen Winery** uses watercolors painted by Jan Haraszthy, one of the count's descendants, on its labels. The originals hang in the tasting room. *1883 London Ranch Rd., Glen Ellen, tel. 707/935–3000. Open daily 10–4:30.*

North of Sonoma, through the Valley of the Moon and in the hills above Glen Ellen, is **Jack London State Historic Park.** The House of Happy Walls is a museum of London's effects, including his collection of South Sea artifacts. The ruins of Wolf House, which London designed and which mysteriously burned down just before he was to move into it, lie nearby, and

London is buried there. *2400 London Ranch Rd., tel. 707/938–5216. Parking: $5 per car, $4 per car driven by senior citizen. Park open daily 8–sunset, museum 10–5. Museum closed Thanksgiving, Christmas, New Year's Day.*

Highway 101 Santa Rosa is the Wine Country's largest city and your best bet for a moderately priced hotel room, especially if you haven't reserved in advance.

The **Luther Burbank Memorial Gardens** commemorate the great botanist, who lived and worked on these grounds for 50 years, single-handedly developing modern techniques of hybridization. Arriving as a young man from New England, he wrote: "I firmly believe . . . that this is the chosen spot of all the earth, as far as nature is concerned." The Santa Rosa plum, the Shasta daisy, and the lily of the Nile agapanthus are among the 800 or so plants he developed or improved. In the dining room of his house, a Webster's Dictionary of 1946 lies open to a page on which the verb "burbank" is defined as "to modify and improve plant life." *Santa Rosa and Sonoma Aves., tel. 707/524–5445. Gardens free, open daily 8–5. Home tours: $1, children under 12 free; open Apr.–Oct., Wed.–Sun. 10–3:30.*

The wineries of Sonoma County are located along winding roads and are not immediately obvious to the casual visitor; a tour of the vineyards that lie along the Russian River is a leisurely and especially bucolic experience. For a map of the area, contact Russian River Wine Road (Box 46, Healdsburg, 95448, tel. 707/433–6782).

For a historical overview, you could start at the imposing **Korbel Champagne Cellars,** with their photographic documents housed in a former stop of the North West Pacific Railway. *13250 River Rd., Guerneville, tel. 707/887–2294. Open Oct.–Apr., daily 9–4:30; May–Sept., daily 9–5.*

Traveling down the River Road east of Guerneville, turn left down Westside Road and follow it as it winds past a number of award-winning wineries.

Davis Bynum Winery, an up-and-coming label, offers a full line of varietal wines that have done well in recent competitions. *8075 Westside Rd., Healdsburg, tel. 707/433–5852. Open daily 10–5.*

The **Hop Kiln Winery** is located in an imposing hop-drying barn built during the early 1900s and used as the backdrop for such films as the 1960 *Lassie* with James Stewart. *6050 Westside Rd., Healdsburg, tel. 707/433–6491. Open daily 10–5.*

Lambert Bridge produces some superbly elegant Cabernet Sauvignons and Merlots. *4085 W. Dry Creek Rd., Healdsburg, tel. 707/433–5855. Open daily 10–4:30.*

The **Robert Stemmler Winery** draws on German traditions of wine-making and specializes in Pinot noir. There are picnic facilities on the grounds. *3805 Lambert Bridge Rd., Healdsburg (Dry Creek Rd. exit from Hwy. 101, northwest 3 mi to Lambert Bridge Rd.), tel. 707/433–6334. Open daily 10:30–4:30.*

Lytton Springs Winery produces the archetype of the Sonoma Zinfandel, a dark, fruity wine with a high alcohol content. There is still dispute over the origin of this varietal and whether it was transplanted from stock in New England, but the vines themselves are distinctive, gnarled, and stocky, many of them over a century old. *650 Lytton Springs Rd., Healdsburg, tel. 707/433–7721. Open daily 10–4.*

In Healdsburg, back on Highway 101, is **Clos du Bois**, wine-making at its most high-tech. You can tour by appointment, but you'd do better to concentrate on sampling the fine estate wines of the Alexander and Dry Creek valleys that are made here. *5 Fitch St., tel. 707/433–5576. Open daily 10–5.*

South of Healdsburg, off Highway 101, are the **Piper Sonoma Cellars,** a state-of-the-art winery that specializes in champagne. *11447 Old Redwood Hwy., Healdsburg, tel. 707/433–8843. Open daily 10–5.*

Time Out In case you've had enough wine for the day, **Kozlowski's Raspberry Farm** (5566 Gravenstein, Hwy. N. 116), in Forestville, makes jams of every berry imaginable. Also in Forestville, **Brother Juniper's** (6544 Front St., Hwy. 116, tel. 707/887–7908) makes a heavenly *Struan* bread of wheat, corn, oats, brown rice, and bran. *Open Mon.–Sat. 9–4:30.*

What to See and Do with Children

In the **Bale Grist Mill State Historic Park** there is a flour mill powered by a 36-foot overshot water wheel, erected by Dr. Edward Turner Bale in 1846 and since restored. Hiking trails lead from the access road to the mill pond. *3 mi north of St. Helena on Hwy. 29, tel. 707/942–4575. Day use: $2 adults, $1 children 7–18. Open daily 10–5.*

Old Faithful Geyser of California is a 60-foot tower of steam and vapor that erupts about every 40 minutes; the pattern is disrupted if there's an earthquake in the offing. One of just three regularly erupting geysers in the world, it is fed by an underground river that heats to 350° F. The spout lasts three minutes. Picnic facilities are available. *1299 Tubbs La., 1 mi north of Calistoga, tel. 707/942–6463. Admission: $3.50 adults, $2 children 6–11. Open daily 9–6 during daylight saving time, 9–5 in winter.*

In the **Petrified Forest** volcanic eruptions of Mount St. Helena 6 million years ago uprooted the gigantic redwoods, covered them with volcanic ash, and infiltrated the trees with silicas and minerals, causing petrification. There is a museum, and picnic facilities are available. *4100 Petrified Forest Rd., 5 mi west of Calistoga, tel. 707/942–6667. Admission: $3 adults, $2 senior citizens, $1 children 4–11. Open daily 10–6 in summer, 10–5 in winter.*

A scale steam train at **Train Town** runs for 20 minutes through a forested park with trestles, bridges, and miniature animals. *20264 Broadway, 1 mi south of Sonoma Plaza, tel. 707/938–3912. Admission: $2.40 adults, $1.80 children under 16 and senior citizens. Open mid-June–Labor Day daily 10:30–5; Sept.–mid-June, weekends and holidays 10:30–5:30. Closed Christmas.*

Howarth Memorial Park, in Santa Rosa, has a lake where canoes, rowboats, paddleboats, and small sailboats can be rented for $3–$4 an hour. The children's area has a playground, pony rides, petting zoo, merry-go-round, and a miniature train. Fishing, tennis, and hiking trails are also available. *Summer-*

field Rd. off Montgomery Rd., tel. 707/539–1499. Amusements: 25¢–50¢. Park open daily; children's area open Wed.–Sun. in summer, weekends in spring and fall.

Off the Beaten Track

You'll see breathtaking views of both the Sonoma and Napa valleys along the hairpin turns of the **Oakville Grade,** which twists along the range dividing the two valleys. The surface of the road is fine, and if you're comfortable with mountain driving, you'll enjoy this half-hour excursion. Trucks are advised not to take this route.

Robert Louis Stevenson State Park, on Highway 53, 3 miles northeast of Calistoga, encompasses the summit of Mount St. Helena. It was here, in an abandoned bunkhouse of the Silverado Mine, that Stevenson and his bride, Fanny Osbourne, spent their honeymoon in the summer of 1880. The stay inspired Stevenson's "The Silverado Squatters," and Spyglass Hill in *Treasure Island* is thought to be a portrait of Mount St. Helena. The park's 3,000 acres are undeveloped except for a fire trail leading to the site of the cabin, which is marked with a marble tablet, and then on to the summit. Picnicking is permitted, but fires are not.

Shopping

Most wineries will ship purchases. Don't expect bargains at the wineries themselves, where prices are generally as high as at retail outlets. Local residents report that the area's supermarkets stock a wide selection of local wines at lower prices. Gift shops in the larger wineries offer the ultimate in gourmet items—you could easily stock up on early Christmas presents.

Sports

Ballooning This sport has fast become part of the scenery in the Wine Country, and many hotels arrange excursions. Most flights take place soon after sunrise, when the calmest, coolest time of day offers maximum lift and soft landings. Prices depend on the duration of the flight, number of passengers, and services (some companies provide pickup at your lodging, champagne brunch after the flight, etc.). You should expect to spend about $150 per person. Companies that provide flights include **Balloons Above the Valley** (Box 3838, Napa 94558, tel. 707/253–2222 or 800/464–6824 in northern CA); **Napa Valley Balloons** (Box 2860, Yountville 94599, tel. 707/253–2224 or 800/253–2224 in CA); and **Once in a Lifetime** (Box 795, Calistoga 94515, tel. 707/942–6541 or 800/722–6665 in CA).

Bicycling One of the best ways to experience the countryside is on two wheels, and the Eldorado bike trail through the area is considered one of the best. Reasonably priced rentals are available in most towns.

Golf Though the weather is mild year-round, rain may occasionally prevent your teeing off in the winter months. Call to check on greens fees at **Fountaingrove Country Club** (1525 Fountaingrove Pkwy., Santa Rosa, tel. 707/579–4653); **Oakmont Inn and Golf Course** (7025 Oakmont Dr., Santa Rosa, tel. 707/539–0415 or 548–2454); or **Silverado Country Club** (1600 Atlas Peak Rd., Napa, tel. 707/257–0200).

Dining

by Bruce David Colen

A number of the Wine Country's kitchens are the domains of nationally prominent chefs. The emphasis everywhere on the freshest ingredients goes hand in hand with local bounty: vegetables and fruits, seafood, lamb, and poultry. While some of the restaurants are expensive (dinner at Auberge du Soleil or the Silverado Country Club may run more than $50 per person), wonderful local foods are available for picnics.

With few exceptions (which are noted), dress is informal. Where reservations are indicated to be essential, you may need to reserve a week or more ahead during the summer and early-fall harvest seasons.

The most highly recommended restaurants are indicated by a star ★.

Category	Cost*
Very Expensive	over $35
Expensive	$25–$35
Moderate	$16–$25
Inexpensive	under $16

per person, excluding drinks, service, and 6.5% sales tax

The following credit card abbreviations are used: AE, American Express; D, Discover; DC, Diners Club; MC, MasterCard; V, Visa.

Calistoga
Moderate

Calistoga Inn. With the atmosphere and appeal of a village tavern (but the talents of a big-city chef), this restaurant has nicely prepared California cuisine and excellent fish dishes. First-rate local wines are also featured. *1250 Lincoln Ave., tel. 707/ 942–4101. Reservations advised. Dress: informal. Wine and beer. MC, V.*

Alex's. This family-style restaurant features prime rib and New York steaks. If you're not in the mood for steak, try one of the several fish entrées or the daily seafood special. Don't pass up the family-recipe cheesecake. *1437 Lincoln Ave., tel. 707/ 942–6868. Full bar. AE, MC, V. Closed Mon. Dinner only.*

Geyserville
Very Expensive
★

Château Souverain Restaurant at the Winery. There is a gorgeous view of the Alexander Valley vineyards from the dining room and terrace. The California/Continental menu is imaginative: Sonoma lamb loin with soy mustard ginger glaze; black peppercorn rosemary lamb essence and Japanese eggplant; grilled marinated quail with smoked pear puree, pancetta, and basil quail essence. *400 Souverain Rd. (take Independence La. exit west from Hwy. 101), tel. 707/433–3141. Reservations advised. Jacket required at dinner. Wine. AE, MC, V. Dinner Thurs.–Sat., lunch Tues.–Sat., Sun. brunch.*

Healdsburg
Very Expensive

Madrona Manor. The chef uses a brick oven, smokehouse, orchard, and herb and vegetable garden to enhance other fresh produce and seafood on his California menus. Dinners and Sunday brunch are served in the dining room and terrace of an 1881

Victorian mansion on a hilltop west of town. À la carte and prix fixe. *1001 Westside Rd., tel. 707/433–4231. Reservations advised. Jacket required. Wines. AE, DC, MC, V.*

Moderate **Jacob Horner.** California cuisine with an emphasis on locally grown vegetables ("no more than 2 miles from the restaurant") and fresh seafood, lamb, and duck from near at hand is the focus here. An enthusiastic owner-chef has put together a comfortable, good-looking restaurant on Healdsburg's charming town plaza. There is an extensive, award-winning wine list with 17 wines served by the glass. *106 Matheson St., tel. 707/433–3939. Reservations advised. Full bar. AE, MC, V. No dinner Mon. Closed Sun.*

Plaza Grill. Mesquite-grilled meats, fresh fish (orange roughy en papillote), espresso, and cappuccino are served at a small, attractive wine bar on Healdsburg's pretty town plaza. *109–A Plaza St., tel. 707/431–8305. Reservations advised. Beer and wine. AE, MC, V. No lunch Sat. Closed Mon. and 1st week in December.*

Napa **Silverado Country Club.** There are two dining rooms and a bar
Very Expensive and grill at this large, famous resort. Vintner's Court, with California cuisine, serves dinner only; there is a seafood buffet on Friday night and a champagne brunch on Sunday. Royal Oak serves steak, seafood, and lobster for dinner; in summer, it also serves lunch. The bar and grill is open for breakfast and lunch year-round. *1600 Atlas Peak Rd., 707/257–0200. Reservations advised. Jacket preferred at dinner. Full bar. AE, DC, MC, V.*

Inexpensive **Jonesy's Famous Steak House.** This longtime institution at the Napa County Airport is popular with private pilots throughout the West and with local people. Steaks are prepared on an open grill, with large hot rocks placed on top of them while cooking. The building is nothing special: plain and businesslike. *2044 Airport Rd., tel. 707/255–2003. Reservations accepted for groups of 6 or more. Full bar. AE, MC, V. Closed Mon., Thanksgiving, a week at Christmas, New Year's Day.*

Rutherford **Auberge du Soleil.** Sitting on the dining terrace of this hilltop
Very Expensive inn, looking down across groves of olive trees to the Napa Val-
★ ley vineyards, is the closest one can get to the atmosphere and charm of southern France without needing a passport. The mood is enhanced by a menu centered around light Provençal dishes, using the fresh produce of nearby farms. The Auberge features a fine list of wines from California, France, and Italy. It is also a 48-room inn (*see* Lodging, below). *180 Rutherford Hill Rd., tel. 707/963–1211. Jacket and tie preferred. Reservations advised. Full bar. AE, MC, V.*

St. Helen **Starmont at Meadowood.** Three-course prix-fixe dinners and an
Very Expensive extensive Napa Valley wine list with some French wines are served in this elegantly casual 65-seat restaurant that turns to the outdoors, maximizing the view over the golf course and the stands of pine trees beyond. There is terrace service in warm weather and a piano bar. Lunch and Sunday brunch April–November. *900 Meadowood La., tel. 707/963–3646. Reservations required. Jacket preferred. Full bar. AE, DC, MC, V.*

Moderate– **Abbey Restaurant.** Greek specialties, seafood, beef, lamb
Expensive shanks, and pastitsio are served at lunch and dinner; next door to Freemark Abbey. *3020 N. St. Helena Hwy. (Hwy. 29), tel. 707/963–2706. Reservations accepted. Full bar, wine. V. No*

dinner Mon.–Tues. Closed Easter, Christmas, New Year's Day.

★ **Terra.** The delightful couple who own this lovely, unpretentious restaurant, in a century-old stone foundry, learned their culinary skills at the side of chef Wolfgang Puck. Hiro Sone was head chef at LA's Spago and Lissa Doumani was the pastry chef. The menu has an enticing array of American favorites, prepared with Hiro's Japanese-French-Italian finesse: addictive baked mussels in garlic butter; sautéed Miyagi oysters with jalapeño salsa; home-smoked salmon with golden caviar; grilled quail and polenta; and sweetbreads with asparagus and wild mushrooms. Save room for Lissa's desserts. *1345 Railroad Ave., tel. 707/963–8931. Reservations advised. Jacket required. Wine and beer. AE, MC, V. Closed Tues.*

Tra Vigne. This Napa Valley fieldstone building has been turned into a barn of a trattoria, serving good pizza; pastas; and traditional Italian grilled meats, fish, and fowl. Tra Vigne has terrace dining, weather permitting. This is a meeting place for locals and tourists. *1050 Charter Oak Ave., tel. 707/963–4444. Dress: casual. Reservations advised. Full bar. MC, V. Closed July 4, Thanksgiving, Christmas.*

Moderate **Fairway Grill and Bar.** California specialties include Meadowood sandwich (with chicken-apple sausage and roasted bell pepper) and roasted breast of chicken stuffed with goat cheese. This is a light, airy, casual restaurant at the Meadowood Resort, where large windows and an outdoor terrace overlook the golf course and croquet lawns. Antique croquet mallets and tennis rackets decorate the walls. *900 Meadowood La., tel. 707/963–3646. Reservations advised. Full bar. AE, DC, MC, V. No dinner in winter.*

Inexpensive **French Laundry.** Long a favorite of surrounding wine-makers
★ for its tasty blend of French and California cooking, French Laundry is one of the most attractive wine bars in the Wine Country. *Washington and Creek Sts., tel. 707/944–2380. Reservations advised. Dress: casual. Wine and beer. MC, V. Dinner only, Wed.–Sat.*

Santa Rosa **John Ash & Co.** The thoroughly regional cuisine here emphasizes
Expensive sizes beauty, innovation, and the seasonality of food products
★ grown in Sonoma County. In spring, local lamb is roasted with hazelnuts and honey; in fall, farm pork is roasted with fresh figs and Gravenstein apples. There are fine desserts and an extensive wine list. Two dining rooms are in a vineyard setting next to Vintner's Inn. The restaurant also offers Sunday brunch. *4330 Barnes Rd. (River Rd. exit west from Hwy. 101), tel. 707/527–7687. Reservations advised. Jacket preferred. Wine. AE, MC, V. Closed Mon.*

Moderate **Equus.** In this handsome restaurant, the equestrian theme is carried out in redwood carvings, murals, and etched glass. A gallery of Sonoma County wines features nearly 300 bottles hand-picked by their makers. *101 Fountaingrove Pkwy., tel. 707/578–6101. Reservations advised. Jacket preferred. Full bar. AE, DC, MC, V.*

Los Robles Lodge Dining Room. The elegant 120-seat dining room specializes in tableside presentations of chateaubriand, lamb, and flaming desserts. Seafood and sautéed dishes are also featured. This 28-year-old restaurant has a loyal local following. *9255 Edwards Ave. (Steele La. exit west from Hwy. 101), tel. 707/545–6330. Reservations advised. Jacket preferred. Full bar. AE, DC, MC, V. No lunch on major holidays.*

Inexpensive **Omelette Express.** At least 300 omelet possibilities are offered in an old-fashioned restaurant in historic Railroad Square. *112 4th St., tel. 707/525–1690. No reservations. Wine and beer. MC, V. No dinner. Closed Thanksgiving, Christmas.*

Sonoma
Expensive
Sonoma Mission Inn. There are two dining rooms as well as a poolside terrace for alfresco meals at this attractive, "contemporary country" resort. The inn is also a spa, so the menu has a wide assortment of light dishes, with the accent on fresh salads, fish, and poultry, prepared in nouvelle-California style. The annual Sonoma Wine Auction is held on the inn's grounds, so the extensive wine list comes as no surprise. *18140 Hwy. 12, Boyes Hot Springs, tel. 707/938–9000. Reservations advised. Jacket preferred at dinner. Full bar. AE, DC, MC, V.*

Moderate–
Expensive
★
L'Esperance. The room is small and pretty, with flowered tablecloths to the floor, burgundy overcloths, and burgundy chairs. There is a choice of classic French entrees, such as rack of lamb, plus a "menu gastronomique" that includes hot and cold appetizers, salad, entree, dessert, and coffee. *464 1st St. E. (down a walkway off the plaza, behind the French Bakery), tel. 707/996–2757. Reservations advised. Wine and beer. AE, MC, V.*

Piatti. On the ground floor of the recently remodeled El Dorado Hotel, a 19th-century landmark building, this is the Sonoma cousin of the Napa Valley Piatti (*see* below). This very friendly trattoria features a nice selection of grilled northern Italian items. *405 1st St. tel. 707/996–3030. Dress: casual. Full bar. MC, V.*

Moderate
Gino's Restaurant and Bar. This relaxed, friendly eating and drinking establishment on Sonoma's plaza specializes in fresh seafood and pasta. *420 1st St., tel. 707/996–4466. Reservations advised on weekends. Dress: informal. Full bar. AE, V.*

La Casa. "Whitewashed stucco, red tile, serapes, and Mexican glass" describes this restaurant just around the corner from Sonoma's plaza. There is an extensive menu of traditional Mexican food: chimichangas, snapper Veracruz, flan for dessert, sangria to drink. *121 E. Spain St., tel. 707/996–3406. Reservations advised. Full bar. AE, DC, MC, V.*

Sonoma Hotel Dining Room. Seasonal produce and homemade ingredients are featured in this restaurant with antique oak tables and stained glass. The saloon boasts a magnificent old bar of oak and mahogany. Service in garden patio in summer. *110 W. Spain St., tel. 707/996–2996. Dress: informal. Reservations advised. Full bar. AE, MC, V. Closed Tues. and Wed. in winter.*

Yountville
Expensive–
Very Expensive
★
Domaine Chandon. Nouvelle seafood, pasta, beef, and lamb are prepared imaginatively and presented beautifully. The architecturally dramatic dining room has views of vineyards and carefully preserved native oaks. There is also outdoor service on a tree-shaded patio. *California Dr. (no number), tel. 707/944–2892. Reservations essential. Jacket and tie required. Wine. AE, DC, MC, V. No dinner Mon.–Tues. year-round; no lunch Mon.–Tues. Nov.–Apr.*

Moderate–
Expensive
Anesti's Grill and Rotisserie. Rotisserie-roasted lamb, duck, and suckling pig are specialties of this small, cheerful restaurant with two mesquite grills. *6518 Washington St., tel. 707/944–1500. Reservations advised. Full bar. AE, DC, MC, V.*

California Cafe & Grill. This is the Wine Country link of a small upscale chain serving bar and grill dishes, plus roast game and a variety of good pastas and salads. Also on the menu: chicken breast with red-pepper jam, tapas, warm apple crisp, and an extensive wine list all in a large, square room with an open kitchen. There is outdoor service on the terrace. Sunday brunch is also served. *6795 Washington St., tel. 707/944-2330. Reservations accepted. Full bar. AE, DC, MC, V.*

Mama Nina's. This homey and old-fashioned restaurant serves homemade pasta and fresh grilled fish. There's a children's menu. *6772 Washington St., tel. 707/944-2112. Reservations advised. Full bar. MC, V. Lunch weekend only. Closed Easter, Thanksgiving, Christmas Eve, Christmas Day.*

★ **Mustard's Grill.** Grilled fish, hot smoked meats, fresh local produce, and a good wine list are offered in a simple, unassuming dining room. It's very popular and crowded at prime meal times. *7399 St. Helena Hwy. (Hwy. 29, 2 mi north of Yountville), tel. 707/944-2424. Reservations essential. Dress: informal. MC, V.*

Piatti. A small, stylish trattoria with a pizza oven and open kitchen, this cheery place is full of good smells and happy people. Its authentic, light Italian cooking—from the antipasti to the grilled chicken to the *tiramisu*—is the perfect cure for a jaded appetite. The pastas are the best bet. *6480 Washington St., tel. 707/944-2070. Reservations advised. Jacket required at dinner. Full bar. MC, V.*

Inexpensive **The Diner.** This is probably the best-known and most-appreciated stop-off in the Napa Valley, especially for breakfast. Be sure to have the local sausages and the house potatoes. At night, many of the specials are Mexican. *6476 Washington St., tel. 707/944-2626. No reservations; expect a wait for seating. Wine and beer. No credit cards. Closed Mon.*

Lodging

Make no mistake, staying in the Wine Country is expensive. The inns, hotels, and motels are usually exquisitely appointed, and many are fully booked long in advance of the summer season. Since Santa Rosa is the largest population center in the area, it has the largest selection of rooms, many at moderate rates. Try there if you've failed to reserve in advance or have a limited budget.

Highly recommended hotels are indicated by a star ★.

Category	Cost*
Very Expensive	over $100
Expensive	$80–$100
Moderate	$50–$80
Inexpensive	under $50

All prices are for a standard double room, excluding 7% tax.

The following credit card abbreviations are used: AE, American Express; D, Discover; DC, Diners Club; MC, MasterCard; V, Visa.

Calistoga
Expensive–
Very Expensive
★

Brannan Cottage Inn. This exquisite Victorian cottage with lacy white fretwork, large windows, and a shady porch is the only one of Sam Brannan's 1860 resort cottages still standing on its original site. The restoration is excellent and includes elegant stenciled friezes of stylized wildflowers. All rooms have private entrances. Full breakfast is included. *109 Wapoo Ave., 94515, tel. 707/942–4200. 6 rooms. MC, V.*

Mount View Hotel. This refurbished 1930s hotel provides live music and dancing on weekends. Continental breakfast in the lobby is included, and the restaurant features northern Italian cuisine. *1457 Lincoln Ave., 94515, tel. 707/942–6877. 34 rooms with bath. Facilities: pool, Jacuzzi bar, restaurant. MC, V.*

Moderate–
Expensive

Dr. Wilkinson's Hot Springs. This hot springs spa resort has been in operation for more than 40 years. Reserve ahead for weekends, when there are separate fees for mud baths, massages, facials, and steam rooms. Mid-week packages include room and full spa services. *1507 Lincoln Ave., 94515, tel. 707/ 942–4102. 42 rooms. Facilities: 3 mineral pools. AE, MC, V.*

Moderate

Comfort Inn Napa Valley North. All the rooms in this recently opened motel have one king- or two queen-size beds, and many have vineyard views. Continental breakfast is included. There are rooms for nonsmokers and handicapped guests, and there are senior citizen discounts. *1865 Lincoln Ave., 94515, tel. 707/ 942–9400 or 800/228–5150. 54 rooms with bath. Facilities: natural mineral-water pool, spa sauna, steam room, movies. AE, D, DC, MC, V.*

Mountain Home Ranch. This rustic ranch, built in 1913, is set on 300 wooded acres, with hiking trails, a creek, and a fishing lake. There is just one TV, in the dining room, and no phones. Families are welcome and there are special children's rates. In summer, the modified American plan (full breakfast and dinner) is used; otherwise Continental breakfast is included. Six simple cabins without heat are available from mid-June to Labor Day. They have a separate shower facility, and you must bring your own linens. *3400 Mountain Home Ranch Rd., 94515 (north of town on Hwy. 128, left on Petrified Forest Rd., right on Mountain Home Ranch Rd., to end; 3 mi from Hwy. 128), tel. 707/942–6616. 14 rooms with bath, 6 cabins with half bath. Facilities: 2 pools, tennis. MC, V. Closed Dec.–Jan.*

Healdsburg
Very Expensive

Madrona Manor. A splendid, three-story, 1881 Gothic mansion, carriage house, and outbuildings sit on eight wooded and landscaped acres. Mansion rooms are recommended: All nine have fireplaces, and five contain the antique furniture of the original owner. The approach to the mansion leads under a stone archway and up a flowered hill; the house overlooks the valley and vineyards. Full breakfast is included, and there's a fine restaurant on the premises that serves dinner. Pets are allowed. *1001 Westside Rd., Box 818, 95448, tel. 707/433–4231 or 800/258–4003. 21 rooms with bath. Facilities: pool, restaurant. AE, DC, MC, V.*

Moderate–
Very Expensive

Healdsburg Inn on the Plaza. This renovated 1900 brick building on the attractive town plaza has a bright solarium and a roof garden. The rooms are spacious, with quilts and pillows piled high on antique beds and clawfoot tubs complete with rubber ducks. Full breakfast, afternoon coffee and cookies, and early evening wine and popcorn are included. *110 Matheson St., Box 1196, 95448, tel. 707/433–6991. 9 rooms. MC, V.*

Moderate **Best Western Dry Creek Inn.** Movies, Continental breakfast, and a complimentary bottle of wine are included at this three-story motel in Spanish Mission style. There is a 24-hour coffee shop next door. Small pets are allowed; discounts are available for senior citizens. Direct bus service from San Francisco Airport is available. *198 Dry Creek Rd., 95448, tel. 707/433–0300 or 800/528–1234; in CA, 800/222–5784. 102 rooms with bath. Facilities: pool, spa, laundry. AE, D, DC, MC, V.*

Napa **Clarion.** This modern, comfortable, and immaculately main-
Very Expensive tained motel has a restaurant and lounge on the premises, live music in the lounge, movies, and rooms for the handicapped. Pets are allowed with a $10 fee. *3425 Solano Ave., 94558 (1 block west off Hwy. 29; take Redwood-Trancas exit), tel. 707/ 253–7433 or 800/333–7533. 191 rooms. Facilities: pool, spa, lighted tennis courts. AE, D, DC, MC, V.*

Silverado Country Club. This luxurious 1,200-acre resort in the hills east of the town of Napa offers cottages, kitchen apartments, and one- to three-bedroom efficiencies, many with fireplaces. There are also two dining rooms, a lounge, a sundries store, seven pools, 20 tennis courts, and two championship golf courses designed by Robert Trent Jones. Fees are charged for golf, tennis, and bike rentals. *1600 Atlas Peak Rd., 94558 (6 mi east of Napa via Hwy. 121), tel. 707/257–0200 or 800/532–0500. 277 condo units. Facilities: restaurant. AE, D, DC, MC, V.*

Expensive **Chateau.** There's a French country inn atmosphere at this modern motel which provides Continental breakfast and a social hour with wine. Movies, in-room refrigerators, facilities for the handicapped, and senior citizen discounts are available. *4195 Solano Ave., 94558 (west of and adjacent to Hwy. 29; take W. Salvador Ave. exit), tel. 707/253–9300 or 800/253–6272 in CA. 115 rooms. Facilities: pool, spa. AE, D, DC, MC, V.*

Moderate– **Best Western Inn Napa.** This immaculate modern redwood mo-
Very Expensive tel with spacious rooms has a restaurant on the premises and same-day laundry and valet service. There are suites, as well as rooms for nonsmokers and the handicapped. Small pets are allowed. *100 Soscol Ave., 94558 (Imola Ave. Hwy. 121 exit east from Hwy. 29 to junction of Hwy. 121 and Soscol), tel. 707/257– 1930 or 800/528–1234. 68 rooms. Facilities: pool, spa. AE, D, DC, MC, V.*

John Muir Inn. Continental breakfast and in-room coffee are included at this new, well-equipped, three-story motel that has kitchenettes, refrigerators, movies, valet service, and some whirlpool tubs. Senior citizen discounts and rooms for nonsmokers and handicapped guests are available. *1998 Trower Ave., 94558 (adjacent to Hwy. 29, east at Trower exit), tel. 707/ 257–7220 or 800/522–8999 in CA. 59 rooms. Facilities: pool, spa. AE, D, DC, MC, V.*

Rutherford **Auberge du Soleil.** This luxurious French country–style inn has
Very Expensive an excellent restaurant and a spectacular view over vineyards and hills. *180 Rutherford Hill Rd., 94573, tel. 707/963–1211. 48 rooms. Facilities: pool, spa, tennis, masseuse. AE, MC, V.*

Rancho Caymus Inn. Early California-Spanish in style, this inn has well-maintained gardens and large suites with kitchens and whirlpool baths. There are home-baked breads and an emphasis on decorative handicrafts, and there are unusual beehive fireplaces, tile murals, stoneware basins, and llama blankets. There is a two-night minimum stay April 1–Nov. 30. *1140 Rutherford Rd., 94573 (junction of Hwys. 29 and 128), tel. 707/*

963–1777 or 800/845–1777. 26 rooms. Facilities: restaurant. MC, V.

St. Helena
Very Expensive

Meadowood Resort. The resort is set on 256 wooded acres, with a golf course, croquet lawns, and hiking trails. The hotel is a rambling country lodge reminiscent of turn-of-the-century Rhode Island, and separate bungalow suites are clustered on the hillside. Half of the suites and some rooms have fireplaces. *900 Meadowood La., 94574, tel. 707/963–3646 or 800/458–8080. 82 rooms. Facilities: 2 restaurants, lounge, room service, 2 pools, saunas, 9–hole and par golf courses, tennis, masseuse, wine school. AE, DC, MC, V.*

Expensive–
Very Expensive

Harvest Inn. This English Tudor inn with many fireplaces overlooks an active, 14-acre vineyard and an award-winning landscape. The furnishings are antique, but there are also wet bars, refrigerators, fireplaces, and a wine bar and dance floor in the lobby "Great Room." Dogs are allowed for a $5 fee. *1 Main St., 94574, tel. 707/963–9463 or 800/950–8466. 55 rooms. Facilities: 2 pools, 2 Jacuzzis. AE, D, MC, V.*

Hotel St. Helena. This restored 1881 stone hostelry, furnished with antiques and decorated in rich tones of burgundy, aims at Old World comfort. Continental breakfast is included. Smoking not encouraged. *1309 Main St., 94574, tel. 707/963–4388. 14 rooms with bath, 4 rooms with shared bath. AE, DC, MC, V.*

Moderate–
Expensive

Cinnamon Bear Bed and Breakfast. Built in 1904 as a wedding gift, this house is decorated with a period flavor, from the antique quilts and toys to the clawfoot tubs. Full breakfast is included. Rooms for nonsmokers are available. *1407 Kearney St., 94574 (from Main St., Hwy. 29, turn west on Adams St., then 2 blocks to Kearney), tel. 707/963–4653. 4 rooms with bath. MC, V.*

Moderate

El Bonita Motel. This old-fashioned roadside motel was recently remodeled in the Art Deco style. The decor is white and gray, with streaks of flamingo and blue; a neon calla lily graces the north side. The small rooms have soft, smart furnishings. There are 16 rooms in the main motel and six garden rooms with kitchenettes. *195 Main St., 94574, tel. 707/963–3216 or 800/541–3284. 22 rooms. Facilities: pool. AE, MC, V.*

Santa Rosa
Very Expensive

Vintner's Inn. Set in 50 acres of vineyards, this recently built inn has large rooms, French Provincial furnishings, and wood-burning fireplaces. Movies and breakfast are included, and there is an excellent restaurant on the premises. Rooms for the handicapped are available, as are VCRs, for a small fee. *4350 Barnes Rd., 95403 (River Rd. exit west from Hwy. 101), tel. 707/575–7350 or 800/421–2584 in CA. 44 rooms. Facilities: spa. AE, DC, MC, V.*

Expensive
★

Fountaingrove Inn. This new, elegant, and comfortable inn boasts a redwood sculpture, *Equus III*, and a wall of cascading water in the lobby. Rooms have work spaces with modem jacks. Buffet breakfast is included, and there's an exceptional restaurant. Senior citizen discounts and rooms for nonsmokers and the handicapped are available. *101 Fountaingrove Pkwy., 95403, tel. 707/578–6101 or 800/222–6101 in CA. 85 rooms. Facilities: lap pool, spa, room service, movies. AE, DC, MC, V.*

Moderate–
Very Expensive

Doubletree Hotel. Many rooms in this large, modern, multi-story hotel on a hilltop have views of the valley and vineyards; the Burgundy, Cabernet, Chardonnay, Chablis, and Riesling buildings have especially fine views. The spacious rooms have work-size desks and functional, comfortable furnishings. There are rooms for nonsmokers and the handicapped, and patio rooms overlooking the pool. Golf and tennis are available at the adjacent Fountaingrove Country Club for additional fees; there's a courtesy shuttle to Santa Rosa airport and a jogging path. *3555 Round Barn Blvd., 95401 (Old Redwood Hwy., exit east from Hwy. 101), tel. 707/523–7555 or 800/833–9595. 252 rooms with bath. Facilities: restaurant, bar, lounge, pool, spa, room service, valet service. AE, D, DC, MC, V.*

Moderate–
Expensive
★

Los Robles Lodge. This pleasant, relaxed motel has comfortable rooms overlooking a grassy, landscaped pool. Rooms for the handicapped and nonsmokers are available. Pets are allowed, except in executive rooms, which have Jacuzzis. *925 Edwards Ave., 95401 (Steele La. exit west from Hwy. 101), tel. 707/545–6330 or 800/255–6330. 105 rooms. Facilities: restaurant, coffee shop, lounge with nightly entertainment, pool, outdoor Jacuzzi, laundry. AE, D, DC, MC. V.*

Inexpensive

Best Western Hillside Inn. Some rooms at this cozy, nicely landscaped, small motel have balconies or patios. Kitchenettes and suites are available. Pets are allowed. *2901 4th St., 95409 (at Farmers La., 2 mi east off Hwy. 101 on Hwy. 12), tel. 707/546–9353 or 800/528–1234. 35 rooms. Facilities: pool, restaurant, sauna, shuffleboard. AE, DC, MC, V.*

Sonoma
Very Expensive

Sonoma Mission Inn. This elegantly restored 1920s resort blends Mediterranean and old-California architecture. It's early Hollywood—you half expect Gloria Swanson to sweep through the lobby. The location is unexpected, off the main street of tiny, anything but posh, Boyes Hot Springs. The grounds are nicely landscaped and the accommodations include suites. This is the home of the *Spa Food* cookbook, and there are extensive spa facilities (fee for fitness classes and treatments). *18140 Sonoma Hwy. (Hwy. 12 north of Sonoma), Box 1447, 95476, tel. 707/938–9000 or 800/358–9022, 800/862–4945 in CA. 170 rooms. Facilities: restaurant, coffee shop, 2 bars, lounge, 2 pools, weight room, steam room, Jacuzzis, sauna, tennis. AE, DC, MC, V.*

Moderate–
Expensive

Best Western Sonoma Valley Inn. Just one block from the town plaza, this new motel features balconies, handcrafted furniture, wood-burning fireplaces, and whirlpool baths. Continental breakfast and a complimentary split of wine are included. Senior discounts, kitchenettes, and rooms for nonsmokers and the handicapped are available. *550 2nd St. W, 95476, tel. 707/938–9200 or 800/334–5784 in CA. 72 rooms. Facilities: pool, whirlpool, laundry. AE, D, DC, MC, V.*

Sonoma Hotel. At the edge of Sonoma's plaza, this hotel, built in 1870, has been carefully restored and each of its rooms furnished with antiques in an attempt to re-create a Victorian country inn. There's no TV, but Continental breakfast and a complimentary split of wine are included. The restaurant specializes in California country cuisine. *110 W. Spain St., 95476, tel. 707/996–2996. 5 rooms with bath, 12 with shared bath. Facilities: bar. AE, MC, V.*

Windsor
Moderate

Redwood Royale Hometel. This clean, no-frills motel is a bargain for an economy-minded family. Each unit has a bedroom, bath, kitchen, and living/dining area, and the rate is the same for one to four persons. Kitchen items are available for rent.

The motel is on 2½ acres, and there is secured parking for RVs. *8900 Bell Rd., 95492, tel. 707/838–9771. 80 units. Facilities: pool, laundry. AE, MC, V.*

Yountville
Very Expensive

Vintage Inn. All rooms have fireplaces, whirlpool baths, refrigerators, private verandas or patios, hand-painted fabrics, window seats, and shuttered windows in this luxurious new inn. Continental breakfast with champagne, a complimentary bottle of wine, and afternoon tea are provided. Bike rental in season and hot-air ballooning are available. *6541 Washington St., 94599, tel. 707/944–1112; 800/982–5539; in CA, 800/351–1133. 80 rooms with bath. Facilities: lap pool, spa, tennis. AE, DC, MC, V.*

Napa Valley Lodge. Spacious rooms overlook vineyards and valley in this hacienda-style lodge with tile roofs, covered walkways, balconies, patios, and colorful gardens. Freshly brewed coffee is provided in rooms, as well as Continental breakfast and the morning paper. Some rooms have fireplaces. Kitchenettes and rooms for nonsmokers and the handicapped are available. *Madison St. and Hwy. 29, Box L, 94599, tel. 707/944–2468 or 800/368–2468. 55 rooms. Facilities: exercise room, pool, spa, sauna, valet service, refrigerators. AE, D, DC, MC, V.*

Expensive

Napa Valley Railway Inn. This unusual establishment is made of nine vintage railcars on the original track of the Napa Valley Railroad. Each car is now an air-conditioned suite, with sitting area, queen-size brass beds, skylights, bay windows, and full tiled baths. Wine and coffee are provided. *6503 Washington St., 94599, tel. 707/944–2000. 9 rooms with bath. MC, V.*

The Arts and Nightlife

Galleries throughout the Wine Country display the work of local artists: painters, sculptors, potters, and jewelry makers. The **Luther Burbank Performing Arts Center** in Santa Rosa (tel. 707/546–3600, box office open Mon.–Sat. noon–6) has a full calendar of concerts, plays, and other performances, with both locally and internationally known performers. Wineries often schedule concerts and music festivals during the summer.

Nightlife in the Wine Country is best savored in a leisurely, elegant dinner at one of the restaurants for which the area is justly famous. Many of the larger hotels and motels feature live music on weekends.

Index

Personal Itinerary

Departure *Date*

Time

Transportation

Arrival *Date* *Time*

Departure *Date* *Time*

Transportation

Accommodations

Arrival *Date* *Time*

Departure *Date* *Time*

Transportation

Accommodations

Arrival *Date* *Time*

Departure *Date* *Time*

Transportation

Accommodations

Personal Itinerary

Arrival	*Date*	*Time*
Departure	*Date*	*Time*
Transportation		
Accommodations		

Arrival	*Date*	*Time*
Departure	*Date*	*Time*
Transportation		
Accommodations		

Arrival	*Date*	*Time*
Departure	*Date*	*Time*
Transportation		
Accommodations		

Arrival	*Date*	*Time*
Departure	*Date*	*Time*
Transportation		
Accommodations		

Personal Itinerary

Arrival *Date*   *Time*

Departure *Date*   *Time*

Transportation

Accommodations

Arrival *Date*   *Time*

Departure *Date*   *Time*

Transportation

Accommodations

Arrival *Date*   *Time*

Departure *Date*   *Time*

Transportation

Accommodations

Arrival *Date*   *Time*

Departure *Date*   *Time*

Transportation

Accommodations

Personal Itinerary

Arrival *Date* *Time*

Departure *Date* *Time*

Transportation

Accommodations

Arrival *Date* *Time*

Departure *Date* *Time*

Transportation

Accommodations

Arrival *Date* *Time*

Departure *Date* *Time*

Transportation

Accommodations

Arrival *Date* *Time*

Departure *Date* *Time*

Transportation

Accommodations

Personal Itinerary

Arrival *Date*   *Time*

Departure *Date*   *Time*

Transportation

Accommodations

Arrival *Date*   *Time*

Departure *Date*   *Time*

Transportation

Accommodations

Arrival *Date*   *Time*

Departure *Date*   *Time*

Transportation

Accommodations

Arrival *Date*   *Time*

Departure *Date*   *Time*

Transportation

Accommodations

Personal Itinerary

Arrival *Date*   *Time*

Departure *Date*   *Time*

Transportation

Accommodations

Arrival *Date*   *Time*

Departure *Date*   *Time*

Transportation

Accommodations

Arrival *Date*   *Time*

Departure *Date*   *Time*

Transportation

Accommodations

Arrival *Date*   *Time*

Departure *Date*   *Time*

Transportation

Accommodations

Addresses

Name	*Name*
Address	*Address*
Telephone	*Telephone*
Name	*Name*
Address	*Address*
Telephone	*Telephone*
Name	*Name*
Address	*Address*
Telephone	*Telephone*
Name	*Name*
Address	*Address*
Telephone	*Telephone*
Name	*Name*
Address	*Address*
Telephone	*Telephone*
Name	*Name*
Address	*Address*
Telephone	*Telephone*
Name	*Name*
Address	*Address*
Telephone	*Telephone*
Name	*Name*
Address	*Address*
Telephone	*Telephone*

Addresses

Name	*Name*
Address	*Address*
Telephone	*Telephone*
Name	*Name*
Address	*Address*
Telephone	*Telephone*
Name	*Name*
Address	*Address*
Telephone	*Telephone*
Name	*Name*
Address	*Address*
Telephone	*Telephone*
Name	*Name*
Address	*Address*
Telephone	*Telephone*
Name	*Name*
Address	*Address*
Telephone	*Telephone*
Name	*Name*
Address	*Address*
Telephone	*Telephone*
Name	*Name*
Address	*Address*
Telephone	*Telephone*

Addresses

Name	*Name*
Address	*Address*
Telephone	*Telephone*
Name	*Name*
Address	*Address*
Telephone	*Telephone*
Name	*Name*
Address	*Address*
Telephone	*Telephone*
Name	*Name*
Address	*Address*
Telephone	*Telephone*
Name	*Name*
Address	*Address*
Telephone	*Telephone*
Name	*Name*
Address	*Address*
Telephone	*Telephone*
Name	*Name*
Address	*Address*
Telephone	*Telephone*
Name	*Name*
Address	*Address*
Telephone	*Telephone*

Fodor's Travel Guides

U.S. Guides

Alaska
Arizona
Boston
California
Cape Cod, Martha's Vineyard, Nantucket
The Carolinas & the Georgia Coast
The Chesapeake Region
Chicago
Colorado
Disney World & the Orlando Area
Florida
Hawaii

Las Vegas, Reno, Tahoe
Los Angeles
Maine, Vermont, New Hampshire
Maui
Miami & the Keys
National Parks of the West
New England
New Mexico
New Orleans
New York City
New York City (Pocket Guide)

Pacific North Coast
Philadelphia & the Pennsylvania Dutch Country
Puerto Rico (Pocket Guide)
The Rockies
San Diego
San Francisco
San Francisco (Pocket Guide)
The South
Santa Fe, Taos, Albuquerque
Seattle & Vancouver

Texas
USA
The U. S. & British Virgin Islands
The Upper Great Lakes Region
Vacations in New York State
Vacations on the Jersey Shore
Virginia & Maryland
Waikiki
Washington, D.C.
Washington, D.C. (Pocket Guide)

Foreign Guides

Acapulco
Amsterdam
Australia
Austria
The Bahamas
The Bahamas (Pocket Guide)
Baja & Mexico's Pacific Coast Resorts
Barbados
Barcelona, Madrid, Seville
Belgium & Luxembourg
Berlin
Bermuda
Brazil
Budapest
Budget Europe
Canada
Canada's Atlantic Provinces

Cancun, Cozumel, Yucatan Peninsula
Caribbean
Central America
China
Czechoslovakia
Eastern Europe
Egypt
Europe
Europe's Great Cities
France
Germany
Great Britain
Greece
The Himalayan Countries
Holland
Hong Kong
India
Ireland
Israel
Italy

Italy 's Great Cities
Jamaica
Japan
Kenya, Tanzania, Seychelles
Korea
London
London (Pocket Guide)
London Companion
Mexico
Mexico City
Montreal & Quebec City
Morocco
New Zealand
Norway
Nova Scotia, New Brunswick, Prince Edward Island
Paris

Paris (Pocket Guide)
Portugal
Rome
Scandinavia
Scandinavian Cities
Scotland
Singapore
South America
South Pacific
Southeast Asia
Soviet Union
Spain
Sweden
Switzerland
Sydney
Thailand
Tokyo
Toronto
Turkey
Vienna & the Danube Valley
Yugoslavia

Wall Street Journal Guides to Business Travel

Europe   International Cities   Pacific Rim   USA & Canada

Special-Interest Guides

Bed & Breakfast and Country Inn Guides:
Mid-Atlantic Region
New England
The South
The West

Cruises and Ports of Call
Healthy Escapes
Fodor's Flashmaps New York

Fodor's Flashmaps Washington, D.C.
Shopping in Europe
Skiing in the USA & Canada

Smart Shopper's Guide to London
Sunday in New York
Touring Europe
Touring USA